1

NEW
DIMENSIONS
IN
RELIGIOUS
EXPERIENCE

alba house • DIVISION OF THE SOCIETY OF ST. PAUL
STATEN ISLAND, N.Y. 10314

GEORGE DEVINE

Editor of the Proceedings of the
College Theology Society

NEW
DIMENSIONS
IN
RELIGIOUS
EXPERIENCE

Library of Congress Catalog Card Number: 76-158566

SBN: 8189-0206-X

Copyright 1971 by the Society of St. Paul, 2187 Victory Blvd., Staten Island, N.Y.
10314

Designed, printed and bound in the U.S.A. by the Pauline Fathers and Brothers of
the Society of St. Paul, 2187 Victory Blvd., Staten Island, N.Y. 10314 as part of their
communications apostolate.

Also by George Devine:

Our Living Liturgy. Chicago: Claretian Publications, 1966.
Why Read the Old Testament? Chicago: Claretian Publications, 1966.
To Be A Man (ed.) Englewood Cliffs, N.J.: Prentice-Hall, Inc., 1969.
Theology in Revolution (ed.) Staten Island, N.Y.: Alba House, 1970.

Acknowledgments

The editor of this volume wishes to thank all who have contributed to the successful publication of this volume of the College Theology Society Proceedings, based on the Society's last annual Convention in Boston, March 29-31, 1970, especially our President, Prof. James Wieland; our Vice-president, Sister Francis Regis Carton, S.S.N.D.; our Secretary, Sister M. Gertrude Anne Otis, C.S.C.; and our Treasurer, Brother C. Stephen Sullivan, F.S.C. Also instrumental in the success of this volume are some of our officers who retired at the Boston Convention: Rev. Mark Heath, O.P. (President); Rev. Berard Marthaler, O.F.M., Conv. (Vice-president); and Sister Maura Campbell, O.P. (Secretary); and the other Directors of the CTS.

Thanks should also go to those who assisted the editor during and right after the presentation of the papers at Boston, especially Professors Patricia Ahern and Thomas Wangler. And the editor's burden has been lightened and his task made more enjoyable by numerous individuals who have, in myriad ways, aided in various aspects of the Proceedings project, including Sister Katherine T. Hargrove, R.S.C.J.; Mr. William J. Toohey; Mr. Peter R. Flynn; Miss Anne M. Buckley; Mrs. Sally Gran; Mr. John T. Smith and Rev. Michael Mullen, C.M. Valuable reactions to this book, at various stages of its formation, were received from the CTS Board of Directors and from the editor's students and colleagues at Seton Hall University, especially Prof. Gerald Pire. The physical production of the book and its appearance are due to the fine work of Alba House, the publishing division of the Society of St. Paul.

Also, production of this book was facilitated by and through the resources and facilities of the Main Branch (42nd Street), New York Public Library; Duane Library, Fordham University; McLaughlin Library, Seton Hall University; Richard A. Gleeson Library, University of San Francisco; and the firm of H. Reader & Co., New York City, as well as by Mrs. Margaret Chaing, and her staff in the Department of Religious Studies at Seton Hall University.

Lastly, the editor wishes to thank all those who have been around and with him throughout this endeavor, but especially his wife Joanne, and his son George IV.

— George Devine

Contents

II The Diversity of Religious Experience

NEW
DIMENSIONS
IN
RELIGIOUS
EXPERIENCE

I Man and His Religious Experience

1   Religious Experience and Doctrinal Statement

GREGORY BAUM

Recent developments in the theological understanding of divine revelation enable us to take seriously the Church's religious experience in accounting for doctrinal development. We have come to affirm divine revelation as on-going. While we continue to insist that God's self-revelation was complete, definitive, and unconditional in Jesus Christ—and that he is, therefore, Lord and Word—we have come to look upon divine revelation as continuing in the Church. God continues to address his people. The Church's faith does not lean simply on the divine witness of the past; the Church's faith, rather, is evoked by God's Word addressed to her in the present.

Where does God's Word address the Church? This takes place through the scriptures, the liturgy, the ecclesiastical witness of the past; and this takes place, secondly, through the experience of Christians in the present. Since God's Word sounds in the hearts of men and in their history, the Church continues to be addressed by him through the experience of the present generation. But since Christians have many experiences, the question arises how they can discern among these the truly significant ones. How can they be sure that a special experience contains a divine message? The answer to this is simple. It is the Church's possession of scripture and past tradition (which may be called the *memoria Christi*) that enables her to sift her experience and detect the message addressed to her in the present.

There is a dialectical relationship between *memoria Christi* and the Church's present experience. They interact and affect one another. In the first place the *memoria Christi criticizes* present Christian experience. By this I mean that Christians submit their experience to the scriptures, to the sensitivity created in them through the liturgy and ecclesiastical teaching, and test if their experience will stand up under this critique. It may turn out to be spurious. It may be necessary to correct or modify it. It is possible, for instance, that the testing reveals that certain aspects of the experience lead to destruction and hence have no religious significance, or that other aspects deserve to be stressed since they strengthen divine grace in the faithful. In this manner the *memoria Christi* affects the sensitivity of Christians and enables them to detect the Word of God addressed to them in their present experience.

What is the effect of present experience on the *memoria Christi?* The Church's religious experience specifies the inherited witness in scripture, liturgy, and doctrine. The religious questions and concerns of the Church make concrete the divine message and hence give it a specific meaning for the present. The Church's experience brings out the aspect of the Gospel that is central and crucial today, and enables Christians to proclaim divine revelation as the Good News, addressed to the contemporary world, dealing with the problems people actually have.

This dialectic between *memoria Christi* and present religious experience, described here in terms of *critique* and *specification,* goes on in the entire Christian community, slowly achieves a consensus in the Church, and ultimately leads to a new doctrinal formulation on the part of the ecclesiastical magisterium.

A typical example for this process is the new Christian conviction, confirmed by the doctrine of Vatican II, that the supernatural brotherhood of man is not confined to the Church but embraces all men. Christians are bound to other men not simply by a sort of natural brotherhood, based on a common creation, but by the ties of the Holy Spirit, who summons all men and leads them on the path of the common, divine destiny. This doctrine is not on the surface of scripture and the Church's tradition: the stress, in the past, has usually been quite different. Yet the new experience of the Church (a new sense of universality, reconciliation, and responsibility for others), tested by the scriptures and the sensitivity produced through liturgical worship, has led to the ever-growing conviction that all men are brothers in the supernatural sense. What has taken place here is the dialectic between doctrine and experience: and we know that this dialectic has eventually influenced the Church as a whole through the documents of Vatican II.

We conclude that the Church's experience deserves to be taken seriously, that it affects the understanding of divine revelation, and ultimately contributes to the development of doctrine.

Religious Experience Yesterday and Today

It is my view that the Church's self-understanding is changing at this time and that, therefore, the religious experience of Christians is undergoing significant modification. Some Christians are, in fact, deeply troubled by the fact that the pious practices which meant so much to them in the past have almost lost their meaning. Prayer does not work for them as it used to. What has happened? As we shall see, there is no need for alarm, for as one set of religious experiences disappears, other experiences assume greater importance and communicate to us the strength and the grace of God.

First I wish to mention the typical religious experiences of the past, namely, the two classical experiences of the holy and of total dependence. There is no need to give an ample description of these. The holy produced awe and affection in men; it separated them from the ordinary aspects of life; it divided reality into the sacred and the profane. The experience of total dependence, typical of Christian piety, made men aware that they belonged to another and that despite the threats to their salvation they were in the hands of a power transcending them, who was in their favor and would not permit them to get seriously hurt. This experience impelled men to surrender themselves more wholeheartedly to God in faith, hope and love.

I have the impression that these traditional religious experiences are not as frequent among Christians today as they were in the past. Something has happened to us through recent developments in the Church: at least in many cases, particularly among priests, nuns and others occupied full-time with religion, the piety which produced fruits in the past does not seem to work any more. Many Christians who loved prayer in the past find that it does not do anything for them now: nothing happens to them any more as they turn to God in the customary way.

Why is this? I wish to give two reasons why the traditional religious experiences occur more rarely today and why they have less power over men. First there is a trend or process established in the consciousness of Western society which may be called functionalization. Sociologists have analyzed this process in detail. There is the trend among us to achieve greater critical awareness, to subject the details of life to a critique, to organize the life of society as rationally as possible in order to increase efficiency and production, and to enlist all of man's energies and talents for the building of a better world. In other words, in the present culture men try to unify their life and orientate it towards the transformation of their environment and the creation of their future. Valuable to man is only what participates in this process of greater humanization. If, therefore, the sacred is experienced as separating, as bringing man in touch with another world, as making him withdraw from the building of the present world, then it becomes dys-functional—and men refuse to deliver themselves to it. Total dependence, too, becomes dys-functional. For the effort of man in Western culture is to assume more and more responsibility for his environment and his future, and he fears therefore that the stress on dependence, even on divine dependence, may encourage his passivity and strengthen his own inner resistance to grow up and become himself.

Another reason, related to the first, why traditional religious experience has become a rare thing for many men of the present culture, is the new awareness of self-alienation. Parts or aspects of man can become estranged from him; as he grows and wants to become truly himself, he may discover that these aspects or parts no longer belong to him, that he has been damaged, that he cannot recover his humanity anymore. Some human relationships may alienate a man from himself. The particular, traditional religious experiences appear to many of our contemporaries as a form of alienation. The sacred separates certain aspects of life, declares them to be more than human, severs them from ordinary life situations and the building of the human world. The sacred creates an island in the world, which is not part of human development and history. Similarly many people feel that the experience of total dependence tends to be alienating. For what man needs, above all, is the strengthening of his sense of responsibility. He is too inclined to rely on mother and father and, as he grows up, on substitutes for these. He is too prone to shirk responsibility and let others make decisions for him. The experience of total dependence would tend to alienate man from his powers of self-creation.

While traditional worship and piety have become more difficult, more problematic, and for some Christians an empty form, there are other, "new" experiences that are precious to them. There is new religious experience. I wish to describe in particular two experiences which are of greatest significance to modern men and which are for them the encounter with the absolute.

The first of these experiences I shall call *conversion*. Many Christians, along with other men of our culture, have learned how to listen to others, be open to what is being said to them in conversation, in literature, in other forms of human witness, and be ready to be unsettled by the word addressed to them. People realize that they have many blind spots. We do not see the truth about ourselves and the situation to which we belong, because we do not want to see. Since we are so eager to defend our interests, our various castles, personal or social, we do not make ourselves sensitive to the aspect of reality that threatens us in our safe possession. Yet in conversation with others, we may begin to detect some of the deceptions we have entertained about ourselves and society. We may be shaken, we suddenly see; the truth challenges us; and we may discover in us the freedom to leave self-deceptions behind, face reality, and enter creatively into the future. This experience of conversion has become precious to modern man. He exposes himself to this in the dialogue with others and even in the conflict with groups that offer a radical critique of the present society.

This experience of conversion or truth has a religious quality. The summons addressed to man is not due to his own insight, it is not produced by him, it transcends him; moreover the summons to truth, though present in conversation with others, is gratuitous, it is experienced as a gift. No man is proud of the conversions through which he moves; he, rather, marvels at the extraordinary things that have happened to him.

Recent developments in the Catholic Church have made Catholics particularly sensitive to this experience of truth. The movement of renewal has introduced them to discussions and dialogue and taught them many times that a group of people is changed through conversation, comes to see things in a new way, and eventually finds a new way of acting. Priests and nuns, in particular, have opened themselves to this experience of truth through the very effort of renewing their institutional life.

The second religious experience I wish to mention is that of *reconciliation*. This refers to the creation of fellowship across many barriers of estrangement. These experiences may be had in the creation of intimate friendship, in a small community that becomes an extended family, or in the wider political arena of reconciliation between races, classes, and nations. Community and interpersonal relations have begun to count for Christians in a new way. There is no need to develop this at length. This experience, I insist, has a religious quality. It is regarded as a supreme value, as an absolute: in other words, Christians are ready to evaluate the rest of life in terms of reconciliation. This is the norm in the light of which they judge political action, social policies and personal behavior. Reconciliation, moreover, is experienced as gratuitous. It is a marvel when it takes place. Despite the hostilities, fears and suspicions in regard to others which, as sinners, we have inherited and endorse, fellowship does become possible at certain moments. A new element enters here, an element that transcends the powers of man—namely divine grace. Again the social movement in the Catholic Church makes Catholics particularly open to this experience.

These are two principal experiences of the present generation of Christians. They may find traditional piety difficult or even empty form: but they are not devoid of religious experience. According to the remarks made above, it would not be necessary to test this experience by the scriptures. It is easy to see and to establish by a careful study that both the experience of conversion and that of reconciliation are in harmony with the Bible, in fact express a central concern of the Gospel. For this reason, it is possible to conclude that in these new experiences God's Word is addressing the Church.

In the light of this new experience, tested by scripture and more and more approved by the entire Church (the Vatican II documents are already profoundly influenced by it), it is possible and necessary to re-interpret the sacred and man's dependence on God. The sacred is no longer experienced as separating, it does not divide life into two sections, the holy and the profane. The sacred, rather, is a pivotal moment in man's humanization. Man grows as a human being and becomes progressively reconciled to himself and the rest of mankind, through many crucial experiences by which sin is conquered in him and grace heals and renews his consciousness. Here the sacred has become "functional," in the sense that it is a moment of the redemptive process, in which God is gratuitously present to man. The sacred, thus experienced and understood, no longer alienates. The division it introduces, is between the superficial and the profound. The sacred is the depth dimension of human life. It is here that God is redemptively present to man. The sacred, in other words, is not localizable. It is present in all aspects of life as the deepest dimension. The mystery of God, experienced and understood in this new way, delivers man from his bondage, frees him to assume responsibility for himself, and enables him to dedicate himself more and more to the building of the human world and creation of his future. The living God, understood in this new light, is therefore the mystery of man's de-alienation. The presence of God is the humanization of man.

The above paragraph suggests that the new experience of the Church, tested by scripture and approved by a growing consensus, specifies or concretizes the Church's message in a new way and hence will ultimately lead to a reformulation of doctrine. We have here doctrinal development according to the dialectic described above. It should be possible to speak about God and his self-revelation in Jesus Christ, in terms and concepts that correspond to the *present* experience of Christians. If the Church offers the Good News in terms of a past experience, which has little weight in the present, then doctrine will appear abstract and unreal. It will not deal with what people experience in fact, with their deep fears, their concerns, their actual aspirations. In order to proclaim the Good News in power, it is necessary to express it as the answer to the questions which people actually have and the clarification of the profound experiences which make life precious for them. This sort of formulation is the effort of contemporary theology.

The Good News God has revealed in Jesus Christ is that wherever people are, marvellous things happen despite the awful games in which they are involved. Sin, or the destructiveness alive in us, affecting every aspect of life, personal and social, is not the only reality: there is another, the ground for hope, and the source of new truth and love, namely the divine mystery of redemption, God's self-gift, operative in the lives of all men, even though proclaimed and sacramentally celebrated only in the Church. This mystery of man's humanization gains power over us as we open ourselves to it in faith.

These few sentences are samples of what a reformulation of doctrine might look like, identical with the revelation once for all received and yet a message addressed to man's salvational questions today.

Contemplation

I have mentioned only two "new" religious experiences. Both of them, we recognized, were in a sense secular. They take place in ordinary life, among the religious and non-religious. What about the contemplative side of man, by which he is in more direct touch with the divine?

It is my view that because of the change in man's self-understanding, prayer has become very difficult today. The traditional experiences of the holy and of total dependence are rare. The new religious experiences I have described shake up people, nourish them, and rebuild them, yet they do not constitute what is usually called prayer. True enough, if prayer is defined as man's listening and responding to the divine Word, then the experience of conversion is, properly speaking, prayer. For here men reflect on the meaning of their life and the content of their experience, and seek to detect in these a message or summons addressed to them. Without this sort of contemplation, no man can become a truly human being, whether he be a Christian or not. Without this kind of listening to the divine, no man can grow in his humanity.

But do we find today a new kind of contemplation, based on the two "new" experiences I have described? There is some evidence that some people who have experienced the mystery of redemption in conversion and reconciliation many times and have followed the course of action inspired by these experiences, begin to develop a familiarity with this mystery, present to them at crucial moments of the past, so that they are able to remain with it, be linked to it, and to be aware of it, even when they are alone. Having experienced the mystery in their association with others, either in secular or liturgical community, they are able to abide with this mystery and focus on it, as they are by themselves. This is contemplation. But the model for this is not that of traditional prayer, where we projected God ahead of us, imagined him to be our invisible friend, and then talked to him and surrendered ourselves to him. The model of contemplation here is different. It is not man's withdrawal from ordinary life and association with people, in the effort to turn to the invisible God; it is rather a being more closely present to ordinary life and the association with people, and a touching of the mystery alive in oneself and in others as source of new consciousness. The inner gesture is here not of turning away from oneself to the invisible other, but rather of being in touch with all of oneself, with all layers, in reconciliation, and thus, opening oneself to the mystery alive at the source of one's being.

2   The Social Setting of the Experience of Religion

THEODORE M. STEEMAN

In line with the general orientation of the scientific study of religion, the sociology of religion tries to understand religious behavior in terms of its human reality and takes, therefore, its explanatory framework from the human sciences. Sociology accepts religion as a real fact of life, and tries to understand it as such, without making statements about the validity or invalidity of forms of religious behavior and expression. The central concern, rather, is to understand why people do, or do not, believe in God, what kind of God they believe in, why they engage in specific religious activities.

The sociological study of religion has much more to say to both Church and theology than simply statistics on church membership and religious practices or other such information that might be helpful to the theological-ecclesiastical enterprise. The sociological enterprise is genuinely and deeply involved in the effort at understanding man as a religious being. It tries to get to the human roots of religious thought and action. It is, therefore, able to reach insights into the structure of religious phenomena which theology, working within that structure, cannot reach. Part of this undertaking is to understand the theological enterprise in its social and cultural context. It also analyzes the Church as an on-going institution and the specific social dynamics that are at work in the religious institutions.

This does not mean that sociology would try to diminish the value of the theological enterprise. But sociology does relate the concrete forms religion takes to the socio-cultural environment. It also has its eyes open to discern the social consequences of religious beliefs and practices or of styles of theological thinking. It relates religious phenomena not to a transcendent, immutable God, but to a historically variable and historically developing human situation and tries to discern what religion does in that situation. It has to do this because the observation of man's religious history cannot be understood except if one agrees that changes in the situation of man and in his self-understanding do lead to different forms of religious articulation and expression, liturgical, ethical, and in a very broad sense, theological. In pointing out what is actually happening on the religious scene the sociology of religion can formulate better than theology or church officials what the religious problem is, so that both Church and theology may be better attuned to the situation as it actually presents itself.[1]

Experience [2]

By "experience" I mean here the primary awareness of the world one lives in, or the primary givenness of the world to the self. The emphasis is very much on "primary." It does not matter that much what one becomes aware of—physical objects, other human beings, total situations, oneself—as long as it is a primary awareness. In this sense experience is the root form of man's awareness of himself and the surrounding world, the most original way of becoming aware of being in a world, the event by which man realizes that he is present to himself and to the world—and the world to him. This is pre-reflective, immediate,

1. For an interesting appraisal of the value of sociology for theology by a theologian, see Gregory Baum, "Personal Testimony to Sociology," *The Ecumenist* (November-December, 1969).
2. The discussion of experience which follows is very much based on Alfred Schütz, *Der Sinnhafte Aufbau der sozialen Welt,* 2nd ed. (Wien: Springer Verlag, 1962). See the use that Peter Berger and Thomas Luckmann have made of Schütz's work in *The Social Construction of Reality* (New York: Doubleday, 1966), and more specifically in Luckmann's *The Invisible Religion* (New York: Macmillan, 1967), pp. 41ff. Leslie Dewart's works *The Future of Belief* (New York: Herder & Herder, 1966) and *The Foundations of Belief* (New York: Herder & Herder, 1969) were very helpful in developing this understanding.

uncritical, spontaneous, and at the same time very much "alive." It is active participation in the world of being.

Every experience is at the same time a self-experience. I am not just aware of the object before me or of the sound that I hear, but I am aware that it is I who see the object or hear the music. Therefore, even in its Religious experience I am involved with the Sacred, and the experience not only reveals the Sacred to me but also myself. I become aware of my being related to the Sacred and in that sense discover who I am. I am given to myself in a different way once I have experienced that I am related to or stand in a relationship with the Sacred Beyond.

Exactly insofar as the experience reveals me to myself, it entails or even constitutes a dimension of human self-transcendence. In experience one becomes aware of involvements that are given, are part of the givenness of life. The experience does not create my involvement in the world of being, but the awareness of it. Experience, therefore, changes the nature of my involvement in the world of being insofar as it makes me know that I am involved and thereby creates in me the possibility to respond freely and actively to my being involved and to the being with which I find myself involved. Without experience I may be affected by my actual involvement in the world of reality but only experience makes me aware of it and makes it possible that I react freely.[3] Experience lifts man above life as a process that runs its natural course in its environment exactly by making him aware of this process and by initiating the possibility of taking distance from it and of a free response.

The third point follows from the second: the type of self one becomes is dependent on the type of awareness one reaches, or the content of the self as self-aware is dependent on the experience one has. Only those things one becomes aware of in experience can become an object of knowledge and of free initiative, but at the same time one becomes what one is as a self in these experiences. That is: I can stand as free self in this world only to the extent that I am aware of this world

3. Dewart, *The Foundations of Belief*, p. 271, and *passim*.

and of myself as standing in this world. My self-awareness as a free self is therefore related to my awareness of the world as it is given to me in my experiences. This is not to say that the Self is only a product of its experiences, the outcome, as it were, of a random set of experiences that happen to happen to me. By virtue of the structure of self-awareness the self can reflect on its experiences, order them and come to some kind of patterned view of the world, during which process it also defines itself in relation to the world and to itself.

Fourth: experience is selective. We see much more than we become aware of and we do not see the same object in quite the same way. There are also occasions when we know that we do not want to see or to look at something, or more generally, to go through a certain experience. There is a correlation between the self and the experiences it is likely to be open to. In other words: the relationship between the self and the world as mediated by experience is dialectical in experience, and experiences the world in terms of its self-definition. This is not to say that this is a closed system, though it may be in certain cases, but that we have to conceive of experience as a kind of conversation between self-aware man and his world, a conversation in which man can become more and more aware of both himself and the world and of his relationship with the world.

A fifth point: experience as analyzed here is a process by which *meaning* is established.[4] That is: those objects, persons, or situations of which we become aware and which, therefore, become part of the world we can and must relate to as self-aware humans, acquire by that fact itself meaning, or significance, for the relation of man to himself and to the world. This meaning is not always established or disclosed at the very entrance of a specific awareness into the orbit of self-conscious presence to the world and to himself, and in that sense can remain problematic or create a problem of meaning. Not all experience is necessarily relevant to the problem of the ultimate meaning of life, but even the act of classifying experiences

4. Schütz, *op. cit.,* pp. 72ff.; cf. Luckmann, *The Invisible Religion,* pp. 41ff.

in terms of the frames of reference in which they find meaning is an act by which meaning is established. Even if some fact is classified as meaningless or absurd, this constitutes an establishing of meaning. Experience puts man in the position where he has to make sense out of this world and his own existence. It demands interpretation.

I want to add here that, at least in some usages of the term, this element of interpretation in terms of meaning is part of what is called experience. When we speak of "the Catholic Religious Experience," or "the Eastern Religious Experience" we quite clearly do not simply refer to the religious experience as the primary awareness of the presence of the Sacred. The terms refer to the experience as understood or interpreted. I do not want to raise the question, at this point, whether this use of the term is correct or incorrect. But I do want to point out, taking a more or less phenomenological approach, that this use of the term suggests apparently, the interpretation of what we do experience—that is, actually given in a primary fashion. I presume, at least, that what is called "the Catholic Religious Experience" is not meant to describe a Catholic interpretation of religious experience, but rather the givenness of a Catholic interpretation as part of the mind-set with which Catholics, formed by their religious community, would experience and understand the presence of the Sacred.

We come here to a simple and rather basic fact which throws some light on the concept of the "social setting of experience": The individual self, in its experiential conversation with itself and the world, is also in conversation with the community of man.[5] The process by which meaning is established, including religious or ultimate meaning, is a process that takes place in a community of selves. The self-experience of the individual self is, both in its selectivity and in its ability to articulate itself, dependent on, or at least heavily influenced by, the thought

5. The point is basic to the philosophy of George Mead. See his *Mind, Self and Society* (Chicago: University of Chicago Press, 1934; many subsequent printings). Mead's influence on American sociological theory is tremendous. Berger and Luckmann draw heavily on him. See, e.g., Luckmann, *The Invisible Religion,* pp. 43-45.

patterns and meaning structures that are laid down in the language in which it has learned to think—with all the limitations that every language has.[6]

The "Catholic Religious Experience" the typical ways Catholics interpret their religious experience insofar as the Catholic community has a formative influence on the experiencing self, gives it, on the one hand, the means to interpret its experiences, on the other hand, a principle of selectivity. To the extent that we do not become aware of the structure of the self that comes out of our social involvement, and of the limitations the structure of the self puts upon the openness to the world of experiences, we can consider these limitations as conditioning the primary awareness of the givenness of the world around us. In that sense they are part and parcel of the experience as a complex process. At the same time we have to say that, to the extent that this mind-set becomes part of our self-awareness, the experience leads to a better self-understanding, and thereby to the possibility of transcending it. This process leads, then, to a restructuring of the self in terms of new experiences, notably a new self-experience. The important thing is to see that the conversation between man and world is an open conversation, which allows for a continuous process of reformation and new developments. Transcendence does not mean that man is less involved in the world of being, but rather that in human experience the world becomes available to man as a world in which he is involved. He is given the freedom to interpret and understand it and to act freely in it. Basically this means that man is the bearer of meaning in the world and by virtue of his possibilities also responsible for it.

Experience in Religion [7]

Even if one would, as I am sure one should not, make the affirmation of God's existence the criterion by which to separate religious from irreligious people, or believers from unbelievers,

6. The importance of language is somehow a commonplace in present-day sociological thought, among others, in Talcott Parsons. For a useful and short discussion, see Dewart, *The Foundations of Belief*, pp. 120ff.

7. The literature is indeed enormous. Very interesting from the sociolo-

the question for the human sciences is how to explain religious convictions and attitudes and activities in terms of the human subject.[8] Phrased in this way the question of the definition of religion takes a very different, non-theological turn: we have to understand and define religion in terms of human dynamics. In this perspective, I would propose that we take religion to be the basic motivational, expressive and cognitive structure by which we find and articulate meaning to human life as a whole. That is: religion has to do with convictions and activities that give life meaning or make living a meaningful enterprise. Religious conceptions should explain the meaning of life; religious celebration should give this apprehension of life's meaning an expressive form in self-articulation; religious ethics should provide a way of life that fulfills this apprehension of life's meaning.

I would rather like to insist on this approach: the grounding of religious phenomena as human phenomena in the problem of meaning as their experiential basis. The point is that, even if we have to assert that the fact of human life requires that it be meaningful, this meaning is not given in the structure of human life as it is given to us, as we experience it in primary givenness. It is exactly the structure of self-awareness that is basic to the typical human experience and self-experience, that makes human life problematic. The fact that we rise above our involvement, thereby attaining freedom vis-à-vis the world and our involvement in it, puts us in charge of living our life as more than a natural process —but at the same time makes life itself and

gical point of view is Clifford Geertz, "Religion as a Cultural System," in William A. Lessa and Evon Z. Vogt, *Reader in Comparative Religion*, 2nd rev. ed. (New York: Harper & Row, 1965), pp. 204ff. Cf. also Bellah, "Religious Evolution," in the same volume, pp. 73ff. See also Milton Yinger, *Religion, Society and the Individual* (New York: Macmillan, 1957), pp. 49ff.

8. Cf. Th. M. Steeman, "What Is Wrong with God?," in Michael Taylor, ed., *The Sacred and the Secular* (Englewood Cliffs, N.J.: Prentice-Hall, Inc., 1968), pp. 154ff, and "Psychological and Sociological Aspects of Modern Atheism," in *Concilium*, March, 1967 [Vol. 23: *The Pastoral Approach to Atheism* (Glen Rock, N.J.: Paulist Press)]. In these articles I have explained more fully the sociological approach to the definition of religion. See also my study, *The Study of Atheism* (Rome: IDO-C, 1967).

how we should live it problematic. And religion is exactly the function that deals with this problem: how to give and find meaning to human existence. Religion provides man with an understanding of what has been called the general order of existence, so that he can see the meaning of life and really live it.

Now with respect to the experiential dimension of religion, let me first say that the openness to the Religious Experience in Otto's and James' sense presupposes this problematic nature of the human condition. I, for one, do not see how we could explain the fact that man can have experiences of that kind, and be open to a reality totally different from his own, and find meaning in the intrusion of a Wholly Other into his life, if we do not see this fact in the light of the problematic nature of human existence. Or, in other words, it is the fact that life as given in experience does not make sense, which creates man's openness to a transcendent source of meaning. And it matters little, for the moment, whether this transcendent source of meaning is given in a full-fledged religious peak-experience or in a vague awareness of the kind "there must be something," or as the apprehension of an overriding value to which one can be totally committed. The point is that religious belief and commitment are possible only because man is incomplete, and is given to himself as incomplete.

Thus it follows that the Religious Experience is not the only experiential factor in religion. Also involved is the human self-experience, more specifically man's self-experience as incomplete or man's becoming aware of the problem of the meaning of his life. That is: the human basis for response to and searching for religious meaning is self-experiential in nature. More than that, this self-experience is indeed an integral and constitutive part of the religious attitude as a human attitude. It is precisely insofar as the transcendent source of meaning is adhered to out of the self-experience of man as calling for a meaning structure that is not given in his experience of life as primarily given, that we can say that life becomes truly religious. For it is only then that the transcendent can be experienced as actually giving meaning to life.

We have to push this analysis a bit further. What I have called the problem of meaning is obviously not experienced in the same way by every human being, nor is the experience of incompleteness interpreted in the same way by all cultures. And I submit that the major source of explanation we have for the variety of religious expressions is exactly that the problem of meaning is indeed experienced and interpreted in different ways. Or, to use a slightly different terminology which I take from Max Weber: doctrines of salvation differ because the conceptions of what one has to be saved from are different.[9]

The Social Setting of Experience in Religion

When we try to understand the present religious situation in the West we have to look at it in an historical-comparative perspective, exactly with respect to changes in man's self-experience and self-awareness.[10] That is: modern man is not the same kind of man as, e.g., primitive or archaic man insofar as he conceives of himself differently and relates differently both to himself and to the world. This basic difference can perhaps best be described in terms of a larger degree of self-awareness and self-knowledge and of an increase in rational and scientific knowledge of the world of nature and the ensuing possibility of technological control over the conditions of human life. In fact, this means a larger degree of transcendence of man with respect to his involvement in the cosmos.

Now, I am not willing to say that in the course of history man has been able to change the basic structure of human existence, or the basic problem of life. But I would say that man's perception of his contingency, and as a consequence, the experience of his own powerlessness, has indeed changed. Which then leads to or is related to a different way of experiencing the

9. Cf. Max Weber, *Gesammelte Aufsätze zur Religionssoziologie,* I (Tübingen: J. C. B. Mohr, Paul Siebeck, 1947). This is the fourth edition; the first was in 1920. The essay I am quoting from has been translated under the title, "The Social Psychology of the World Religions," in H. H. Gerth and C. Wright Mills, ed., *From Max Weber* (New York: Oxford University Press, 1958), pp. 267ff. The whole essay is extremely important for the sociological study of religion.

10. The following discussion is heavily influenced by the reading of Bellah's important article, "Religious Evolution," as quoted in note 7 above.

problem of meaning and to a difference in the way in which the transcendent is articulated or symbolized.

The literature about primitive religion [11] suggests that primitive man experienced himself not so much as standing above or over against nature, but rather as someone who had to come to terms with his natural and social environment. The tendency of mythology and ritual is very much to help man acquiesce in his predicament, to attune himself to the natural environment and the social order, and to find peace in the acceptance of what seems to be the natural order of things. The social order, more especially, and the relationship between man and nature are conceived as static, as an unchangeable order once and for all laid down by the Great Founders, *in illo tempore*. There is no place here for real history or development, no place for changing the order of society or the way of life. Man remains involved in the order of things, natural and social. The religious system serves to keep things as they are. When and where man's sense of powerlessness becomes overwhelming, he resorts to magic, to attempts at controlling the sacred forces in order to ascertain his feeling of security in potentially threatening situations. The Sacred, therefore, is perceived as an immanent, natural, but hidden and mysterious force over which man can exercise some kind of influence, thus giving man the possibility to face danger. But if magic serves, on the one hand, to keep man going in situations which without magic might cause despair or loss of nerve, on the other hand, it keeps man exactly where he is: in a state of acceptance of the world as he finds it.

There is, of course, no reason to look down upon primitive religion. That certainly is not the intention of the remarks I made. But this short description should somehow help us to see the gulf that separates the primitive and his religion from our modern self-experience. Life is very much seen as a one-possibility

11. I am relying here very much on Bellah, *ibid.*, and on Stanner, "The Dreaming," in Lessa and Vogt, *op. cit.*, pp. 158ff. Cf. also Emile Durkheim, *The Elementary Forms of the Religious Life* (New York: The Free Press, 1967), translated from the French by J. W. Swain; and Bronislaw Malinowski, *Magic, Science and Religion* (New York: Doubleday, 1948).

thing,[12] to be accepted as it comes. One does not ask too many questions. This is not to say that the problem of life and death, and the question about the why of the natural and social order, do not arise. Rather, they have been taken care of in mythology and ritual. The problem of meaning is not absent, it is answered by saying that this is how things have to be because that is how they are. And this is not so amazing an answer either, when one realizes that primitive societies are indeed very stable, with little social change and little internal history. They persist in time, over a long period, without the experience of history in the sense of change and development.

We get a quite different picture when we look at the Jews of the Old Testament.[13] The social experience of the Jews was one of not having a country of their own, of a traveling people. I don't have to go through the materials again. But I do want to suggest that there is a relationship between this social experience of the Jews as a people and the problem of meaning it creates, and the acceptance of Yahweh as the transcendent Lord of history. What the prophets are saying is, if I may take the freedom to express it in more or less colloquial terms: "Our god is the Lord of History and has his own plans for us. You had become too domesticated anyhow, too much like the others, with your kingship and your temple cultus and your economic prosperity. That is not what we were meant to be. Remember your history. It is the same Yahweh who led Abraham out of Ur of the Chaldeans, and who led you out of Egypt, who is now doing a new thing and asking you to move on."

There is indeed ample evidence that the self-experience of modern man is different, not only from the primitive or even the Jewish, but from the kind of self-experience and self-aware-

12. The term is used by Stanner, *op. cit.*, p. 164.
13. My main reference for this topic is Eric Voegelin, *Israel and Revelation* (Baton Rouge, La.: The University of Louisiana Press, 1969), 3rd ed. Also cf. G. E. Wright, *God Who Acts*, 5th ed. (London: S. C. M. Press, 1960); Bernhard W. Anderson, *Understanding the Old Testament*, 2nd ed. (Englewood Cliffs, N.J.: Prentice-Hall, Inc., 1966); Walther Eichrodt, tr. J. A. Baker, *Theology of the Old Testament*, Vol. I (London: S. C. M. Press, 1961).

ness that is presupposed by most of the Western Christian tradition. I am not saying that the two are necessarily irreconcilable, but the fact of a real and serious gap cannot be denied. It may be difficult to formulate exactly what this gap is but the general awareness is there. There is a widespread rejection of the God of the Christian tradition, the churches are not really speaking to modern man and have lost their power to really influence our culture, there is also the widespread disaffection vis-à-vis the churches among our young people. Basically we have to say that the religious institutions of Western society, the Churches, have become marginal institutions.[14] But it is precisely therefore that an exploration of the modern self-experience and the modern experience of the problem of meaning is important. It is not so much that the self-experience should become normative for the theological enterprise, but that the theological enterprise should be able to speak to the modern self-experience in the light of the Christian tradition, with all the differences of discerning what really is the core of that tradition and what it had to say to modern man.

Perhaps the most pervasive element in the modern self-awareness is man's sense of power and responsibility.[15] We know, in our self-experience, that we are in charge of this world and of our lives, we are able and called upon to take responsibility for the quality of life in the community of man. Of course, we have here an awareness that certain natural conditions have to be fulfilled for human life to be possible on this planet, and in that sense a sense of dependency, but it does not become a matter of respect for the mysterious ways of nature or a feeling of dependence on the gifts of nature. It is much more a concern for *our* environment, our resources—ultimately ourselves. And there is very much an awareness that we have to solve this problem and can solve it—by scientific means. In the religious dimension this means that modern man cannot accept, really and

14. Cf. Luckmann, *The Invisible Religion;* he has summarized the evidence very neatly.

15. This discussion of modern man summarizes the broader statement I gave in the articles quoted in note 8, above. An extended bibliography is given in the IDO-C paper.

wholeheartedly, a God of nature. Basically, I believe, the God of modern man is a God who commissions us to live, who puts us in charge, who demands us to make life worthwhile. Life in this world becomes a sacred duty, to be taken seriously as a God-given task.

The experience of powerlessness is, in a kind of parallel development, increasingly located within man. If powerlessness means the incongruity between what is and what can be and should be, then modern man has overcome his powerlessness vis-à-vis nature, but not vis-à-vis himself. That is: it is the incongruity between what man knows he can and should be and what he in fact is, that constitutes the problem of life. I would think that this is but another way of saying that man knows himself as sinful, as not responding to God's call to build the Holy Community, or to rise to the level of what really should concern him most. What is seen, therefore, as a religious duty, is to combat evil. This may sound familiar to people steeped in the tradition of Western Christianity, but I think there are some changes in this area too. First of all, it would seem that modern man is little salvation-minded, in the sense of relying easily on God's forgiveness. Overcoming evil is not to wait upon God's grace, nor is the primary concern one's soul. Overcoming evil is to do good, to live the good life, to be honest. Modern man is pragmatic in this respect: he wants to see the fruits of the religious commitment, and the test put to the Christian Church is whether or not it is able to promote the good life. Life is to be lived in this world, not toward a hidden beyond that may serve as an alibi for serious involvement in this world. Religious practices which do not have relevance to man's life are suspect. More important perhaps, because more novel, is that the experience of incongruity is more and more located in the social realm. We know that our social arrangements are below standard and that something can and should be done about it. We can and should build a holier community than we have. I emphasize this because it seems to characterize very much the present scene. I trace the phenomenon back to Marx. It is, at any rate, very much at work in the labor movement which we can hardly separate from the Marxist protest. And it is no sheer coincidence that in both the feminist movement and in the present young generation Marxism is claimed to be the philosophy behind it.[16] If sometimes, much to the displeasure of the social scientist, the knowledge of what Marxism is about is rather deficient among our young protesters, it cannot be denied that there is at least a basic affinity between the experiences that are at the basis of these three movements: the protest against a society that does not really make the welfare of all people, in equality and justice, its basic concern. And it is no wonder that to many of our young this society just does not make sense. It is not only incongruous, it becomes the embodiment of evil. And evil has to be fought.

These short remarks sum up, more or less, what I think is most central to the modern self-experience. Man in charge of and responsible for the welfare of the human community had taken it upon himself, as a sacred duty, to combat evil. It is in this area that he most forcefully experiences the limitations of his finite existence, but at the same time sees the challenge to his creativity. It is in this area also that modern man most clearly differs from his ancestors. Therefore, it is in this area too that we find modern man estranged from the religious tradition of the West, which, at least up till very recently, maintained a concept of God that was more likely to create an alibi for man's own responsibility or to presuppose a self-conception of man that shortened man's self-experience as responsible.

16. I should add the black movement as another case of this awareness of social evil. That I do not mention it in the text is because I do not see as clearly a connection with Marxism.

4 Revelation and Religious Experience

In speaking of the notion of revelation in past decades and centuries, great stress was laid on the verbal communication and the concept. The intellect was primary, and according to Vatican I, revealed truths were those which surpassed the created intellect.[1] At times it seemed the traditional view would almost look upon public revelation as a series of infusions of revealed concepts given by God from time to time in human history. No point of contact was indicated between God and man, and the guarantee of the validity of these conceptual revelations was to be found in external signs and miracles. It is therefore necessary to delve deeper to discover the source of revelation. In other words, how exactly does God make himself known? We wish to search for the point of contact between God and man, that zone where infinite Mystery touches a finite creature who somehow is able to be receptive to that touch. Of course, one possible view is that there is no contact point between God and man and therefore revelation is impossible.

Some attempts at providing an answer to the possibility of revelation are unacceptable. For example, to stress the role of man too far might imply that revelation is what man on his own can know unaided about God and therefore is basically a human creation.[2] To paraphrase Barth, such an approach is

1. See Karl Rahner, "The Concept of Mystery in Catholic Theology," *Theological Investigations,* trans. by Kevin Smyth, (Baltimore: Helicon Press, 1966), Vol. IV, pp. 39-41.
2. See Karl Rahner, *Hearers of the Word,* trans. by Michael Richards, (New York: Herder and Herder, 1969), p. 113.

to speak about God by speaking about man with a loud voice. On the other hand, an approach that would stress the transcendence of God too much will cause difficulties in explaining how God and man ever do encounter each other. Karl Barth, for example, preserves the mystery and transcendence of God, but it seems to me that he does not offer an adequate explanation of how humans can verify that it is God who is speaking when revelation is claimed to have occurred, since according to Barth there is no place in man as man that is congenial to God's revelation.

I shall attempt to preserve the transcendence of God and yet speak of a point of contact between God and man. This will be done by grounding revelation in religious experience. I am using the term religious experience in a generic sense, namely, any pre-cognitive and therefore unthematic and unreflected awareness of absolute transcendence in a graced situation. Such an approach is justified since it would seem that post-Kantian philosophical and theological thought, with its stress on the self-constituting subject, is agreed that the original knowledge that man has of God is not in the form of objectified concepts but is rather non-objective. For example, Schleiermacher speaks of the "whence" of absolute dependence. Although the later Heidegger speaks about Being rather than God, he announces the end of metaphysics and opts for primal language to disclose Being. Bultmann rejects any mythological representation of God because he sees it as endangering God's absolute transcendence. For him, we must believe in God in spite of appearances.[3] Tillich declared that the only literal statement that we can make about God is that all religious statements about God are symbolic. Karl Rahner speaks about the "whither" of our pre-cognition of transcendence, and Bernard Lonergan declares that God exists because "absolute intelligibility exists." It will be my contention that if the original experience[4] of God is non-objective, then

3. See Rudolf Bultmann, *Kerygma and Myth*, trans. by Reginald Fuller, (New York: Harper and Row, 1961), pp. 210-211.

4. It is necessary to note that the term "experience" when used here does not refer to emotional experience or even to the later stages of religious experience. Rather we are speaking of that point of pre-cognitive

it must be on a level of experience different from that of reason, and possibly at the level of the pre-cognitive. Once we have indicated that the original experience of God is pre-cognitive, then we will try to show that the original experience of God in a graced situation is also pre-cognitive. And therefore, the source of revelation as such is religious experience. Conceptual revelation is a thematization and articulation of this original religious experience. In developing this approach, we will rely heavily on the writings of Karl Rahner.

In order to understand what Rahner means by the pre-cognition of the absolute, I shall briefly describe his theory of knowledge. Man is spirit in the world. Knowing is not a going out of the knower to the object, not some contact with the object outside of the knower, but a being-present-to-himself of the knower, which constitutes his subjectivity. The intelligible species is a determination of the knower within himself. Rahner sees abstraction as the liberation of the species from the phantasm and as the act universalizing the species so as to be found possibly in an infinite number of individuating subjects. Abstraction makes possible the objectification of the datum of sense experience. But in order to grasp and universalize a potential object of knowledge, man must have an absolute horizon against which to contrast the potential object of knowledge, as limited and hence capable of repetition in an infinite number of singulars. Since this is a horizon of knowledge, it is pre-apprehended. Rahner reasons, especially, by analyzing the implications of judgment, that man's pre-apprehension of an absolute horizon is in reality a pre-apprehension of absolute Being.[5] In every judgment a universal *esse* is simultaneously grasped in a pre-apprehension. Writing in *Hearers of the Word,* he says ". . . the *affirmation* of actual finitude of an existent, requires, as condition for its possibility, the affirmation of the existence of an *esse absolutum.* . . .[6] "Every statement is a statement about some spe-

---

awareness which is the source of all subsequent revelatory and religious experiences.

5. Karl Rahner, *Spirit in the World,* trans. by William Dych (New York: Herder and Herder, 1968), pp. 117ff.

6. Rahner, *Hearers,* p. 64.

cific existent thing and is made against the background of a
previous although implicit knowledge of being in general."[7]
In his article on the "Concept of Mystery . . . " Rahner describes
the human spirit as dynamically pushing beyond the object of
knowledge to an "anticipatory grasp of the absolute."[8]

The pre-concept is not an *a priori* knowledge of an object
but the *a priori* horizon of knowledge.[9] Rahner goes on to say
that this absolute is indescribable because it is non-objectivated
and is in a "region beyond all categories" not even grasped by
reflection. However, it is because of this transcendental horizon
that categorical knowledge is possible. Therefore, this "whither"
of transcendence, as Rahner calls it, is distant and beyond our
grasp. It is to this "whither" of transcendence that Rahner gives
the name God. He says:

> . . . it is also obvious that the most primordial, underivative
> knowledge of God, which is the basis of all other knowledge
> of God, is given in the experience of transcendence, insofar
> as it contains, implicitly and unobjectivatedly, but irrecusably
> and inevitably, the "Whither" of transcendence, which we
> call God.[10]

Interestingly, Rahner seems to prefer "Whither" to the term
"God," since he notes that to use an objective word for God
might imply that God is known objectively whereas the whole
point is that God is experienced in the transcendence that is
prior and concomitant to the knowledge of finite concepts. The
"whither" of transcendence is in no way an object. Rahner goes
on to say that the only way to speak accurately of God is not
in finite concepts but by continually referring to the infinite
transcendence which delimits concepts. Also, merely to remove
the limits from finite concepts gives us only a negative knowledge
of God and does not tell us what infinite means in a positive
sense.[11]

7. *Ibid.*, p. 35.
8. Rahner, "Concept of Mystery . . . ," p. 42.
9. Rahner, *Hearers*, p. 143.
10. Rahner, "Concept of Mystery . . . ," pp. 49-50.
11. *Ibid.*, p. 50.

We must now consider whether this philosophical basis can serve to shed light on how revelation takes place. As we have mentioned, when speaking of the mysteries of revelation, too often we apply the term "mystery" to statements or propositions rather than to the reality itself. Overstressing the role of the intellect, we sometimes mean by mystery that which is mysterious to reason. We might ask whether this is not too narrow and superficial a notion. Rahner asks if it is not possible that a primordial unity of the spirit exists prior to the division of faculties into intellect and will, and whether perhaps it is to this primordial unity that the Divine Mystery is directed and related.[12] He answers his own question by stating that since man is one spirit and since his intellect and will are faculties of the one spirit, this one spirit must have an original relationship to itself and to absolute being—there must be "a basic act, whose components are the interrelated and independent acts of knowing and willing, of insight and love. . . ."[13] In another place, he speaks about the state of being where "reality and one's consciousness of reality are still unseparated from each other. . . ."[14]

Writing in *Hearers of the Word,* Rahner states very clearly that he is seeking the place of encounter between man and God who may possibly reveal himself, and that this place is the transcendence of man in its specifically *human* character.[15] Revelation takes place in man's pre-cognition of absolute transcendence. It is this point which is elevated by grace and divinized. Man's horizon of knowledge and freedom become graced. Rahner states:

> And that grace-given fundamental subjective attitude of man, which is directed towards the God of triune life, can quite definitely be regarded as a word-revelation, provided the notion of word is not reduced to that of a phonetic utterance. . . .[16]

12. *Ibid.,* p. 38.
13. *Ibid.,* pp. 42-43.
14. Karl Rahner, "Dogmatic Reflections on the Knowledge and Self-Consciousness of Christ," *Theological Investigations,* trans. by Karl H. Kruger (Baltimore: Helicon, 1966), Vol. V, pp. 208-209.
15. Rahner, *Hearers,* p. 120.
16. Karl Rahner and Joseph Ratzinger, *Revelation and Tradition,*

Rahner also refers to the scholastic notion of formal and material object. It is the material objects that are immediately known under the *ratio* of the formal object. Therefore, in revelation the formal object, the horizon within which individual objects are distinguished and known is changed by grace. Just as this horizon in a natural state cannot be reflected upon immediately, neither can the horizon in a graced state. This revelation of the divine is not, then, a communication of concepts and propositions. "It is, however, a revelation in the sense of a change of consciousness ... which originates from a free personal self-communication of God in grace." Also, just as the natural horizon constitutes the concepts and propositions within it, so the graced horizon constitutes the concepts and propositions of expressed revelation.[17]

We can also speak of God as the ground of the revelation which takes place in man. For example, when explaining God's activity in evolution we say that he is not a finite cause along side of other causes but is the transcendent ground of the dynamic of creative evolution. The same can be said of God's action in revelation since here we are again speaking of a mutual act of God and creature.[18] If this be the case, we cannot view the events of revelation and their subsequent expression as disparate irruptions of God in the normal course of human history. We will note later that in view of the universal salvific will of God, we must admit that all human beings are addressed by revelation in the pre-cognitive experience of transcendence. Question may arise as to how public revelation is to be distinguished from general private revelation. Would it be stretching our analogy to God's activity in creative evolution too far to say that just as leaps take place from species to species and even in the conception of every human being, and just as these leaps are accounted for by a more intense activity on both the part of creatures as secondary causes, and on the part of God as first cause, so the same process takes place in public revelation?

trans. by W. J. O'Hara, (New York: Herder and Herder, 1966), p. 16.

17. Karl Rahner, "History of the World and Salvation History," *Theological Investigations,* Vol. V, pp. 103-104.

18. Rahner, *Revelation and Tradition,* p. 12.

Note, however, that in this perspective, public revelation is not due to arbitrary interventions of God but to a complex of circumstances where man must play a crucial part. Just as God encourages nature to take its course, so he encourages human history and development to provide the atmosphere for the appearance and surfacing of public revelation. To take this position is not to limit the freedom of God, but rather to view Divine freedom as taking into consideration the whole cosmic plan, freely chosen by God himself.

It is not enough to speak of the graced self-communication of God to man's transcendence; it must also be received by man. Man's subjectivity is also elevated by grace. In other words, for Rahner, the self-communication of God would be synonymous with uncreated grace, and the disposition of man to be receptive to it, to be hearer of the word, would be synonymous with created grace. The difference in man's condition before and after the event of grace is summarized by Rahner in. this way:

The contrast [grace as opposed to pre-grace] is between immediate sight of the mystery itself and the merely indirect presence of the mystery after the manner of the distant and aloof. Grace does not imply the promise and beginning of the elimination of mystery, which is not eliminated by its proximity, but really presented as mystery.... Grace and beatific vision can only be understood as the possibility and the reality respectively of the immediate presence of the holy mystery as such.[19]

In this approach faith takes on a different perspective. Traditional theology has stressed the authority of God as the formal object or motive of faith. However, this expressed authority of God was mediated through human words and therefore was determined by the horizon of human knowledge. The question then is how to preserve the Word of God as truly divine. Therefore, if we view the original divine self-communication as taking place on the level of the transcendent horizon itself, and the horizon as the limit of the human spirit itself, then the problem

19. Rahner, "The Concept of Mystery . . . ," p. 55.

of the motive of faith disappears.[20] Therefore, the original act
of faith takes place at the point where faith and the reception
of revelation still form a unity. Man's graced transcendence is
constituted by God's self-communication. He accepts this constitution in the radical freedom of faith although this may as yet
be quite unsystematic. The act of faith is directed immediately
without the mediation of words to uncreated grace, to the Trinity.
Rahner says that one believes "into God."

Since propositions cannot of their nature give an adequate
presentation of the Divine Mystery, faith must break through
these propositions. Therefore, the language of revelation must
of necessity have a secondary role. Both kerygma and dogmatic
statements provide a means of experiencing being beyond them.
In this sense, Rahner claims that explicit faith lives by implicit
faith, and not merely vice versa.[21]

A very important implication from all the above is that the
kerygma is primarily addressed not to the intellect of man
but to his experience of transcendence which is already divinized by grace and joined to the reality of God—to that experience
of transcendence which experiences the depths of love and death
along with the absolute divine mystery. Such a view is reminis-
cent of Schleiermacher's view of Christian preaching. He says
that such preaching must always be a testimony to one's own
experience, which shall arouse in others the desire to have the
same experience. In his view, the whole mark of Christ himself
was to communicate his self-consciousness by preaching.[22]

A possible option (although certainly only a possibility)
would be to put aside conceptual language as a vehicle of communicating religious experience and to turn to symbol and image.
The symbol would be an attempt to represent the whole of transcendence. The role of these symbols would be not so much
to give knowledge as to evoke a religious experience in the
hearer similar to the one had by the person formulating the

20. Rahner, *Revelation and Tradition,* p. 23.
21. Rahner, "Dogmatic Notes on 'Ecclesiological Piety,'" *Theological
Investigations,* Vol. V, p. 345.
22. Frederich Schleiermacher, *The Christian Faith,* trans. by H. R.
Mackintosh and J. S. Stewart, (New York: Harper and Row, 1963),
Vol. I, pp. 69, 77.

symbol. The prophet experiences the Divine and tries to express this in language. What is important to others is that through this language they are able to experience the Divine the same way that the prophet experienced it. Otherwise we are dealing with merely descriptive finite words and narrations which may be of passing interest but are not the opening to Divinity. The hearer must try to re-enact the original experience of the prophet, he must put himself in the position of the prophet, or for the Christian in the position of Christ, when Christ experienced Divinity. The evocative words of the prophets are preserved in the sacred books. A religious community is a group of members who try to share and re-enact the same religious experiences.[23]

To sum up this section we may say that the actual event of revelation takes place deep within the person and this applies both to the prophet and the ordinary layman. Every conceptual objectification is secondary in comparison, although it may be accepted later as part of public revelation. An analogous case is that of the mystic. Rahner states:

". . . A clear distinction must be made in mystical experience between the actual experience of God in the core of the person and the conceptual communication, interpretation and reflex objectification of that experience which the mystic undertakes for himself and then also for others with the aid of concepts, means of understanding, etc. available to him from elsewhere. . . ."

". . . it is nevertheless quite justifiable to conceive the actual and original central experience of the original bearers of revelation in the original event of revelation analogously to this central mystical experience."[24]

Granting that this original revelation is unthematic, the next point of consideration is: what exactly is the content of this

23. See Herbert Richardson, "Three Myths of Transcendence," in *Transcendence*, edited by H. W. Richardson and D. R. Cutler, (Boston: Beacon Press, 1969), pp. 101-104.

24. Karl Rahner, "Theology in the New Testament," *Theological Investigations*, Vol. V, p. 40.

original revelation? Rahner claims that there are only three mysteries in Christianity, if we are to apply the term mystery in the strictest sense—these are the Trinity, Incarnation, and grace and glory. However, the revelation of these three mysteries reduces itself to one theme, namely, that we not only have a negative knowledge of God existing in distant aloofness and unapproachableness, but that God is present in absolute and radical proximity. We can portray how these three mysteries express the one reality of radical proximity in the following way: God the Father as origin has radically imparted to us His Logos and Spirit as seen in Christ, and thus we being intimately joined to the Trinity respond in transformed knowledge and love.[25] If one accepts that all Christian mysteries can be summarized in the one theme of radical proximity of the Divine, it is not too difficult to reconcile this theme of radical proximity with man's unthematic consciousness. The real question though is whether the pre-cognitive awareness of Divine proximity does in fact result in the articulation of these three mysteries. Since these mysteries are already in possession, it is difficult to verify the Rahnerian thesis. However, this thesis does provide us with a point of contact between God and man, and shows us that these articulated mysteries are only feeble attempts to touch the Divine Reality.

In spite of our viewing of the conceptual expression of revelation as secondary, transcendental revelation must be objectified in historical categories. This is true because even on the philosophical level the transcendent horizon is manifested only concomitantly with the knowledge of individual objects. This is the only way the human spirit can understand itself and communicate with others. Also, objective propositions are needed if revelation is "to become the principle of man's concrete behavior in his objective reflex consciousness. . . ."[26] Since man is spirit in the world, he must rely on appearances for knowledge, and appearances put man in history. Therefore the objectified expression of revelation must also take place in history.

25. Rahner, "The Concept of Mystery . . . ," p. 72.
26. Karl Rahner, *Theological Dictionary,* trans. by Richard Strachan, (New York: Herder and Herder, 1965), pp. 409-411.

In other words, the importance of objectified revelation is two-fold. First, while man's transcendental horizon is essential to his make-up, he is only a being-present-to-himself through objective knowledge. His consciousness becomes awareness only through the thematization of reflection. Second, man can only fulfill himself by going out to others and recovering himself. The experience of others communicated to him is essential. If he is to achieve a deep religious experience, then, he must rely on the religious experience of others as made known to him. The revealed proposition therefore can either stimulate and guide him to look into himself and discover God within, or to show him that he has truly discovered God, or to help him articulate to himself and to others the event he has experienced.

Public revelation can refer to that series of the best and most original articulations of the human spirit of the Divine Mystery in grace. Christ experienced the fullest and ultimate event of encounter with the Trinity and by articulating this experience through the action of God within him is the prophet par excellence. The Christian Church is the community where the experience of Christ continues to be relived by the power of the Spirit and is transmitted to others. The New Testament is the original translation of the religious experience of the primitive Christian community.

A confirmation of our thesis that revelation is primarily precognitive and that verbal revelation is a means to an end can be seen in the teaching on the anonymous Christian. Whether one follows the view of Rahner or the traditional theological view on baptism of desire, the fact remains that the act of faith of the non-Christian is in the Triune God of revelation and not in the God of reason. It is more likely that this revelation is an internal affair rather than some external private revelation as some have held in the past. Nor is an infused illumination likely since this would imply almost continuous interruptions of God in the world since non-Christians constitute the majority of the world's population.

As an example of how the teaching on the anonymous Christian supports our position, we will again turn to Rahner. In view of the universal salvific will of God and man's supernatural destiny intended from the beginning, we should hold that man has lived in a graced situation from the start. Therefore, the "whither" of man's transcendence has always been the Divine self-communication of the Trinity. For the Christian, this un-thematic consciousness of God has been made explicit by the interpretation of the Gospel. For the non-Christian, it remains unreflexive. The non-Christian becomes an anonymous Christian by assenting to this transcendence as it expresses itself in his daily life—for example, through unselfish love and fidelity to his goals. Missionary preaching, therefore, can strike a harmonious response in the anonymous Christian since it is the expression in objective concepts of what he has already experienced within the depths of his being.

Rahner even extends the possibility of internal revelation to the atheist. He claims that one can have a transcendental experience of the Divine and assent to it in faith, and yet in-correctly objectify and interpret it. The result is an atheism on the level of categorical reflection co-existing with a transcen-dental theism.[27] It might be noted that this explanation shows very clearly the primary position Rahner gives to internal reve-lation and the secondary role given to categorical revelation. In fact, it is interesting that Rahner goes on to say that such atheism should not be approached by the Christian with cate-gorical concepts but by making the atheist aware "of his own transcendental experience of God by a kind of 'mystagogy.'"[28]

Finally, a model of how revelation is grounded in religious experience is found in the knowledge of Christ as a result of the Hypostatic Union. Rather than viewing the Beatific Vision in Christ as a supplement to the Hypostatic Union, it can be under-stood as the very point of contact. Therefore, the basis for the union itself would be the Beatific Vision in the human spirit of Christ. Because of this contact the human nature of Christ is divinized. However, the term vision is misleading and the Divine Mystery will always remain Incomprehensible Mystery to the created finite mind of Christ. According to our thesis, God's total self-communication to Christ was that of his radical

27. Karl Rahner, "Atheism and Implicit Christianity," *Theology Digest* (February, 1968), p. 50.

28. *Ibid.*, p. 52.

proximity. Therefore, in Christ the Divine Presence was experienced in his pre-cognitive transcendent horizon. All of Christ's actions would then be informed by this graced horizon. In such a view, the preaching of Christ would be an objectification and articulation of this primal experience. Since the presence of the Divine Mystery was most intimate and proximate in Christ, it is logical that his expressed revelation would be the most extensive and complete.

The fact that Christ's external revelation is gradual is also understandable. A man must grow and mature in the community of others before he can fully recover himself and be able to articulate his transcendental experience. It takes time to carry out a thematization of the unobjectified experience.

To summarize briefly: our thesis has been that in order to speak about Divine revelation, it is first necessary to speak of a point of contact. We have taken as our philosophical basis Rahner's thesis of pre-cognitive experience of transcendence and the "whither" of transcendence. In view of God's universal salvific will, we have claimed that this "whither" is none other than uncreated grace and the pre-cognitive horizon of man is disposed to receive the Triune God through created grace. Therefore, the point of contact for revelation is established since grace and revelation become one experience and faith is the response. The purpose of the kerygma is to evoke this religious experience in others and to articulate and confirm that the experience has taken place. Conceptual revelation plays a role second in importance albeit indispensable since the human spirit can communicate and live only by concepts. Such a thesis in no way diminishes the life of Christ and its impact on men, nor does it question the role of the Christian community. Rather, it has been our purpose to seek the origins of revelation and religious experience, and we have pointed out that man's pre-cognitive awareness of God can never be sought in itself but is concomitant with the ordinary and extraordinary experiences of man.

5   The Experience of Self as the Beginning of Systematic Theology

For the purpose of this chapter and without prejudging its wider applicability, I accept H. Ott's definition of systematic theology as reflection upon the hermeneutical in theology as a whole.[1] This definition considers;

(1) that theology, at least in the present situation, is hermeneutical from exegesis to preaching. This means it considers both the understandability of certain specific contents and the understandability of the witness to these contents;

(2) that there are things that are not said in individual texts or dogmas but rather said through their totality and to see and say them is the task of systematic theology.

For example, when Rahner says that Catholicism prohibits only one thing, the denial of *homo capax infiniti,* it is the voice of systematic theology coming through. This stand excludes the rigid unchangeability of dogmas; the demand of the understandability of both the *extra ecclesiam non est salus* and the presence of efficacious grace outside of the Church transformed the meaning of the former with the introduction of the unthematic or prepredicative acceptance of Revelation and of the anonymous Christian.

The first thesis maintains that the actual self-experience of the subject, especially in its transcending movement, is capable to give experiential anchorage and meaning to the organizing concepts of theology. In another formulation: we gain our

1. Heinrich Ott, "What is Systematic Theology?" in *New Frontiers in Theology,* Vol. I, ed. by James M. Robinson and John B. Cobb, Jr. (New York: Harper & Row, 1963), pp. 76-111.

systematic concepts by extrapolation and intensification of notions culled from self-experience and which for the sake of understandability, we frequently need to refer back to their origin. This occurs even in case of such concepts as omnipotence which has reached almost mathematical purity. This procedure is going to be exemplified by referring to the systems of Rahner and Macquarrie.

The second thesis is concerned with the specific difficulties of this procedure within the British-American tradition and I will suggest some strategy to meet them. It is here I have in mind those students who are exposed to logical empiricism, to a strong behavioristic psychology, and a marked positivistic sociology. Such courses are becoming more and more frequent in the Catholic colleges.

First, it seems to be revelant and advantageous to give a short survey of those efforts which, without actually applying the notion of self in theology, busy themselves with the groundwork and try to show the possibility of theology and metaphysics exactly through the analysis of self.

The continental theologians too easily assume that the life of the self cannot be explained within the horizon of the world— that it demands different categories than were used, or ever will be used, in science. For the English speaking theologian and metaphysician, the Humean tradition, the long shadow of Professor Ryle, the success of the neo-behavioristic psychology, the projected efficiency of cybernetic simulations, prohibit such optimism.

In many essays Ian Ramsey showed that the odd logic of the first person "I" language is parallel to the God-language, and, in principle, is impervious to the scientific method.[2] (See also Poteat.[3]) Others prefer to point out the parallelism between the knowledge of the other self and the knowledge of God. Alvin Plantinga, relying on the analogical knowledge of the other

2. Ian Ramsey, ed., *Biology and Personality: A Symposium* (New York: Barnes and Noble, 1965), pp. 174-206.

3. William H. Poteat, "God and the 'Private I'" in *New Essays on Religious Language,* ed. Dallas H. High (New York: Oxford University Press, 1965), pp. 127-137.

minds [4] and H. P. Owen espousing the direct though mediated knowledge of other selves find the structure of the theological discourse similar to the interpersonal discourse.[5] Owen also takes advantage of the later writings of A. J. Ayer—a really unexpected ally. S. Strasser convincingly takes out the self, i.e., "soul," from the jurisdiction of empirical psychology and so makes the theological avenues open and clear.[6] J. Wild, besides giving an excellent undergraduate introduction and sensitization to the problem of self, makes clear the difference between the dynamism of desires and needs on one hand, and the self-transcendence of the other hand.[7] Before Christian theology consciously turned to self as hermeneutical starting point, the English speaking atheists and agnostics instinctively felt the role of the self for metaphysics and theology. Therefore, their efforts to discredit theology and metaphysics went hand in hand with the reduction of self to an accidentally concatenated mental phenomenon or to a categorical mistake. The philosopher-apologetical defense of the reality of self is a special task for us and one not faced by the transcendental or existential theology of Europe.

Due to its simpler and more compact form, the system of Macquarrie, though later in time and in some respects (perhaps only for encouragement—indebted to Rahner) offers sharper exemplification of the role of self. The maximum of selfhood is equivalent with christhood; it is in the Christology that anthropology most strikingly turns into theology. (Note: for Rahner, the maximum of self-transcendence is the maximum of God's self-communication.) The self is "existence," i.e., it stands out from the rest of creation due to its concern for what it is and that it is. The *presence to oneself* is differently exploited by Rahner and Macquarrie. For Rahner the level of self-possession sets the particular being in the hierarchy of beings; the analogy

4. Alvin Plantinga, *God and Other Minds* (Ithaca, New York: Cornell University Press, 1965), pp. 187-272.

5. H. P. Owen, *The Christian Knowledge of God* (London: Athlone Press, 1969), pp. 123-153.

6. Stephen Strasser, *The Soul in Metaphysical and Empirical Psychology* (Pittsburgh: Duquesne University Press, 1962).

7. John Wild, *Existence and the World of Freedom* (Englewood Cliffs, New Jersey: Prentice-Hall, 1963), pp. 199-218.

of being appears an analogy of self-possession. Consequently, the notion of freedom becomes very central.

Macquarrie makes the relation to oneself the basis of the experience of responsibility for one's own existence. Man finds himself in charge of a task he cannot master, but unless being grants what it commands it does not make sense. Thus, the very fundamental dynamism of self forces a choice of faith or unfaith. The demands emerging from self-transcendence always outstrip the actual resources. The alternatives are clearly set: either I call this situation absurd and the subjectivity useless passion as Sartre did, or I consent to the dynamism of the self with trust that sooner or later there must be resources from 'outside,' in one or other context, I then have faith. The concern with what I am and what I am responsible for is completed with the concern that I am and that I may not be. This ontological anxiety, the object of which is nothingness, evokes the affirmation of Being.

The ontological analysis, since the experiential-existential approach is insufficient here, exhibits being as letting be, the meaning of which is more active than the linguistic formula suggests — something like enabling to be. The self stretches towards the mysterious reality that lets it be—lets things be at all—and finds its most authentic mode of existence in letting, enabling another to be in self-giving love. The hierarchy of being is arranged according to the level of letting-be. The source of reality of particular beings, the letting-be, is called God if apprehended as holy. In Christ, the self-giving, letting others be, reaches its peak. Even death is affirmed as life, i.e., being. The acceptance of limitations of the historical context, in existential terminology: facticity (cf. *kenosis*), did not lessen his commitment to Being, i.e., possibilities, future, 'existence.' The self-hood becomes christhood on the cross by the affirmation of death as the absolute form of letting-be. We can see that the identification of the meaning of Being with letting-be involves risk even for God; the presence of evil is not an anomaly. The categories of self-experience—not in an introspective isolation, but those already involved in the world—are detectable in Trinitology too. The Father is the ultimate energy or act of letting-be (cf. Rahner's "unoriginate origin of plenitude of being and life, communicated yet undiminished"). The Son is the "expressive"

Being or the Logos expressing Being in the beings (cf. Rahner's "God's historical expressibility"). The Spirit is the "unitive" being, uniting beings to Being (cf. Rahner's "yearning and welcoming love"). These are evidently 'analogical projections,' intensified and purified from the dynamism of the self. The attributes of God are also reinterpreted in terms of religious experience. Omnipotence means that God is the horizon and also the source of all possibilities.[8] Besides the criticism the dogmatic theologian is likely to make—the suspicion of Adoptianism, despite Macquarrie's protest, the achieved christhood and sinlessness, the 'risk' involved in creation—there is a more fundamental problem to face especially in the present hermeneutical situation. How can we show that what our concepts mean is not exclusively the self, my own self? Should we be contented with saying that the vague prepredicative synthetic *a priori* of the Self recognizes its confirmation and correction in the historical Revelation? Or should we resume the epistemological struggle for the transition from the existential-ontological level to that of the metaphysical, speculative-theological level? Can we say meaningful things about non-experienceable realities on the basis of existential experience?[9] (Cf. also, B. Lonergan[10]).

Rahner refers to self (according to the different aspect it is called spirit, person, *reditio subjecti completa in seipsum*, transcendental subject) as a "drive," a motion open to all being and in final analysis to God. Such radical openness is due to its anticipatory grasp, *excessus* as Vorgriff terms it, which reaches farther than the boundaries of the particular, and exactly for this reason, perceives it as object as limited. So far it is quite traditional.

The next step is central to Rahner's systematic theology. The self-transcendence *is* God's self-communication, self-giving. What appears as ever greater, ever more demanding horizon, mystery in the experience of self-transcendence, is proposed in the Reve-

8. John Macquarrie, *Principles of Christian Theology* (New York: Scribner, 1966), esp. pp. 54-74, 97-105, 174-193, 272-279.

9. W. Norris Clark, "The Self as Source of Meaning in Metaphysics," *Review of Metaphysics* XXI (June, 1968), pp. 598-614.

10. Bernard Lonergan, *The Subject* (Milwaukee: Marquette University Press, 1968), pp. 32, 33.

lation as God's self-communication. Consequently, pure human nature actually does not exist since self-communication represents "grace" in one or other level. Human nature is abstraction from the concrete existence which is in an incipient sense already graced, i.e., the supernatural existential. The supernatural existential is not merely openness to the infinite God, but to his historical manifestation.

Since self is a precondition of even the simplest human perception, it is not the result of achievement as in Macquarrie. The consent to this movement of self-transcendence is an acceptance of God even preconceptually. Self-transcendence is also self-performance. The pragmatic concern in objects and deeds is animated by the concern in self-performance. I am interested in the morally good result on the basis of being concerned with my being good. The feed-back of the deed is as important, if not more so, than the object of the deed.

Furthermore, the self is *reditio subjecti in seipsum,* a retro-active act, not merely a reflective act. This means that when the self-transcendence reaches the boundary of a particular, it falls back upon itself, feeding back so to speak. Therefore before my act returns to me it has been modified and restructured by what is other. Man, in his self-transcendence, never fully achieves what he intends to be. Both his nature and the world have their structures in which, and through which, man disposes of himself.

The juridical, extrinsicist interpretation of salvation is rejected and salvation is reinterpreted in the terms of continuous ontological self-determination. The Christian proposition that man's salvation or damnation depends on the free decision makes sense only if freedom coincides with man's substantial ground, if it disposes the very core of person. Freedom is self-transcendence. Man does not have freedom, he is his own freedom. The ontological freedom does not operate intermittently. It cannot be under constraint as the freedom of choice. It reacts to constraints precisely because subjectivity always has relation to what it is not. Since my freedom is I myself, I cannot take a real distance from it, not even in reflection. One cannot know his salvation or damnation, and ambiguity cannot be taken out from moral judgments.

Some theological consequences are the following:

1. Since self is towardness, openness to God as horizon, God remains mystery even in heaven. His self-giving is the movement of the self. If the beatific vision were to mean the end of the mystery of God, there would be no further motion of the self which is tantamount to say that there would be no self at all. (Cf. in the oriental systems: the possession of the absolute is the extinction of the self.) The structure of love admits fulfillment and still desires to move ahead. Besides, only mystery can be loved. The known can only be appreciated. Mystery, therefore, is not something that can be eliminated.

2. The greatest possible human self-transcendence is God's greatest self-communication. By this, the hypostatic union gains partial reinterpretation and conceptual enrichment. In his maximal self-giving God becomes man. Both 'becomes' and 'man' are to be taken literally. God not only loves man, but also loves to be man besides remaining God. The divinity of Christ is the humanity of God. In Rahner's system it is more consistent to say that God is man (i.e., non-god) besides remaining God than to say Christ (=man) is God (beside remaining man). Rahner never states this as sharply, but it follows and explains his very understanding and mild criticism concerning panentheism.

3. Rahner applies the category of self-transcendence to the whole gamut of creation. Matter transcends itself (in evolution). Spirit is the self-transcendence of matter become present to itself, conscious of itself, disposing itself, self-possession of the transcendence of matter. Consequently, there cannot be anything such as disembodied, dematerialized soul. Since even the self-transcendence of matter (evolution) is self-communication of God, the causality of God must be seen as inner moment of the material creation though not "part" of it. The concept of "quasi-formal" causality (very roughly: catalytic causality) is to be extended in an attenuated version to the subpersonal region of reality.

A number of felicitous solutions of Rahner depend on the distinction between thematic and unthematic knowledge. The salvation of the non-Christian, importance and rank of pagan religions, the consciousness of Christ and so on are examples of this. This distinction also is rooted in the dynamism of self. Prior to affirmation and negation there is the questioning. Questioning entails not only the lack of knowledge but also a vague, indistinct knowledge of what I am making the question about. The total lack of could not even question.

Questioning means expecting answer. The questions that arise from one's experience of self-transcendence are answered in the historical Revelation. The transcendental subject recognizes the answers in the categorically explicit events of salvation history. Though such event-answers cannot be analyzed out from the nature of the questioning self-transcendence, when they occur they can be recognized as such.

So man is the hearer of the word. The scholastic *objectum formale* turned into a dynamic principle of self that keeps us moving in ever greater appropriation of being and value.

Metz's criticism [11] maintains that such a transcendental experience is conditioned by history, especially by the history of a particular philosophical and theological climate. Modern man less and less can avail himself of it. However, the flourishing of interest in oriental philosophies, psychologies of peak-experiences and a host of similar phenomena militate against his diagnosis.[12] Furthermore, his horizontal transcendence of the future kingdom of God is as much *beyond* as the vertical transcendence. Unless we find transcendence within we fall short of our hermeneutical task. As a starting point, the self as transcendence *within* seems to be fruitful. The step from the transcendence within to the transcendence *without* demands more than the analysis of the self.

Dewart speaks of the increase of the consciousness of consciousness as the condition of modern theologization. The Presence of the Reality which transcends both noun and verbal naming, and there it cannot be called Being, constitutes the open background against which man becomes conscious of his transcendence (i.e., self). Since this Presence transcends transcendence, or self, it must be beyond the category of the personal.

11. Johannes B. Metz, *Theology of the World* (New York: Herder and Herder, 1969), pp. 81-141.

12. Herbert Richardson and Donald R. Cutler, *Transcendence* (Boston: Beacon Press, 1969).

God is not a compelling force but "fuel" (Cf. Plotinus' and Dumery's potentiality God); not the horizon "ahead of" as in Rahner, but rather the background, expansive force which impels persons to go out and beyond themselves.[13] Dewart's challenge demands us to face an epistemological dilemma: (1) Is the explanatory principle of a system (in this case beings, persons) something radically different from the most fundamental categories of the system? or: (2) Is the explanatory principle the highest exemplification of the fundamental categories of the system?

If epistemologically we were forced to accept the first— and we are not—Dewart would be right.[14] If we were compelled to accept the second we would find ourselves in process theology. If we take both one and two we are back to good old *analogia entis*.

Ray L. Hart approaches the problem of human self-hood from the side of *imagination* which he regards as the clue to both the proper ontology of the agent self and to the problem of Revelation. The self-transcendence in the terms of imagination proffers a very intricate, unsuspectedly rich structure.[15] If I understand him correctly, despite his side-tracking penchant for the elaboration of the ramifications of the question, the openness of the human being to Being can be laid on broader foundation than ontological anxiety.

The overuse of anxiety, disquietude, and similar notions, springing from the confrontation with nothingness, have lost their illuminating function. At least this is my impression from teaching. One may sympathize with Hans Urs von Balthasar's plea for "splendor" as a central theological category. Perhaps it could be shown that praising also is an inner moment of transcendence and as such may qualify as a subjective correlate to

13. Leslie Dewart, *The Foundations of Belief* (New York: Herder and Herder, 1969), pp. 209-334.

14. Note: Even in Scholasticism if the most universal characteristic of the world is motion, the explanatory principle will be unmoved mover, i.e., the explanation of a system transcends the system.

15. Ray L. Hart, *Unfinished Man and the Imagination: Toward an Ontology and a Rhetoric of Revelation* (New York: Herder and Herder, 1968), esp. pp. 109-179.

the splendor of being. The centrality of the personal categories tends to do away with the category of cause in theological discourse. This is especially marked in the case of Marcel[16] and Dewart. But even Rahner's quasi-formal causality may be regarded as a kindred move. Pannenberg's intriguing suggestion is that the self-experience is not prior to religious experience but has its origin in it.[17] This needs further investigation. The anthropological evidence, notwithstanding Pannenberg's competency, is not as strong as he thinks.

Generally, one should not speak of religious experience but of a religious dimension of varied experiences since the self-transcendence is quite detectable in all cultural phenomena.[18]

Any theology which takes self, self-transcendence, consciousness of consciousness, and religious experience or something similar as a starting point, finds itself in an unenviable position. Our students learn in the social sciences that the self is not reality but a theoretical construct at best.

For Critical Naturalism, self cannot represent more than the intersection of various conscious activities, which, if it were linguistically viable, should be used in adjectival form and not in noun form, thereby suggesting an entity. The agent self is denied. Here, the expression 'agent self' intends to avoid both the static connotation of the substantive self especially in the Lockean tradition, and the epiphenomenalist conception of self. Nevertheless, Critical Naturalism acknowledges the novelty of mental life as compared to neuro-physiological events.[19]

The direct accessibility of the self is contested by the Identity Theory. First person present tense utterances presumably do not constitute a class different from the third person observational statements. Self remains on the level of "explanatory fiction" in a very contemptuous sense. The self is, at best, a verbal tool

16. Leo Sweeney, "Marcel's Position on God," *The New Scholasticism* (XLIV: Winter, 1970), pp. 121-122.

17. Wolfhart Pannenberg, *Theology and the Kingdom of God* (Philadelphia: Westminster Press, 1969), pp. 57-58.

18. John E. Smith, *Experience and God* (New York: Oxford University Press, 1968).

19. Harry and Geiger G. Girvetz, *Science, Folklore, and Philosophy* (New York: Harper and Row, 1966), pp. 347-365.

to express the structural-temporal continuity of the neuro-physiological concomitants of behavioral responses.

Skinner's functional analysis of human behavior and the epiphenomenalistic shift of many authors escape the pitfalls of the older Identity Theory. Nevertheless, a minimal inner life and "raw feels," grudgingly admitted, remain inconsequential for motivations. Even if consciousness or awareness are accepted as realities, they are regarded as side-effects of overt behavior, and therefore, negligible for any scientific purpose.[20]

It is good strategy against both trends to pose the question of the agent self in the context of freedom vs. determinism. The Identity Theory is strict determinist; Critical Naturalism is soft determinist.[21] Determinism is on the defensive now, and there is a rising readiness to accept the agent-self.

The following strategy is specifically directed against Critical Naturalism. One should keep in mind that Critical Naturalism is not against religious experience which allegedly makes one open to the emergence of new qualities of life and to the "order of splendor," nor does it deny the emergence of really novel qualities in a pluralistic and evolutionary world. However, Critical Naturalism is against faith. The combined insistence on the reality of new qualities emerging in the world and on atheism drives it to the denial of the principle of sufficient reason; or to put it in ontological terms instead of logical, it is driven to the denial of the *ex nihilo nihil fit*.[22]

The proper strategy is to press the question of the whence of the novel entities and qualities. The typical answer from this quarter that this is the way things are, or that the descriptively ultimate is also the explanatory ultimate, relinquishes the essential drive of mind for total intelligibility which is given in the *implications* of the descriptive ultimate.

According to Critical Naturalism, consciousness does not contain more than its content; it does not transcend it. Since the Critical Naturalism is willing to consider at least a limited use

20. See also: Feigl, Feyerabend, Hook, Skinner, Wann, Mackinnon. in bibliographic citations.

21. Cf., Castell, Hampshire, Jonas, Macmurray, Smart, Taylor as listed.

22. Girvetz, *op. cit.*, p. 353.

of introspection, one can call the attention to the prepredicative, *a priori* form of the consciousness which aims always at more than the actual content. The transcendent affirmation is co-given with limited affirmation of the content and explained from the latent affirmation of the infinite. This, in turn, renders possible the affirmation of the limited as limited.

We come now to a brief consideration of the *Identity Theory*. This theory is still more widely represented than any other trend in the places of higher learning. The word 'identity' is to be taken strictly. It does not mean correlation of the conscious with the physical—but identity. Neither does it mean mere genetic dependence. On the linguistic level it maintains the reducibility of the phenomenal, i.e., mentalistic language to the physicochemical language. The language of psychology, at least in principle, can be reduced to the language of biology. The latter, in turn, is reducible to the language of chemistry, etc.; finally love equals an electrical overcharge of the cortex. To avoid the accusation of pursuing metaphysics, the authors prefer to pose the question on the linguistic level. But do not be mistaken, they mean more. The old question if there is anything like soul reappears as the question concerning first person statements. Since science must speak third person language, for the representative of the Identity Theory, it is imperative to reduce the first person language to third person language. Once this reduction is made, he has good enough chances to reduce the third person mentalistic language to biological, then later, to physicochemical language. The third person language admits of such reductionism.

"I am now excited" has the same content, according to the Identity Theory, as "my body is now in that condition which, both under my observation and that of others, exhibits such and such characteristics of excitement." "I am going to mail a letter," according to Skinner, is not in a different class from similar statements made by others who have observed his behavior upon fewer occasions.[23] "I was about to go home" equals "I observed events in myself which precede or accompany my going home."

23. Burrhus F. Skinner, *Science and Human Behavior* (New York: Macmillan, 1953), p. 88.

In other words, there is no direct access to my inner (private) life; my statements are inferences.

What does the Identity Theory gain by this procedure? On this ground, and only on this ground, it can asseverate that the mentalistic concepts, not only the self, but also the purpose, intent, meaning and so on, are theoretical constructs, or, in Skinner's intolerant language—"explanatory fictions." To concede the direct experience of "I" would mean to acknowledge the empirical basis of metaphysics and theology.

In counter-strategy we have to emphasize the *direct, though mediated,* accessibility of self and inner life, thereby dispelling the superstition of "theoretical construct." Note the role of self-experience. I experience myself only "sidewise," "alongside"— with experiencing something else than me; i.e., the self-experience is mediated, but I am not making inferences from observation. I am directly aware of myself. The old identifications: direct = immediate; mediated = indirect = inferential just do not hold good. The logic of a direct mediated though not inferential discourse is going to be, in principle, different than the logic of scientific discourse.

It can be pointed out that the self-transcending toward the "ever more" of being and value is not a need in the ordinary sense. Needs are system bound. Their aim is adaptation to a system, whereas the movement of the self transcends any system, even any conceivable system.

A more intricate but logically elegant argument is provided by Ayer.[24] He shows that the "I" is *not describing* properties of any kind, nor their combinations. It *refers,* rather, to something else which cannot be put in predicate position as properties can be. This argument takes the "I" out of the competence of science, be it physical or psychological, since science deals with properties.

Ayer, due to his positivistic commitment, cannot think of an agent-self. He thinks that the non-property like reality emerges alongside the psychic, etc., qualities as if it were coproduced. This standpoint is similar to that of Critical Naturalism. It cannot answer the problem of the continuity of self which is expe-

24. Cf. A. J. Ayer, *The Problem of Knowledge* (Baltimore: Penguin Books, Inc.).

rienced. Nor can it solve the problem of why we are aware of the succession of mental contents when the theory should demand succession of awarenesses as its logical conclusion.

The *Identity Theory* and similar trends seemed to have become defunct before the second World War. But the development of cybernetics imparted a new vitality to it. The frequently heard slogan in Catholic circles that "behaviorism is out, or materialism is out" is just simply not true.

In the confrontation with cybernetics which purports to be the science of control and information (information also conceived as control) one must remember that only behaviors describable in finite number of words can be produced by the cybernetic articrafts.[25] The task remains to show that faith, moral decision, etc., are not such. The distinction between awareness and behavior also is to be underlined, since awareness cannot be "fed in"—only behavior can.

It remains imperative for the theology of self and experience to show that some kind of necessary, though incomplete knowledge, may be derived from direct experiences, and that they may serve as the basis of certitude.[26]

It must be emphasized that it is not the content of the experience but the form, the dynamic structure thereof, which constitute a good starting point for systematic theology. Any content of experience is vulnerable to sociological and psychological attacks. Only the transcendental form, structure of experience which is co-given with the content promises to stand up against the attacks of the sociology of knowledge.

Also, it is to be stressed that in the defence and characterization of the agent-self, the British-American scholarship offers such a sophistication which one can not find in the continental scholarship where the reality of self is taken for granted.

There is a pedagogical task also, namely, the education of "consciousness of consciousness," or the promotion of the awareness concerning the formal, structural elements of experiencing instead of the content elements.

25. Neville Moray, *Cybernetics* (New York: Hawthorne Books, 1963), chap. 6.
26. Kenneth T. Gallagher, *The Philosophy of Knowledge* (New York: Sheed and Ward, 1964), chaps. 9, 11.

II   The Diversity of Religious Experience

6   The Ways of West and East

In order to expose with a certain order the core, and obviously only the core, of the question, we shall consider, first the meaning of *experience*, second, what *Supreme* can possibly mean in this case and thirdly, some of the different ways of expressing it. If we were to follow a more congenial way of putting the problem I would simply say: *The Myth*, the *Logos* and the *Spirit*.

The Problem of Experience. The Myth

Prolegomena

The question about the nature and value of experience arises at the very moment when we begin to think about our experience. But then we no longer experience: we think. Or even more generally expressed: the awareness of an experience is not the experience. Experiencing, unlike thinking, does not allow for self-reflection. That is its greatness and its weakness at the same time.

By experience we may understand any immediate contact with reality. The perfect experience would mean no difference, no distinction whatsoever between the experiencing subject and the experienced object.

For the sake of situating the place of experience in human life and not with the claim of stating a full-fledged anthropological theory, we may assume that man has three organs, or

---

1. The bibliography is so immense that we are forced to renounce writing a footnote after every line. The references and echoes scattered throughout the essay, could be found in the notes of my course at Harvard (Spring 1969), *Some Metaphysical Categories for a Hindu Christian Theology* and in my Seminar (Spring 1971) on *Comparative Mysticism*.

groups of organs, relating him with reality. The *Sensuous* consciousness relates us by means of our sense organs, to what we could call the material part of reality. The *intellectual* consciousness opens us up to the intelligible world, to that web of relations which give consistency to the material world and which we cannot equate with mere matter. The *mystical* consciousness identifies us in a very special way to the very reality which it opens up to us. With whatever name we may like to describe these facts there seems to be no doubt about the existence of these three stages of consciousness whatever interpretation we may give to the 'reality' opened up in each case. There would not seem to be much disagreement in saying that those three degrees of consciousness are ultimately not independent windows but three dimensions of one and the same primordial consciousness, of which the sensual, intellectual and mystical consciousness are different forms.

The senses are not only 'knowing' instruments, they are also acting tools. This is to say that they are also part of the same reality which they disclose. The intellect is not only a knowing mind either; it is an acting will also. This is to say that the intellectual web of reality is not just a private property of the individual, but a common feature in which men participate. The mystical consciousness is not mainly a source of knowledge, but an aspect of reality itself, which discloses itself when it becomes patent to a particular subject.

There is no need to interpret what has been said so far in an epistemic realistic sense; it has meaning and validity also within other epistemologies and within more than one metaphysical system. We do not affirm here what reality is or whether those human experiences have 'objective' truth or not. We only offer a general pattern capable of being interpreted in many different ways. What has been stressed however is the unitarian character of this trinity. i.e.; the fact that any human act of consciousness has to a greater or lesser degree the three above mentioned dimensions. When we call a human act a sensory activity or an intellectual action or a mystical awareness we are actually abstracting, i.e., considering only one aspect of a more complex and unitarian fact, which includes all in one the sensual, the intellectual and the mystical.

In this light we may call consciousness that bridge between the two shores of reality, the subject and the object. This bridge connects these two shores by means of one of the three ways of that unique bridge: an upper level of a sensorial two-way-traffic, a lower intellectual level, predominantly a one-way track, and the very columns of the bridge itself connecting the two shores. On the first we act, on the second we understand, on the third we are.

Whereas the concept of consciousness may be used to stress the overall character of this process and the supraindividual aspect of the same phenomenon, the concept of experience stands for the peculiar distinctive feature of the individual having or sharing in that consciousness. Whereas consciousness is something in which we share, experience is something peculiar to and particular to every one of us. We may almost say that by definition experience is the individualistic and peculiar way of sharing in a given state of consciousness. With these clarifications we may now proceed to our task of describing what can be understood by Supreme Experience.

The Empirical, the Experiment and the Experience

The history of human civilization could be considered under the perspective of one or the other of these three variations of the same basic concept, the basic concept being personal realization or, following the common etymological root, the attempt at integrating ourselves into reality by passing through whatever process is needed.[2] We could call them *kairological* moments, for obviously there is no question of considering them as chronological divisions.

There is a first period in the history of mankind and one is tempted to say that there is equally a first period in the develop-

---

2. *Peraô* and *peiran* in Greek, both at the basis of our three words, come from the root *per* (in Sanskrit *par* [cf. *pi-parmi*]) meaning to conduct, to pass through, to test. Cf. the latin *porta, peritua, periculum,* the German *fahren* (from where *erfahren*), the English fare, ferry, etc. The empirical is the proven reality, because it has passed through our senses; the experience is the same reality submitted to our testing and trying capacities; experience is again the same reality which has already passed through.

ment of human consciousness, in which given data are uncritically assumed and taken as bare facts. That which is given, especially what is given to our senses, is taken as real. The empirical here does not mean only sense-knowledge. The philosophically uncritical mind takes equally for granted that what appears to it as a given. And the spiritual vision is also unreflective. It is the ecstatic vision, the overwhelming presence of the object, with forgetfulness about the subject; it is the awareness of presence without the slightest cloud of self-awareness. In religion, philosophy and art we could substantiate this period re-calling the beginnings of almost any culture.

The second moment is represented by the predominance of the experiment. A certain doubt about the value of objectivity has crept in; man has become more conscious about himself and realizes that he cannot leave the external subject untouched and unreflected upon. The doubt has to be checked by abandoning the passive attitude of the contemplator and taking a more active and aggressive approach: the experiment, the trial, the test, the intervention in the object itself. It is the period of the critical awareness. This is felt on all the three levels of consciousness. The experimental sciences make their appearance. In order to know what a thing is mere observation is not considered enough. But the experiment is not limited to the object alone; it is also performed on the subject itself: Men begin to analyze the human mind and the whole spiritual organism. To the physical experiment in the natural sciences corresponds the internal experiments of critical philosophy and the psychological introspection of the mystics. The European Renaissance offers us a typical example: We have there a flourishing of experimentation on the three levels of consciousness. Not only the human body and the celestial bodies are examined, but also the human mind and spirit are submitted to the scrutinizing process of experimentation. There is one and the same wind blowing in Leonardo da Vinci, Luther, Servet, St. Theresa, Galileo and Descartes, to quote only a few names.

The third moment is the obvious result of the same continuing process. Man has lost confidence in his first empirical data; he asks for criteria of truth, of verification and is ready to accept only that which he sees for himself. But the experiment is still too impersonal, too objective, too reliant on the objective methods of the experimentor, it requires still a certain confidence in the skill, awareness and judgments of others. He shall not be satisfied until he experiences it by himself. Only individual experience cannot err, only if he makes the experience for himself shall he be convinced that such is the case. The empirical is pure objectivity, the experiment blends the object with subjectivity, the experience abolishes any kind of objectivity not assumed and integrated in the subjectivity. Anybody today asking for an experience of whatever kind, biological, psychological, scientific or religious is saying that he does not care for objectivity or for how others judge, see or sense things. He has to have an individual involvement which can only be had if the experience is there. One cannot have an experience by proxy.

The myth

Experience implies in consequence not only the intransferable and individualistic contact with the experienced object but it excludes also any type of intermediaries, which would be a third party making the experience impossible and reverting it to an experiment, which is always done by means of instruments. This implies, further, that any experience worthy of the name excludes the consciousness of any distance between the object and the subject, that the object is no longer envisaged as such, but as totally united with or plunged into the subject.

The difference between knowing about pain or God or love and experiencing pain, God or love is obvious. My ideas about any object can be correct, checked, eventually abandoned as inaccurate or wrong. There is a distance between the subject and the object, which permits such modifications in the object without endangering the subject. Not so with any experience, as long as it is my experience. When I experience pain it is no doubt possible that I am in pain, even if I am convinced that there is no external or organic cause or intellectual reason for it. I can doubt whether to make this or the other choice as long as I am guided by anything short of experience. I may have to ponder and decide according to reasons, instincts or the like as long as I do not have an experience which renders any further doubt or hesitation impossible. What we have to underscore here is not the analysis of the experience but its mythical character, which amounts to recognizing its primordial and irreducible nature. Any experience, sensory, intellectual or spiritual is, in fact, a myth. It performs, to begin with, the same role and it presents the same structure. The role of myth, as the role of experience, is to allow us to stop somewhere and thus to rest in our quest for the foundations of everything. Otherwise there would be a *regressus in infinitum.* You cannot go beyond a myth as you cannot go beyond experience. If this were possible there would be neither myth nor experience. Both do not allow for further explanations. The moment you explain a myth it ceases to be such; the moment you explain an experience it is no longer an experience. Both do not allow for 'be—causes' and 'therefores,' they are ultimate. Any demythologization destroys the myth as any explanation destroys the experience. Both, myth and experience, are taken for granted when they are actually taken as myth and experience. If one feels the need for some justification they have ceased to be what they were. Neither consciousness nor experiential consciousness allow room for critical self-awareness. They are at opposite poles. If metaphysics implies self-awareness and if philosophy is critical knowledge, then both myth and experience are neither metaphysics nor philosophy; but perhaps both rely and are based on the former pair.

Both myth and experience present the same structure. In the myth as in the experience there is no distance between the subject and the object. You are in the myth as you are in the experience; you believe in the myth as you believe in the experience, without being aware in both cases that you really do believe in them; i.e., you believe in them, but you do not believe that you believe in them. Both present a kind of similar receding structure, i.e., they do not disappear altogether when challenged or endangered. When visited by the logos that questions their validity or justification, they simply retrocede, they recede to a deeper level, to another region still untouched by the invading light of the critical reason or the rational mind. The relations between science and religion offer us constant examples of those strategic retreats. Our main concern, however, is not to draw a sketch of their resemblances, but to point out the fact that

among the many myths, experience is one of them and probably
one of the most important and invariant ones.

No myth can be explained without being explained away.
Mythology, i.e., the approach of the logos to the myth, is a
contradiction in terms, because it destroys the very myth it wants
to explain. Another thing altogether is the telling of the myths,
the 'mythos legein' over against the 'mytho-logy.' Here the original connection between word and myth is brought again to light
and the mythical roots of language appear in the very telling
of myths.

What we can do in this particular case is then to tell the myth
of the experience, i.e., the story of the human being believing
that he has a direct contact with reality, that he can participate
not only in the ontic celebration of beings, but also in the ultimate worship of Being, that he has an immediacy which vouches
for a direct contact with the real and that therefore once he has
reached the experiential level he can stop and rest. The myth
of the experience is another more subtle form of the myth of
heaven and of the celestial paradise.

It goes without saying that myths do not have to be overcome.
Even when we overcome one myth another one creeps in its
place, though perhaps on a deeper level. What really goes on
in the so popular nowadays process of demythologization, is
simply a dynamics of transmythologization, a kind of mythical
metamorphosis, where obsolete and anachronistic myths give
place to more modern and up to date myths. These new myths,
obviously, like the old myths, for those who believed in them,
are not seen as myths by the new believers.

We may sum up this first section by saying that any experience is to be considered ultimate because experience means
immediate contact with the real and thus there is no possibility
of going beyond it without destroying the experience.

The Quest for the Supreme Experience. The Logos.
The Loss of the Subject

Human history, both collective and personal, proves that what
at one certain period was considered to be ultimate or immediate,
later on was discovered to be mediated and, thus, neither final

nor ultimate. Innocence is lost at the moment when one is deceived. What then is the value of experience once you cannot have the conviction that that experience is going to be the last one, the final and decisive one? In other words, what happens to experience once it is demythologized? The process is worth analyzing. No experience which is genuinely an experience can have any criterion of its validity and authenticity outside itself. Any experience is self-validating or it is not an experience at all.

Now we have two logical possibilities. Either we say that the experience is the same, even when we see it changing, or we appeal to the historical dimension of man. In the first hypothesis the change is said to have taken place in the interpretation of the experience, but not in the experience itself. In the second hypothesis we have to pay the price of abandoning any possible objective criterion. In other words, either we say that the experience is atemporal, and thus everlasting, though our interpretation depends on the cultural degree, the historical moment etc., or we affirm that the experience is intrinsically temporal which amounts to saying that man, and eventually the whole reality, is essentially temporal.

The first hypothesis has the obvious difficulty of stating a fact for which there is no direct evidence whatsoever; it is an *a priori* derived from a certain world view. The second hypothesis has the inconvenience that it seems to fall into a total anarchy, for there seems to be no guarantee that the human experiences are going to offer any coherence and continuity along the temporal line. There is no reason why what is experienced today as positive, as valuable and as immediately evident is not going to appear tomorrow as utterly untenable.

Is there any way out of the dilemma between a timeless rigidity of everlasting values and a chaotic revolution of sheer relativism? The quest for the supreme experience seems to be relevant here. If this is the case we shall have another example of how the apparently most abstract and theoretical speculation can have practical and concrete relevance. Are we not asking ourselves, among other questions, whether there is no middle way between a Maoist way of constant revolution and the liberal or capitalistic solution of unchanging abstract principles which take care of themselves if only allowed to develop by them-

selves? Are we not asking if this middle way exists without being
either a betrayal or a compromise? But before engaging ourselves
into such problems we should go back to our philosophical
analysis of human experience.

Let me ask myself the simple question: when do I doubt
the validity of my experience? If our description of what an
experience is is correct, there can only be one answer: I doubt
about the validity of my experience, only when I cease to have
that experience. As long as I have an experience I cannot doubt
it. I begin to doubt when I begin to wonder whether what I am
having is an experience or not. This occurs in the first place
when I realize the experience as experience, for then I am no
longer having the pure experience. When the experience becomes
aware of itself as an experience it ceases to be an experience, and
becomes a reflective consciousness of the experience that I am
having. The experience of prayer, like the experience of pain,
like the experience of love, is incompatible with the awareness
that I am having that experience. In other words, when the
logos enters into the experience so as to make possible the sort
of self-awareness which is peculiar to the intellect, the experience
is no longer pure experience. Let us imagine that we are having
an aesthetic experience contemplating the beauty of a landscape. The moment that I become aware that I am having such
an experience or that it is through the eye, that I am seeing
and having that experience, I have lost the real experience;
I have become aware of an intermediary which I did not consider before. Rather, there was no intermediary until I became
conscious of there being one. The intermediary eye through
which I see is at the same time the means that separates that
which it unites. In a word, no critical awareness is capable of
being an experience, because it belongs to the essence of criticism to be conscious of itself.

Is there any possible experience which does not allow for such
destructive self-awareness? Could there be an experience in
which the self that experiences is the same as the experience
itself? We have already seen that in any real experience the
object is lost. The ultimate experience would be that experience
in which the subject is equally lost. We should not, at this stage,

commit the methodological mistake of trying to describe such an experience by relying on a particular interpretation of its contents, say in a theistic world-view, for instance. We have to remain on purely formalistic grounds.

Yet, we may perhaps describe it by leaning on a particular tradition in as far as the terminology goes, but without implying any allegiance to that particular way. If I see the landscape or smell the flower or think the thought or will the action or understand the situation, I may have an experience of those objects when they merge into me so that there is no longer any distinction. But there is always the possibility of coming back, as a certain mysticism would say, because, whereas in the experience the object is lost in the subject, this latter one is not lost, nor is the identification total in either direction, that of the object to the subject and that of the subject to the object. How can I see (understand, discover) that by seeing (understanding, discovering) which all the rest becomes seen (understood, discovered)?

By what would one know the knower? The difficulty is clear: You cannot see the seer of seeing, you cannot think the thinker of thinking. How can you know the knower? The knower which you might eventually know, by this very fact would no longer be the knower but the 'known' by you. To be sure, there is one way by which this question may be answered. Undoubtedly not by knowing the knower or understanding the understander, but by being oneself the knower and understander. This is the only way in which the experience cannot cancel itself: not by merely reaching identification with the object experienced but becoming the experience itself, the knower, the understander.

The supreme experience is neither supreme nor experience. It is not supreme, because it is not the superior or the first one among many. It is not experience either because there is no subject experiencing an object.

The Experience, its Expression and Interpretation

We should not too easily assume that the supreme experience or any experience for that matter is totally independent of its expression or that its interpretation is equally irrelevant to the experience itself. Even if this be the case it would not be an evident case.

It is one of the most common affirmations regarding this type of problem to repeat time and again that the authentic experience is ineffable, that those who know do not speak and those who speak do not know. It may be that no words can communicate what it is, but not all communication needs to be verbal. To affirm that some reality is unthinkable amounts to recognizing that thinking does not exhaust the realm of being. To assert that the ultimate experience reaches into non-being, because it has left all beings behind, amounts to confessing that beings are a relative reality that the spatial metaphor of the 'beyond' is pointing towards a real non-being, if the word 'real' can still be used in this context.

Secondly, we have to become aware of the implications of the dichotomy between the experience and its expression. We understand by expression the manifestation of the experience, i.e., its first emanation *ad extra*, its first result, as it were, so that the act of the experience could not be said to be a solipsistic act with no repercussion or irradiation outside itself. And finally we must also distinguish the expression from its interpretation, this latter being the intellectual explanation of the experience as it is understood by our intellect.

If we accept those three degrees of consciousness mentioned earlier, we can easily see an interesting correlation between each one of these three stages. On the one side there is a correlation between the interpretation and the intellectual consciousness. The expression or manifestation of the experience would correspond to the sensorial consciousness. We may understand by this latter not only the traditional sense organs but our whole body complex, so that the manifestation of the experience does not need to be a word or even a sound but may be the more primordial expression of it in our whole body, in our terrestrial and temporal life. The experience itself would then correspond to what we called the mystical consciousness. If this were the case, we would then have also met the difficulty of the so-called ineffability of the real experience. It would be inexpressible in terms of our sensorial and intellectual consciousness but it would correspond to pure consciousness which evidently does not translate itself in any other form or take any other name, being itself the act which gives name and form to everything.

But be this as it may, we ought not to distinguish so much as to break the ultimate unity of reality. We should not lose sight of the underlying unity between the three stages of consciousness, and the three modes of realization: the experience, the manifestation and its interpretation. It is here that we should introduce that concept which seems to be an adequate carrier of all the burden of the three worlds: the symbol.

By way of summary, we may state that the symbol stands for the whole of reality as it appears and manifests itself in the manifold way of its structure. A symbol is precisely the thing, but not the thing in itself, which is an abstraction of the mind, but one thing as it appears, as it expresses and manifests itself. The symbol of a thing is neither another thing nor the thing in itself but the very thing as it manifests itself, as it is in the world of beings, in the epiphany of the 'is.' Contemporary philosophy speaks of the ontologic or transcendental difference, that of beings and their entity, of the theological or transcendent difference, that of God and beings, including even the so-called widely ontological or 'transcendentable' difference, that of beings along with their entity and Being. We could, analogously, introduce here the *symbolic difference*, as the *sui generis* difference between the symbol and its reality. The symbol is not another reality, it is not another thing, nor the thing as we may imagine that it is in an non-existent ideal realm, but it is the thing as it really appears, as it really 'is' in the realm of beings. The symbol is nothing but the symbol of the thing, that is (subjective genitive), the peculiar mode of being that very thing, which outside its symbolic form is not and cannot be; because, ultimately, being is nothing but the symbol of its self. To be able to discover the symbolic difference, i.e., to discover me as symbol of myself, or, in other words, to realize that my own being is one of the real symbols of the I (not perhaps of my ego), could perhaps be said to be one of the ways to reach the supreme experience.

The Supreme Experience

If all that has been said so far makes some sense, the supreme experience will be synonymous with pure consciousness and pure consciousness will stand for the core of reality in as much as only consciousness makes room for the plurality of the sense-experience and the multiplicity of the intellectual-experience without tainting the oneness of the mystical-experience. Consciousness and consciousness alone allows the harmonious blending between the many and the one: the many states of consciousness and the fact of being conscious of the multiplicity do not make consciousness multiple; on the contrary it reinforces, as it were, its primordial oneness.

The supreme experience would then be that experience which is so identified with reality itself that it is nothing but the same reality. It is not the highest among the experiences; it does not experience anything. It recovers the lost innocence in a way that is not even comparable to the original one. The original innocence had no knowledge of good and evil, nor properly any experience of the manifold in its excruciating diversity, division and tension; it was a kind of blessed ignorance, what we still today call innocence. The recovery of innocence is properly speaking not a recovery, but a creation, a new state, which is not new, because it does not substitute an old or decrepit one.

The supreme experience is not an experience either in the sense in which we may use the word in all other cases. Not only is the object lost, but also the subject is no longer there as substratum or basis for the experience. No man can *have* pure consciousness. It would be no longer pure if it had a foundation in any subject. It cannot be self-consciousness either, if we understand by this any type of reflective consciousness upon the self. We could call it rather self-unconsciousness, precisely because it is mere consciousness: an awareness that it is not aware that it is aware, an infinite ignorance.

One way of describing the supreme experience with the minimum of philosophical assumptions could perhaps take the following form:

Let us begin with any experience, with perhaps the simplest

of all of them: I am touching an object. I am having the branch of a tree in my hand, I am pressing and caressing it, I may like to bite it and to smell and taste it eventually. My thinking is absent for the moment and my spiritual awareness also. I am lost in that contact with a piece of nature. This is a sensual experience. But this experience does not last for ever. Perhaps an impertinent fly disturbs me in my 'distraction,' or a fleeting thought crosses my mind, or my body reminds me of the hour. I still want to remain in communion with that branch, but I have discovered, first, that neither the object nor the subject were pure, total and exhaustive. The branch is not the whole tree and much less the whole nature; my hands and all my senses are not the whole of my being and much less the whole of all the other possible subjects. I would like to cling to my branch and I may begin to meditate upon it, to concentrate not only my senses but also my mind and even my will upon the branch. If I succeed, I may reach another type of experience in which the identification is much deeper and wider at the same time. For a moment I may be identified with the branch and if I am lost deep enough in the branch my identification may not stop at the branch, which I may no longer experience as branch, but with a great part of nature, with the whole vegetal life eventually. For a moment there may be identification between me and the whole nature. It is not the branch that I touch, but the whole of the world that I embrace.

But my experience does not need to stop here. It may grow in both directions, in the losing of the object until reaching the totality and the losing of the subject until reaching also the other pole of the totality, as it were. Perhaps with the branch it may become a little difficult, but surely not impossible. I may have to leave the woods and throw the branch away, but I may equally go back to the branch though now no longer as branch but as the whole tree and the entire wood and the universe in its totality, which I cannot touch with my hands, nor feel with my sentiments, but somehow enter with my whole being, a concrete mirror and deflection of the whole. I may lose myself in such an experience and perhaps more than one expert will tell me that I have had an experience of nature mysticism. But this is not all. We may assume that I believe in a personal God.

This would allow for another type of experience, which some may call the vision of God. But I do not need to assume, for my general description, that I am a theist or an atheist and I am convinced that the experience may be the same, even if its interpretation differs.

The contact with the branch may be so intense and profound that what I am in contact with is not a bundle of electrons with the configuration of a branch, but that primordial matter in which all material things have their share. Now, entering into immediate contact with this primordial matter, I am also in immediate contact with the very ground of being which gives consistency and existence to that primal matter. Some may call it God, some may not. In any case I am in direct contact with the ultimate reality of that branch, which has to do ultimately with the same reality of everything. We may differ in the use of the word reality, we may disagree in as much as I may think that the reality that matters is the distinctive and not the uniting factor, but there is an experience there, which, as such, i.e., without any claim at metaphysical interpretations, reaches the very boundaries of reality.

This is not yet the supreme experience, because it still has to grow into the total universalization of the subject having that experience. Until now I have been *carried away,* as it were, being lost, in the object, or the object is lost for me, but I have not yet been *carried above* me, such that there is no longer a 'me.' If by concentrating on the branch (disregarding now other possible requirements according to different schools), I can lose myself totally in the entire universe, I need the action of the ultimate reality of the branch upon me, i.e., I need the opposite thrust, in order to totally lose myself, my ego, and realize that the subject of the experience is no longer my senses or my mind or my mystical awareness, but something which overwhelms and overcomes me (about which I can speak only later on) which does not allow room for saying in any way that the experience is mine. In theistic terms I am no longer 'seeing' the branch or the universe, but 'creating' it, calling it into existence because it is no longer my ego which does it but the divine I in which my person is merged and with which my person is united, or however we may prefer to express this process. This would be the beginning of the supreme experience. The explanations, i.e., the interpretations may come afterwards. One thing may still be added: the manifestation of the experience is something which can be detected: it is something which totally transforms my life. The manifestation will not be my words or my recital of the experience, but the expression will be incarnated in my own life, will crystallize in my existence and be visible to those who may care to look.

This is the beginning of the supreme experience. In other words, it has been the supreme experience for the time being. The man who has had such an experience will 'come back' to what mortals call the ordinary life. The supreme experience once it has taken hold of a man has transformed that man totally and he cannot be the same as before. It is a process of death and resurrection. That man will perform the ordinary acts of human life as any other mortal will do. He will not feel distracted, because there is no incompatibility of domains, the supreme experience not belonging to the domain of psychology. Nevertheless it is understandable that most of the mystical schools dealing with these problems distinguish a double degree even at this point: the supreme experience compatible with the mortal life in the visible structures of space and time and that other supreme experience in which time and space have completely been integrated into the experience itself.

The Ways of the East and of the West: The Spirit
The Eastern and Western Values

East and West have been separated for such a long time misunderstanding one another and living worlds apart, that it is understandable that a certain inertia in our ways of looking at things may obscure the fact that East and West are no longer what were traditionally described under these two almost magical names. East and West cannot be considered, to begin with, as purely or mainly geographical features. Not only because already long ago it was discovered that the earth is round, so that all depends on the perspective one adopts, but also because actually those geographical differences are minimal today and to be found in any relatively big geographical unit. East and West cannot be said to be *historical* concepts either. The history of the peoples of the world is no longer an isolated history and the destiny of the West may well be dependent on the battles taking place in the East and the future of the East may depend on the policy of the West. There are no longer closed Eastern and Western histories. For the first time in the world human history is the history of mankind.

Cultural distinctions also fade away or are expressions of not yet totally overcome oversimplifications and ignorances. Not only is the typical Western spirit to be found outside the West, but also the traditional Eastern way of looking at things is gaining more and more ground in the western latitudes. There is not a single cultural difference which could be called specifically Eastern or Western. Surely neither logic, nor mysticism, nor technology, science or metaphysics. Also the *philosophical* idiosyncrasies cannot be divided into Eastern and Western ways of thinking or philosophizing. The East and the West as well are too vast and variegated, to allow for overstatements regarding special features in the philosophical outlook on life. The times in which it could be said that a certain feature is peculiar with exclusivity to the East or to the West are over.

Even *religious* divisions can no longer be credited to East and West. In spite of the still heavy burden of the past, hardly any religion today can be identified with a particular East-West dichotomy. Most of the religions of the world were born in one place and flourished in another and hardly any religion today would identify itself with one particular continent. It is hard to say whether Christianity is more Jewish than Greek or Roman, whether Buddhism is more Indian than Chinese or even Islam more Arabic than Asian, or even for that matter Judaism more Palestinian than Babylonian, eastern European, Spanish or whatever.

Is it, thus, meaningless to speak of the ways of the East and those of the West? We do not believe so. There is still a deep significance, perhaps the deepest and it will seem that only if they are understood as anthropological categories do East and West have their place, justification and value.

In every human being there is an East and a West, as any

human being is in a certain way androgynous, only with the
normal preponderance of one of the two aspects of the human.
It would be monstrous if the world would be becoming geo-
graphically and culturally one and the human persons would
still remain isolated, unconcerned and without that symbiosis,
which is the only hope to more than one world problem today.
But the cross-fertilization is possible because the human being
already has within himself the seeds of both values. Every human
person has an orient, an horizon, always beyond and behind,
where the sun rises and which he never reaches, a dimension of
hope, a dim sense of transcendence, a matutinal knowledge
(*cognitio matutina*) as some tradition would have said. Every
human being has likewise a dimension of West, of maturity,
where the sun sets, where the values materialize, where faith
is felt as a necessity, where the shapes and forms become relevant and the evening knowledge (*cognitio vespertina*) represents the most coveted value, discovering the value of the immanence in the things themselves.

We could go on indefinitely, but this may suffice to apply it
to our problems. The burden of our tale is this: any inter-reli-
gious and inter-human dialogue, any exchange among cultures
has to be preceeded by a intra-religious and intra-human dialogue, an internal conversion within the person. We can only
bridge the gulf between so many abysses, between East and
West in this case, if we realize the synthesis and the harmony
within that microcosm of ourselves.

Four archetypes of the Ultimate

We cannot go on forever avoiding the problem of the contents and overlooking the different ways in which the supreme
experience has been described in the different schools and traditions. But then we must be aware of the limitations of any
particular description. It is here that a study from the point of
view of the History of Religions should prove fruitful and enlightening. Only very tentatively may we submit the following
typology, based not so much on the perhaps too schoolbookish
divisions between religions or cultures but along the lines of
what has been said before of East and West as anthropological

categories. If examples are drawn from the great religious traditions of mankind this should not contradict what we have been saying, but simply witness to the fact that certain emphases are easier to find among certain peoples than others.

We repeat once for all that we do not intend to describe any religious spirituality in particular or deny that within a given religion there are not other trends of thought or even affirm that our typology is a typology of religions. We speak of four archetypes of the human being, though they may be more visible in one place or time than in another. Moreover, a visible trend of our times is to find more and more each one of the four archetypes within the fold of one and the same religion.

It seems that the human spirit in its effort at understanding and expressing the supreme experience has stressed either the transcendence or the immanence of it. In the first group we find again two definite tendencies: the tendency stressing the transcendence and the tendency stressing the immanence. The former is typical of the semitic religions: Judaism, Christianity and Islam. The latter could be said to form the Hindu type and could be represented by the bundle of religious traditions which circulate under the name of Hinduism.

The group more inclined to emphasize the immanence could equally be divided into two: the one underscoring the transcendent character of the immanence and we think of Buddhism and the other laying the accent on the immanent aspect of the same immanence, and here we would see the Chinese religious tradition and curiously enough the modern secular spirit also.

The following scheme sums up what we would like to sketch very briefly:

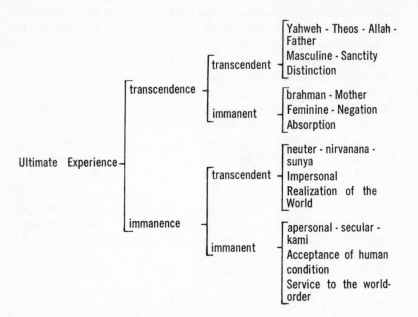

The transcendent transcendence

Its attitude is markedly masculine. Force, Power, Glory are some of its attributes. Be it Yahweh, the Christian *Theos* or Allah, this God is eminently Father and thus creator and evidently outside the world; he is transcendent in such an absolute way that he mainly creates, looks after and judges the world. He does not mix with the world, as it were. The supreme experience is to see this glaring light face to face. Of course, there is the softening effect of the Christian Incarnation like the more mellow tones of the *kabbala,* the hasidic spirituality of *sufism,* but we have already said that we are trying to describe anthropological archetypes more than to elaborate a typology of religions. God is the saint and holiness means here separatedness, lofty segregation. He is utterly transcendent and it is this very transcendence which gives him the sovereign freedom to deal with men. The supreme experience is ultimately not possible for men. It is exclusively reserved for the transcendent God.

We can at most be united with him by love or knowledge, according to the theological trends of different schools. The supreme experience cannot in any way represent an escape from the human condition. It has to be concrete, personal and must preserve our peculiarities. At the same time it has to save us from our limitations. It has to throw us into the arms of the Absolute, but the distinction between both is zealously guarded.

The immanent transcendence

The attitude is here visibly feminine. Brahman is equally transcendent, though not because he is distant, different and above, but precisely because he is below, common, the mere condition for being, the basis of any existence without being itself any existence. Brahman is transcendent because of its own and proper immanence. So immanent that it has no consistence of its own, as it were. It does not even know that it is brahman. This would jeopardise its immanent transcendence, it would then have the necessary distance for any knowledge and could not be so radically immanent to the world. It is the *matrix*, the *yoni*, more like a mother nurturing from below rather than commanding from above. It does not lead, but sustains. The supreme experience would consist accordingly in being immersed in brahman, not perhaps to become brahman, which would posit a certain activity alien to its utter passivity, necessary for its immanent transcendence, but in discovering the brahman that is in me or that I am. The supreme experience is not so much one of keeping with one's own human condition, sticking to a name and form which are only passing and provisional, but to experience the totality, to be the totality from that angle of 180 degrees, as it were, embracing all that is. This way is a negative path of denying all individuality and all differences. One of the criteria of the authenticity of the genuine experience consists in checking whether the candidate has lost fear of disappearing and loosing himself, or if he still sticks to his little ego.

The transcendent immanence

The panorama here changes radically. The attitude is no longer masculine or feminine, but rather neuter (*ne utrum*), neither masculine nor feminine and yet somehow personal in the impersonal sense of the term. There is so radical an immanence that only by transcending all that is built on it can one reach the ultimate. One has to reduce to ashes everything which he can conceive or think of, even every idea or imagination of being has to disappear in order that the pure nothingness (*śūnya*), may emerge, not evidently as something and much less as something else, but as the non-emergence of anything. *Nirvāna* is the supreme experience and is the experience which is no experience at all and at once has realized that *samsāra* is *nirvāna*, i.e., that there is no transcendence other than the immanence, and thus that only by transcending the immanence itself can man somehow fulfill his life.

The supreme experience is obviously not the experience of an Other and not even an experience different from any other of the human experiences. It is underlying all of them and can be reached only by quenching all desire of transcending the human condition. Yet, precisely because this human condition is a negative experience, the negation of it, without wanting to transcend it, is the only way to salvation, to *nirvāna*. The human experience is reached neither by seeing God in all things (first way) nor by seeing all things in God (second way, though expressed in rather foreign terms to this second way), but refusing to divinize anything within the range of our experience. The best criterion to know that one has not got the supreme experience is when one affirms or even doubts whether he has got it. The supreme experience is that there is not such a thing as supreme experience. And yet realizing this is what opens us up to the real liberation.

The immanent immanence

The attitude here is radically terrestrial. The immanence has not to be transcended. If the three other attitudes were, in a personal or impersonal way, still recognizing that the sphere of the immanence has to be somehow corrected, transcended, this attitude does not recognize any escapism of the factual human condition. There is no way out of it. There is no other world than this world and there is no use in sublimating our longings and desires or projecting our dreams outside the realm of sober verification. *Kami* in Japanese means God for the Shinto, but also above, up, or any thing for the matter that is superior to man in any trivial way. The traditional Chinese religiousness will not allow introducing any other factor in the human situation in order to handle it. Religion is ultimate unconcern. The supreme experience is that of the sage full of the knowledge of the trickeries and depths of the human heart. The supreme experience is to renounce any extrapolation and to plunge into the real situation of the world without transcending it, not even negatively. Modern secular spirituality, by pragmatically refusing to speculate about any other experience outside the range of the world, could also be adduced as an example of this attitude. In the concrete it finds the universal and the immanent, in the given, there is all that is needed. . . .

The Spirit

Is there any possible way of finding a certain equivalence to such variegated views and opinions? Have we to conclude that mankind has no unanimity whatsoever? Is the unity of the family of man only a biological factor or a utopian dream? Am I so right that the others are wrong? Nations are at war one with another, religions consider themselves incompatible, philosophies contradict one another and now in the human experience when trying to overcome all pettiness of the systems and ideologies there appear divergencies as deep as any other human reality. Was not the drive towards experience one in order to overcome the discrepancies of sentiments and the divergencies of opinions? If there is no other ulterior judge than our personal experience must one give up all hope for a peaceful understanding of one another, thus preparing the way for new forms of imperialism and world dominion, for otherwise there seems no other way of bringing a certain coherence and unity to mankind. If after two world wars and with several minor, but no less horrible, wars still ravaging men today we cannot trust much in pure reason and particular ideologies, does human experience, supreme or not, offer any better starting point?

All these questions are far from rhetorical and they constitute a real challenge to any authentic theology and philosophy if these disciplines are to be more than mere barren and devitalized brain-juice for the dumbfounding of those men who are still sensitive and sensible. We should not expect everything from philosophy or theology and we must beware of false messianisms, but the one extreme does not justify the other.

Is there any way of understanding and somehow accepting the manifold human experience and even of integrating the variety of expressions of the supreme experience? If we can give a positive answer to this tantalizing query we shall not have solved the problems of the world, but shall have contributed in a very positive and efficacious way to their solution. At least we shall have removed one of the subtle obstacles: lack of mutual confidence because of lack of understanding. This lack of understanding is the cause of considering the other wrong, with all the consequences of this assumption. On the other hand, it would be a negative and lethal service to philosophy and a betrayal to mankind if led by a sentimental and good desire of mutual understanding, we were to blur the issues and to preach harmony and convergence when there is none.

To put it quite bluntly: if there is a God and this is the only possible hypothesis for a fully human and meaningful life, even if we respect the right of the others or acknowledge their good faith, we shall not be able to consider full citizens of academia or of culture or of religion or of mankind all those who deny such a personal God. Or, the other way round: if there is no God and the idea of God is still the 'hang up' of an obscurantist epoch totally incompatible with an enlightened and non-sectarian and fanatical existence, all those who still go on hanging onto such superstition are, to say the least, parasites of society and the greatest obstacles for a better world. We should not minimize or banalize the issue under the guise of academic etiquette. An investigation into the supreme experience cannot bypass this challenge.

Briefly but pointedly I would like to elaborate the direction of my answer. First of all, as the previous analyses may have already suggested, the shift in emphasis from objective values to the experiential truth can only be judged as a positive step toward a more mature conception of the whole and complex human situation. Orthodoxy cannot be the supreme value. Secondly, the distinction between agnostic or sceptical *relativism* and a realistic *relativity* seems to be important. The former is a dogmatic attitude emerging out of reaction against another monolithic dogmatism; the latter is the recognition that nothing is absolute in this relative world of ours, that all depend on the constitutive and intrinsic relationship in which all things are, for isolation and solipsism are the product of particular human hybris. The brotherhood of man is not only an ethical imperative. Thirdly, and this is what we should draw from the foregoing analyses, human experience is not reducible to one single denominator and furthermore the logos element in it is an important factor, which even has the power of veto—nothing against reason can be accepted—but which is not the only power in man nor his highest endowment. Not only can everything not be put into words or concepts, but not even all here on earth is logos.

A real philosophical and theological endeavour today has to integrate in the task not only the exigencies of the logos, but also the realities of the myth and, last but not least, the freedom of the spirit.

7 Religious Experience in Contemporary Judaism

NAFTALI CHAIM BRANDWEIN

The holocaust of European Jewry and the materialization of that ancient dream—the re-establishment of the Jewish State in Israel—are without a doubt the two most shockingly significant historic events that the Jewish people has experienced throughout its lengthy exile.

It is still too early to speak about the conclusions to be drawn from the revolutionary developments, be they social, political, and economical, or the transformation in spiritual relations and values brought about by those historic events. For the stupefying effects of the calamity still linger, reverberating within the Jewish world, beating upon orphaned hearts, demanding comprehension and expression. At the same time, the realization of the ancient dream remains embattled and besieged, fighting for survival. The terror of the reality of the events, as well as the joy of the dream come true, paralyze every attempt at full artistic expression. What is possible, however, is an intermediary evaluation of the revolutionary transformation of values as they are revealed in modern Hebrew literature. In particular, we will concentrate on the religious implications inherent in these changes, as indicated by our topic.

In a general way, we can say that three voices are heard in this Hebrew literature: a furious scream against heaven and man; a joyous, tearful melody; and a stifled mumbling of despair and alienation. Every sensitive listener to these voices, however, can hear in them the struggle for expression and the pangs of birth in conveying the very inability to express the experience of those events. In order to understand the religious implications of these voices, we should examine, however briefly, the religious beliefs and convictions as revealed in Hebrew literature prior to the modern period.

The cry for justice, the sigh of the suffering, the prayer for salvation, and the song of thanksgiving are, as is well known, dominant motifs which are strung like a thread of crimson throughout traditional Hebrew literature. In the center of this ancient literature stands man—praying, pleading with his God, or protesting and arguing:

From:
Shall He who is judge
of all the world,
Not act with justice?
Gen. 18:25

to:
Why do the fortunes of the
wicked men prosper?
Jer. 12:1

to:
Shall I try force?
Look how strong He is.
Or go to court?
But who will summon Him?
Job 9:19

From:
How much longer
shall the wicked, O Lord
How much longer
shall the wicked exult?
Psalm 94:3

to:
O Lord, hear my prayer
Let my cry for help
reach you.   Psalm 102:2

From:
How long, O Lord
Will you eternally
forget me?   Psalm 13:2

to:
The Lord is my shepherd,
I shall not want. Psalm 23:1

Yet in spite of the similarity in motifs between the ancient and modern voices, the essential distinction is in the aura of religiosity and in the beliefs and convictions emanating therefrom. For in the literature of this ancient religious background and its beliefs and convictions we find:

1) the certainty of possible communication and dialogue between man and his God, even though this dialogue and contact be not easily achieved. As the Psalmist has it: "Come, said my

heart, seek his face; your face, O Lord, will I seek. / Turn not your face from me..." (Psalm 27:8-9). Yet possibility of this dialogue does exist, as an unshakable certainty.

2) Nature as well as history are not self-governing; they exist only as reflections of the divine power. All that occurs within the realm of nature and the sphere of history are but processes leading toward realization of the divine purpose.

3) Man, therefore, must measure all life, personal as well as universal, by the criterion of the divine commandments which lead toward this ultimate purpose.

In the Medieval period, as Hillel Bavli writes, "the poet made bold to escape the enchanted divine circle through the narrow gate of delusive art. He took delight in the beauties and bounties of the world, he explored the regions of temporal life probing his own ego, as if seeking some refuge from the guiding hand of Providence. But in the end he succumbed. The song of the Divine within him was all too powerful. It overcame the rebellious, worldly urge." [2]

The Hebrew artist of the Middle Ages, notwithstanding the rich, sophisticated, secular element of his poetry—songs of wine and love, songs of war and vanity, songs of laughter and earthly pleasures, implying motifs of homo-eroticism and anti-traditional-ism—nevertheless is dominated by the spirit of faith, tradition, and religiosity.[3] As Rabbi Abraham Ibn Ezra,[4] the famous poet of the Middle Ages, defined the nature of the Israelites' creativity in his poetical aphorism:

The Ishmaelites, their poems are of love and passion,
And the Edomites, of wars and vengeance,
And the Greeks, of wisdom and forethought,
And the Hindus, of fables and riddles,
And the Israelites, of songs and praise to God Almighty.[5]

1. Psalms 27:8-9.
2. See H. Bavli, "Some Aspects of Modern Hebrew Poetry," Herzl Institute Pamphlets 2 (New York, 1958), p. 32.
3. See H. Schirman, *Toldot ha-Shirah ha-Ivrit b'Sfarad u b'Provence* (Bialik Publications, Tel Aviv), Vol. I, Intro., p. 50. See also A. Mirsky, *Yalkut ha-Piyutim* (M. Neuman, Israel, 1958), p. xi.
4. Born in Spain, 1092, died 1167.

This all-pervasive spirit of faith is beautifully described by S. Y. Agnon,[6] the most prominent Hebrew novelist of our era, in his story, *As Is the Sorrow, So Is the Reward*:

> When Rabbi Zedkiah would take up his pen to write a holy poem, he used to ask permission from the One who possesses all power, and would sit and pluck words with the point of his pen and examine each word to see if it was mentioned in the Bible or in the sayings of the sages. For the Holy One spoke to our fathers only in the language of the Written Law and made a covenant with us only in the Oral Law ... and Rabbi Zedkiah would commune with his creator with no one between them. ...[7]

This relation to words and the artistic act could be possible only on the basis of religious certainty in a world of transcendental holiness.

When this religious certainty was shattered there occurred a fundamental shift full of consequences in the ideology of the Hebrew writer and in his work. This ideological shift may be regarded as a transformation from the theocentric belief to anthropocentric secularity. That is to say, this world, as is, is regarded as self-sufficient, its worthwhileness invested in its own existence. And man, standing in the center of this world, no longer stands praying before or pleading for justice from his God. Man is confident in his own powers to grasp the essence of the world intellectually, to give it expression, and to give meaning to his and the world's existence. As a consequence, man lays down guidelines of life and behavior which he believes can bring him to a world which is humanly moral, good, and worthwhile. This human being, who centers himself in existence, no longer relies upon or expects the divine voice to lead him to a purpose beyond, which would justify his existence.

The essential difference between the Hebrew literature of the last 200 years, and the Hebrew literature prior to that, which extends into antiquity, is that while the latter is a sacred liter-

---

5. Schirman, *op. cit.*, Vol. II, p. 578.
6. 1888-1970.
7. *Ha-Esh Ve ha-Etzim* (Schocken Publications, Tel Aviv, 1966), pp. 7-8.

ature growing out of a world confident in a total sanctity which hovers over every facet of life, the former is a secular literature, sprouting from a world of secularity. This "modern" Hebrew literature reflects, in different modes, the challenge and struggle of the modern Jew with his cultural and spiritual tradition.[8]

A further analysis of modern Hebrew literature reveals three stages: First, the stage of the naive Hebrew literature of the Enlightenment.[9] This literature could not itself grasp the significance of the revolution it was preaching. It lacked the historical insight necessary to fathom the shattering implications of the revolution. Out of a naiveté and superficiality it preached a bridging-of-the-gap, a compromise between two different worlds, where one could exist only at the expense of total ruination of the other.

The second stage is that of the militant Enlightenment literature—that which openly declared war on the old Jewish tradition. This literature, as well, did not yet comprehend the significance of this revolution, but it did realize the strength and deep-rootedness of a tradition which could not be overcome by mere euphemism and superficial rhetoric. To the credit of the writers of this stage, it may be said that they already realized the superficial naiveté of the previous literary generation. A close reader of this literature will discover not a few sharp arrows directed at this superficial naiveté, but at the same time there are a greater number of barbs of irony and satire directed toward the old traditional spiritual world of the Jew.[10]

The third stage might be called the stage of the twofold tragedy. Here, the Hebrew writer reaches the climax of awareness of crisis and struggle with Jewish tradition and culture. The main motifs of this stage are expressed in the outcry arising from the polaric struggle between a world of vision and a world of nihilism, between a world rooted in the values of faith and feeling, and an escape to the abyss of the personal "I," detached,

8. See B. Kurtzweil, *Sifrutenu ha-Chadashah — Hemshekh o Mahapekha?* (Schocken Publications, Tel Aviv, 1959), pp. 13-19.

9. From the eighth decade of the nineteenth century.

10. For further information on the theme, see J. Klausner, *Ha-Historiah Shel ha-sifrut ha-Chadashah;* Daat Publications, Jerusalem, 1954, pp. 1-15. See also B. Kurzweil, *op. cit.,* pp. 49-66.

incapable of return and identification. The scene is one of alienation and strangeness fused with the desire for an unachievable return. The tragedy is created by the quality of awareness the author gives to the heroes of the struggle: the protagonist sees his own world crumbling, as well as the decline of the gradually disappearing world to which he yearns to escape. And over and above stands the writer, as if looking at both worlds and whispering in pained irony:

> Just between you and me, what is broken cannot be repaired, but it is impossible to forget what the broken pieces look like.

There are times when the entire struggle with its two worlds penetrates and becomes confined to the heart of the author himself. One world no longer confronts the other, nor one hero the other. The author, alone, living a defective existence, sadly recalls from its ruins a golden world of childhood. He knows that the struggle is over, that the time has passed, that whatever he sees is only an image of what once was but no longer is, that he has neither a way to return nor a way to flee.[11]

This motif of exposure to a world of exile and alienation and the struggle for a return to the world of mercy is the center and focal point of Agnon's great epic, *The Bridal Canopy*.[12] This wondrous epic is about Reb Yudel, a man pure and innocent as a child, god-fearing, who experiences the problems and anxieties of man without a shadow of hesitation or doubt in the worthwhileness of life.

Reb Yudel is a husband, a father of three daughters, and owner of a rooster. When the time arrives for him to marry off his first daughter, he sets off on a journey to collect charity for a dowry, singing hymns of praise to God. On his way, he experiences many hardships and is torn between despair and hope, humiliation and yearning. He accumulates money and

11. For further elaboration, see my article, "The Conflict of the Generations in Modern Hebrew Literature," *Conservative Judaism*, Vol. XIX, No. 2, 1963, pp. 79-83.

12. Schocken Books, New York, 1967. Translated by I. M. Lask.

squanders it. His name and identity change during the course of his wanderings. And he returns to his town empty-handed, while the aim for which he had set out is still far beyond his reach.

At the end, Yudel Chosid merits a blessed return. In the very last minute a miracle breaks through to his world and turns grief into joy, and converts the tragic ending into a happy, glorious conclusion by virtue of God's mercy and compassion. The *deus ex machina* in this instance is the rooster, Rabbi Zorach, who used to waken Reb Yudel to morning prayers and study. The rooster jumps out of his daughter's hands while being taken to the slaughter house, "climbs mountains and descends valleys," and leads Reb Yudel's family to a cave in which a treasure is hidden. The treasure consists of "golden coins, precious stones and pearls." Reb Yudel succeeds in marrying off all three of his daughters, blindfolds his eyes so as not to see the unclean earth of exile, and merits ascension to the Holy Land of Israel.

In this epic, as indicated, God's mercy intercedes at the last moment to liberate the hero from his agonies. In a masterful sequence of events, Agnon molds the romantic illusion of a world of wholeness and unity, which contains the miracle as a possible and even necessary solution. This illusion is possible because Agnon has so molded his character that Reb Yudel Chosid does not appear out of place, but, on the contrary, actually lives, with his naiveté in a world of his time.

Agnon's artistic intentions in this epic are to remove before him the three generations of enlightenment and Zionistic ideology in order to make a path for himself whereon he may approach and reach out to Reb Yudel. While reaching for him he lets him speak the way he speaks, live the way he lives, feel the way he feels. But from time to time the artist looks inwardly and whispers to himself, murmuring painfully and with a smile, "Look, how gigantic he is, and still, how far away. . . . But I can't help smiling at him." It is for this reason that there is revealed to the reader the story of Reb Yudel and his existence in a world which is composed of a simultaneous blend of two points of view. It is a world which arouses jealousy and excitement by its glory and wholeness—by its love for man and God;

and at the same time arouses smiles and laughter by the grotesqueness of its features and gestures. The total experience of
the reader, like the artist, is, therefore: "I am happy to be wiser
than Reb Yudel, but still, what a pity I can't be like him." The
reader, as the artist, knows that he will never be able to reach
out to the holy world of Reb Yudel, because on his way out
to this world he will not be able to erase the smile of mockery
on his lips.

One observes this world and is astounded—by what virtue was
Reb Yudel saved from a tragic destiny so common in Agnon's
stories? And the answer: by virtue of Reb Zorach the Rooster.
Reb Zorach, who jumps from the hands and discovers hidden
treasures. You repeat to yourself again and again and wonder,
"Reb Zorach the Rooster . . . is not the artist diabolically mocking
me?" No. In the world of Reb Yudel Chosid everything is possible. A miracle suits it no less than a calamity. This miracle
arouses the jealousy and mockery of him who stands outside.
For here comes Reb Yudel, who refuses to lower and shield his
head from the stones of hoodlums. He has said his prayer for a
safe journey and has nothing to fear from rocks. The outsider
smiles and is jealous.

Reb Zechariah the Preacher says in *The Bridal Canopy*:
"That's the reason God created man with two eyes—with one
eye he should see the greatness of the Holy One, Blessed be He,
and with one to see his own lowly state." And it would seem that
in this fashion Agnon has molded his characters. With one eye
he looks at them and sees them as giants planted firmly in their
world, and with the other looks at himself and sees his own
cleverness. He looks again and sees them somewhat grotesque,
but then he looks at himself again and sees the alienated outsider.[13]

The inability of the author to identify with the pure and
simple faith of Reb Yudel, with the world of mercy and miracle
of the always-just God, is implied in many of the parables which
run through the epic. As an example, in the fable of the Jack
of All Trades, God commands his angel to pursue a poor fellow
and save him from starvation, but the poor fellow runs faster

13. See my article, "Alienation and Return," *Jewish Book Council of
America*, Vol. 25, 1967-68, pp. 27-38.

than the angel. When the angel finally catches up with him, the poor fellow is already dead and cold. In *The Bridal Canopy* Agnon contrasts a world of miracles with a world of irony and grotesqueness, in which the miracle comes too late. As the Yiddish proverb puts it, which translates thus: "Before the consolation there comes the expiration." "The poor fellow is already dead and cold."

The outcry against heaven on the miracle which comes too late, and thereby converts the divine world into a demonic world, is the tragic subject of a poem by Bialik,[14] the foremost poet of modern Hebrew literature. The poem is called *Upon the Slaughter*.

> Heavens, beg mercy for me!
> If truly God dwells in your orbit and round
> And in your space is His pathway, that I have not found . . .
> Then you pray for me!
> For my own heart is dead, no prayer on my tongue
> And strength has failed, and hope has passed
> O, how long? O until when?
> Executioner! Here's the neck—come and butcher!
> Behead me like a dog—you have the arm with the ax
> The whole earth is my scaffold
> And we—we are the few
> My blood is outlaw
> Strike the skull and murder's blood will spurt
> The blood of babe and graybeard stain your garb
> It will never be erased, ever!
> If justice there be—let it shine forth now
> For if when I have perished from the earth
> The right shine forth
> Then let His Throne be shattered
> And let the heavens rot
> And you, O murderers, live on your blood
> Cleanse yourself in it.[15]

14. 1873-1934.

15. "Al ha-Shchita, *Kol Kitvei H. N. Bialik* (Dvir Publications, Tel Aviv, 1951), p. 35. For translation, see *Selected Poems of H. N. Bialik* (Block Publishing Co., New York, 1965), pp. 112-113; see also *The Modern Hebrew Poem Itself* (Holt, New York, 1965), pp. 32-34.

The miracle which shines forth after the victim has "perished from the earth" deadens prayer on the tongue. Justice, which does not appear in time, turns innocent blood into purifying water, but paradoxically, the poet, whose heart and prayer are dead and who lives in a godless world, has no other source to turn to than the very heavens which betrayed him. The outcry, "no prayer on my tongue," concludes with the prayerful words of the Psalmist, "O, until when? How long?"

In this literature there are at work contrasting and complex ties to the world of tradition: anger and rebellion against it, and inability to detach oneself from it; shocking uprootedness from any religious certainty, and a painful search for a way to return. Rebellion against the mute heavens and the inability to forget them are the central ideas in another epic of Agnon—*A Guest for the Night*.[16]

In this epic Agnon leaves the clashing worlds of mercy and the too-late miracle which we have seen in *The Bridal Canopy*. From the God who tries to save his creatures and succeeds in bringing about their escape from divine salvation, Agnon proceeds to the God who blocks every path to a human explanation of life. The only gate remaining open to man is to live with the unanswerable questions. For it is better to live in a world ruled by an unfathomable God than in a godless world, which leaves no room either for questions or for answers. All this becomes clear to a close reader of *A Guest for a Night*.

Following is a brief summary of a passage which illustrates this point. The passage concerns a conversation between Daniel, the son, and Reb Shlome, his father, while the author himself listens passively: Daniel refuses to put on his phylacteries and pray to a God who brings about wars, which leave arms scattered in the trenches—arms bound with phylacteries, but without bodies.

"A man can bind himself on the altar and give up his life for the glory of God—cried Daniel—With his dying breath he can pronounce the confessions of faith, 'Hear, O Israel, the Lord is our God, the Lord is One,' and prolong the final 'One' like the great Rabbi Akiba in his torment, until his soul departs. But to

16. Schocken Books Pub., New York, 1968.

be bound every day, every hour, every moment, on seven altars, to have one limb consumed today and another tomorrow—that is something not every man can stand. I'm only a human being, flesh and blood, and when my flesh rots and my blood stinks, my lips cannot utter the praises of the Almighty. And if I do utter His praises, is it to the glory of God if a lump of rotting flesh or a skinful of stinking blood cries out: 'Thou art righteous, no matter what befalls me, and I have been wicked,' and even then—He does not lift His hand from me and continues to afflict me? "[17]

But Reb Shlome, Daniel's father, cannot live in a world without Torah and divine commandments. As Agnon puts it in another passage, fused with naiveté and irony, which explodes at its conclusion as a bitter grotesque, but is nevertheless the only possible answer.

"For what reason did the Holy One, blessed be He, choose us and lay upon us the yoke of the Torah and the commandments, for isn't the Torah heavy and difficult to observe? . . . For it is like a king's crown, made of gold and precious stones and diamonds. So long as the crown is on the king's head, men know that he is a king. Does the king refrain from putting the crown on his head because it is heavy? On the contrary, he puts it on his head and delights in it. The king's reward for the crown being on his head is that everyone exalts and honors him and bows down before him. What good does this do to the king? That I do not know." [18]

For what is life without a crown? What is life for a man who has forgotten he is son of the king? In a world such as this, the pain, and the smile, the poem and the scream are all meaningless. A great muteness stifles them all. In a world like this Reb Shlome cannot even argue with his son Daniel. Man cannot speak to himself nor to his shadow. In the final analysis, man has no other way but to forgive God and submit to him, for only in this way can he live the great pain of the unanswerable question. For it is this pain and this submission which are the essence of the tragi-comic grotesqueness of the worthwhileness of life. This

17. *Ibid.*, p. 34.
18. *Ibid.*, pp. 29-30.

tragic feeling deepens in the light of the holocaust and becomes glorified in the light of a salvation which comes, though late.

Guilt feelings, hopelessness, suffocating silences, inwardly streaming tears, and amazement—amazement at the redemption whose trembling miracle still astounds friends and enemies alike—all these find a powerful expression in the poetry of Uri Zvi Greenberg.[19]

> When the enemy came, what did the Jews possess?
> Millions of men but not one sword!
> The blank mind of the lamb before slaughter,
> Scrolls, synagogues, parchment,
> Foreign flags, prayer shawls, phylacteries,
> And to the Master of the World they sweetly prayed—but
> He was late![20]

But this poetry does not sing only of blood and tears, of chaos and catastrophe. It also envisions the great new hope. Here is another example from Greenberg's poetry:

> To the great return, to the joining in the circle of lights
> Of love of Israel—
> The poet calls to the false dreamers of continued exile
> In this day, the End of days,
> And the God of Israel answers:
> So be it! Amen.
> With faces turned to Jerusalem of the mountains:
> To the Jerusalem of rock, of fire, of gold.
> God will not forsake us then, I do believe."[21]

Yet the calamity of the holocaust, as well as the flaming joy of salvation that came late, still await their fullest expression. The fear about the angel who may be too late still lingers, and the little boy who dreams about the sacrifice of Isaac does not return home with Abraham, but rather turns to sleep with the ram in the thicket.

19. The foremost poet of contemporary Hebrew poetry. Born in 1948 in Eastern Galicia. Lives in Israel.

20. *Rechovot ha-Nahar,* Schocken Publications, Tel Aviv, 1951, pp. 48-50.

21. *Ibid.,* p. 175.

8   Religious Experience in Confucianism and Buddhism

MARY PATRICIA FRANZ

> The world is in great confusion, the virtuous and the sage
> are obscured, morality and virtue have lost their unity, and
> there are many in the world who have seized a single aspect
> of the whole for their self-enjoyment. Everyone in the world
> does what he wishes and is a rule unto himself.[1]

The humanist philosophy developed by Confucius has a tremendous message for this particular period of our own times so
similar to the age of transition in his own era. Ancient institutions
were criticized. Proponents of new systems of thought wished
to revise traditional foundations, and some opposed all institutions entirely. Old establishments had lost their previous authority. New guidelines for the future had not been formulated and
the epoch was one of much variation and incertitude, amidst
the disintegrating feudal society. As a cure for the evils of his
own day, Confucius urged traditionalism—not from a sentimental
attachment to customs of past generations, but to inculcate in his
students a precious philosophical world-view.

Chinese philosophy is concerned primarily with the art of
self-cultivation rather than the seeking of knowledge, that is,
the search for good rather than the search for truth. Oriental
philosophers prefer to apply knowledge to actual conduct and
thus directly obtain happiness, rather than to engage in empty
discussions about it. The Inner Sage is a person who has established virtue in himself. The Outer King is one who has accomplished great deeds in the world. The highest ideal for a man is

1. Fung Yu-Lan, *History of Chinese Philosophy*, Vol. I, p. 14.

at once to possess the virtue of a Sage and the accomplishments of a ruler and so become a Sage-King. Confucius never attained his personal desire to be a philosopher-king, but by promulgating a reverence for learning, the teaching of Confucius re-created the intellectual life of Chinese society and maintained it intact for the next two thousand years.

The Confucian system of education is most simple and reasonable, concerned always with human life and human problems. "In the *Analects* of Confucius we read: 'The wise are free from perplexities; the virtuous from anxiety; the bold from fear.' This anticipates the modern educator who insists on the threefold objective of a modern university: the search for new knowledge, the preservation of existing knowledge, and the application of knowledge to social needs." [2]

> To Confucius, the way of the well educated and superior man is threefold. Only those who are earnest in learning are close to the wise; only those who say little and do much are close to the virtuous; and only those who see the vice of immoderation and apply the Golden Mean in all situations are close to the bold, who will not easily fall to the ground. [3]

Chinese humanism concentrates on certain values. It states that there is a knowledge of essentials and a knowledge of externals. The knowledge of externals is the world of facts. The knowledge of essentials is the world of human behavior. Confucius says, "Be a good son, a good brother, and a good friend. If you have any energy left after attending to conduct, then study books." [4]

Confucianism in its essence is the study of human relations (*jenlun*) through a correct appreciation of human values, by the psychology of human motives, to the end that we may behave as reasonable human beings (*tsuo jen*). Confucianism is also a spiritual discipline. Its dynamic attitudes toward life call forth a truly thorough program for moral reformation of the

2. Paul K. T. Sih, "The Legacy of Confucius," *St. John's University Alumni Magazine,* Vol. xlll, No. 3, (Spring 1967), p. 10.

3. *Ibid.*

4. Lin Yutang, *The Wisdom of China,* p. 571.

world, with one's own moral transformation as the starting point. This is seen in the Confucian treatise called *The Great Learning*.

> The goal of Great Learning consists in the manifestation of virtue, in renewing the spirit of the people, and in resting in the Supreme Goodness. . . . The ancients who wished to spread Virtue throughout the world, first ordered well their own states. Wishing to order well their own states, they first regulated their families. Wishing to regulate their families, they first cultivated their own persons. Wishing to cultivate their own persons, they first rectified their hearts. Wishing to rectify their hearts, they first made their thoughts sincere. Wishing to be sincere in their thoughts, they sought after true knowledge. The attainment of knowledge was found in the investigation of things.[5]

"To put it the other way round, the investigation of things leads to true knowledge. This leads to sincerity in thought. This leads to purity of heart. This perfects the individual man. This produces an ordered family. This helps to make a well-governed State; and this process is a continuous and harmonious movement from innermost harmony to the outermost harmony.[6]

> How abundantly do spiritual beings display the powers that belong to them. We look for them but do not see them; we listen to but do not hear them; yet they enter into all things, and there is nothing without them. They cause all the people in the kingdom to fast and purify themselves, to array themselves in their richest garments, in order to attend their sacrifices. Then like overflowing water, they seem to be over the heads, and to the left and the right of the worshippers. It is said in the Book of Poetry, "The approach of the Spirits you cannot surmise: and can you treat them with indifference? Such is the manifestness of what is minute. Such is the impossibility of repressing the essentials of Ultimate Reality."[7]

5. Paul K. T. Sih, *op. cit.*, p. 11.
6. *Ibid.*
7. Paul K. T. Sih, "The Legacy of Confucius," p. 12.

"In order to know men, one may not dispense with a knowledge of Heaven.... Does Heaven speak? The four seasons pursue their courses and all things are continuously being produced, but does Heaven say anything?" [8]

Kung-Fu-tzu (551-479 B.C.) was born in the province of Lu, Shantung, China. Confucius summed up his own life as follows:

At fifteen I set my mind upon learning. At thirty, I stood firm. At forty I was free from doubts. At fifty I understood the Will of Heaven. [9]

It seems that his personal perfection increased with age for he continues, "At sixty, my ear was an obedient organ for the reception of truth. At seventy, I could follow what my heart desired, without transgressing what was right" (*Analects,* tr. James Legge). Confucius became a wandering teacher, after making a friendly settlement with his wife that they no longer live together. Gradually he gathered some eager followers and obtained government positions by which he was able to substantially reduce crime. Then envious superiors banished him for thirteen years. Finally, when he was called back to his province, he would not accept any political office, but began to edit the Five Classics. The *Shih* describes aims; the *Shu* describes events; Classics. "The *Shih* describes aims; the *Shu* describes events; the *Li* (Rites) directs conduct; the *Yueh* (Music) secures harmony. The *I* (Book of Changes) shows the principles of the *Yin* and the *Yang*." [10] Later Confucius wrote about his own province, Lu, in the *Ch'un Chiu*. The chief aim of Confucius was to transmit unchanged the pure traditions of the ancient day which originated in Heaven. Here are his own words: "A transmitter and not a creator, a believer in and lover of antiquity. Striving unwearyingly in study and teaching others without flagging. I am not one who has innate knowledge, but one who, loving antiquity, is diligent in seeking it therein." [11]

The doctrines of Confucius present a system of ethical, political and social order based on history. Confucianism in the

8. *Ibid.*
9. Fung Yu-Lan, *History of Chinese Philosophy*, p. 58.
10. Fung Yu-Lan, *op. cit.*, p. 47.
11. *Ibid.*, p. 48.

narrowest sense means rituals, propriety, and good manners. In a philosophic sense it means an ideal social order with everything in its place. In a personal sense, it means a holy, religious state of mind, very near to the word "faith," which means a valid unified body of beliefs implicitly accepted, concerning God, and nature, and man's place in the universe. A world without order (Tao) was the result of a breakdown of social institutions and Confucius hoped constantly that the condition might be remedied, so that he said, "When good order prevails in the world, ceremonials, music, and punitive expeditions proceed from the Son of Heaven." The remedy was to be found in the rectification of names: a father should be a father, and a king should be a king. By this, Confucius means that if a father kills his son, he is not a father, that is he does not have the essence of paternity without love for his son. A king is not a king if he starves his people, because the essence of kingship is that a king bring harmony to his domain. Confucius said:

> Neglect in the cultivation of character; lack of thoroughness in study; inability to move toward recognized duty; and inability to correct my imperfections; these are what cause me solicitude.[12]

In explaining the virtue of *chih*, Confucius warned against plausible speech and ingratiating demeanor. An upright man acts according to his own feelings, while the wicked man acts according to the feelings of others, artificially.

In the *Lun Yu*: "The Master said: 'Artful speech and ingratiating demeanor rarely accompany *jen* (I,3). Again; " 'The firm of spirit, the resolute in character, the simple in manner, and the slow of speech are not far from jen' " (XIII, 27). As to the meaning of *Jen*, "the Master replied: 'It is to love your fellow men' " (XII, 22). *Jen* is love of the other with sympathy as its basis. '*Jen* is the denial of self and response to the right and proper (*li*).[13] In the adage: "Desiring to maintain oneself, one sustains others; desiring to develop oneself, one develops others"

12. Fung Yu-Lan, *op. cit.*, p. 45.
13. *Ibid.*, p. 69.

is the Confucian virtue of 'conscientiousness to others' or *chung*. And in the proverb, "Do not do to others, what you do not like yourself," there is the Confucian virtue of *shu* or altruism. Really to practice *chung* and *shu* means genuinely to practice *jen*.[14]

The *chun-tzu*, a superior person, was the product of the instruction given by Confucius who believed that the true manifestations of a man's nature need only be combined with *li* (decorum) to reach the highest excellence. This is possible for all of us to follow and practice. *Li* refers to customs perpetuated in a traditional society and which define an individual's place in the social order. *Yen* applies to the inner quality of a moral being, the creative spontaneity of human kindness:

> To be able wherever one goes to carry five things into practice, constitutes *jen*. They are respect, magnanimity, sincerity, earnestness, and kindness. With respect you will avoid insult; with magnanimity you will win over everyone; with sincerity men will trust you; with earnestness you will have achievement; and with kindness you will be well fitted to command others. (XVII,6)[15]

In following our natural tendencies, we modify our conduct according to time and place. Confucius says: "With me there is no inflexible *may* or *may not*." The Lun Ye states: The Master was entirely free from four things: he had no pre-conceptions, no predeterminations, no obstinacy, and no egoism.[16] Due to his stress on righteousness (*i*), someone said of Confucius: "Is he not the one who knows he cannot succeed and keeps on trying to do so?" Tung Chung-shu, the Han Confucianist said: "Be correct in righteousness without considering the profitableness (of the result of the action); be pure in one's principles without considering whether they bring material return." As to whether one's principles really do prevail or not, this question concerns their profitableness, that is, their material return, and so need not be considered. Confucius says: "The Superior Man is in-

14. Fung Yu-Lan, *op. cit.*, p. 71.
15. *Ibid.*, p. 73.
16. *Ibid.*, p. 74.

formed in what is right. The inferior man is informed in what is profitable."[17] It is here that the Confucian doctrine of righteousness rather than utilitarianism (that which is of profit in itself) clashes with the Mohist school.

Mo Tzu was active between 479 and 381 B.C. He comes very close to Christian teachings in that he taught universal love as the basis of society and peace. He said that Heaven loved people and insisted on the existence of spirits. Mo Tzu believed that to accomplish anything one must have standards, for nothing can be achieved without them. "Neither the parents nor the teacher nor the ruler should be accepted as the standard of government" for there is nothing better than following Heaven.

Heaven is all-inclusive and impartial in its activities, abundant and unceasing in its blessings, and lasting and untiring in its guidance. And so, when the sage-kings had accepted Heaven as their standard, they measured every action and enterprise by Heaven. What Heaven desired they would carry out, what Heaven abominated they refrained from. Certainly Heaven desires to have men benefit and love one another and abominates to have them hate and harm one another. How do we know that Heaven loves and benefits men universally? Because it claims all and accepts offerings from all. All states in the world, large or small, are cities of Heaven, and all people young or old, honorable or humble, are its subjects; for they all graze oxen and sheep, feed dogs and pigs, and prepare clean wine and cakes to sacrifice to Heaven. Those who love and benefit others Heaven will bless. Those who hate and harm others Heaven will curse, for it is said that he who murders the innocent will be visited by misfortune.[18]

To understand the words of Mo Tzu it is necessary to review religious thought prior to Confucius. The primitive Chinese worshipped a single omnipotent Supreme Being in the form of Heaven. There were lesser protective spirits of the stars, mountains and rivers, similar to the Christian angelic hierarchy of

17. Fung Yu-Lan, *op. cit.*, p. 74.
18. Lin Yutang, *op. cit.*, p. 789.

spirits such as the Thrones, Dominations and Principalities who have charge of the government of the world, the Virtues who control the weather, and the guardian angels appointed to take care of each man coming into being. The *Shu Ching* says: "Men must act for the work of Heaven." [19] In the *Kuo Yü* we find the following:

> Sacrifice is that through which one can show one's filial piety and give peace to the people, pacify the country and make the people settled. It cannot be put an end to. For when the desires of the people are given free rein there comes a stoppage; with such a stoppage there comes a wasting away; and when this wasting away continues for long without any stimulus to it, life does not prosper, so that there is no obedience to the commands on high.[20]

The Chinese considered the Emperor not as an idol but as a man especially chosen and sacrosanct because of his relationship with the Divine. Only the Son of Heaven, holding the destiny of the Chinese people, was worthy to offer the sacrifice. Twice a year, clad in a silk robe embroidered with dragons, the sun, moon, and stars, he mounted the steps which to the triply sacred and perfect number of nine, preceded a white marble altar. This lay open to the sky, a round edifice on a square base, its lower circle carved with clouds, the middle with phoenixes, the top with dragons.

> There at dawn, resuming all earthly things in himself, he offered chosen food, bales of silk, a young bull and pieces of lapis lazuli to the mysterious life-giving Heaven. At the summer and winter solstice, in the capital city, at the point of communication between earth and sky the Emperor harmonized man with nature in an astrobiological rite orienting him for another half year to the principles of Yin and Yang.[21]

19. Fung Yu-Lan, *op. cit.*, p. 33.
20. *Ibid.*, p. 39.
21. Vincent Cronin, *The Wise Man From the West*, p. 176.

Mo Tzu said, "To hold that there are no spirits and learn sacrificial ceremonies, is like learning the ceremonials of hospitality when there is no guest, or making fish nets when there are no fish." [22] Probably this is why, in the twentieth century A.D., there is only one religion which truly has the Substantial Presence of God in its offering of sacrifice. Confucius said, "He who sins against Heaven has no place left where he may pray." [23] The words of Confucius when he was at the point of death are as follows:

> When the Master fell ill, Chung Yu asked him to pray, and Confucius answered, "Are there any that can be said?" "Yes. The eulogies read, 'In prayer we turn to the divinities above and here below.'"
> Confucius answered: "My prayer has been in progress for a long time indeed."   (L.Y. VII, 35) [24]

Another profound book which accounts for the mellowness in the social behavior of the Chinese is that of Lao Tzu. In the Book of Tao we find the following:

LXXI. The Way of Heaven

True words are not fine-sounding;
   Fine-sounding words are not true.
A good man does not argue;
   He who argues is not a good man.
The wise one does not know many things;
   He who knows many things is not wise.
The Sage does not accumulate (for himself):
   He lives for other people,
   And grows richer himself;
   He gives to other people,
   And has a greater abundance.
The Tao of heaven
   Blesses, but does not harm.

22. Fung Yu-Lan, *op. cit.*, p. 91.
23. *Ibid.*, p. 57.
24. Albert Verwilghen, *Mencius: The Man and His Ideas*, p. 90.

The Way of the Sage
  Accomplishes but does not contend.[25]

The doctrines of Lao Tzu were developed by Chuang Tzu who was the greatest prose writer of the Chou dynasty due to his brilliance of style. Taoism expresses the Chinese attitude toward life and society. However, Chuang Tzu maintained that if one wished to keep the world in good order, the only way is to govern through non-government. Tso-Chiu Ming produced a standard plan for the writing of history by perfecting Confucius' *Annals of the State of Lu.*

Many schools of Confucianism arose in later centuries of which the greatest thinker in political science was Meng Tzu. His natural law concept greatly influenced the political science of the East. However, his greatest stress was upon the inner qualities of mind and heart, upon growth of the basic virtues, upon Excellence—that which makes the Chun Tzu, the moral man, truly a superior man. "Man's possession of excellence, intelligence, specific arts and devices, or knowledge, constantly depends on his having suffered misfortune" (7A. 18 Ware).[26] The personal program of Mencius is best illustrated in an address to his pupils:

To dwell in the broad house which is the whole world; to stand upright in the right place which is the whole world; to travel the main highway which is the whole world; when ambition is attained to exercise it in cooperation with your subjects; when it is not attained to travel one's own road alone; to be uncorrupted by riches and honors; to remain firm when poor and in low estate; to be unflinching even when threatened with war—this is to be a mighty man. (3B.2)[27]

Mencius himself had to endure many sufferings amid the corrupt officials of Ch'i who enjoyed life without any moral inhibitions:

25. Lin Yutang, *op. cit.*, p. 624.
26. Albert Verwilghen, *op. cit.*, p. 36.
27. *Ibid.*, p. 80.

A great man is differentiated from humanity (other-men) in general by the fact that he preserves his natural heart-and-mind. He preserves it through manhood-at-its-best (Benevolence of Goodness) and Ceremony (Li) also Propriety. Man-at-his-best loves human beings. The ceremonious person reverences human beings. He who loves human beings is always loved by them in return, just as reverence is always reciprocated. (4B 28; W.)[28]

Patiently Mencius points out that man can rid himself of evil:

When a man has been persistently in error, he can later change. When his heart-and-mind have proved utterly powerless and all his foresight has been contraried, then he can rise to prominence. After that, one realizes that life is a function of worries and anxieties, and that death is a function of security and joy. (6B. 16)[29]

Mencius seemed to have a deep understanding of daily problems, a profound sympathy for man's struggles, and a psychological encouragement in a person's endeavors to realize the good of this world. He said: "it is the great duty incumbent upon humanity that male and female should occupy a home" (5A.2). It was the opinion of Mencius that if any soul survived after death, it was not because of its nobility by birth, but because of the decree of Heaven (T'ien Li).

Mencius took Confucius as his model and seems to have lived always in the ways of righteousness, for at any moment he would have preferred death to the abandonment of the ways of virtue:

I am fond of both life and justice. If I cannot have both at the same time, I will forego life and take justice. Life is indeed something that I desire, but there is something that I desire more, so that for the sake of life I will not aim at a foolish goal.

28. Albert Verwilghen, *op. cit.*, p. 39.
29. *Ibid.*, p. 37.

Death is indeed something that I hate, but there is something that I hate more, so there are anxieties which I will not flee. (6A. 10)[30]

Buddhism moved across the frontiers of India and has also greatly affected the religion of China. Its founder, Siddhartha Gautama, had been a prince who was protected from contact with any unpleasant thing during his early life. At thirty years old, while out riding one day, he was so shocked at the sight of people who were old, sick, or impoverished that he began to wonder about the meaning of life. He was attracted at the sight of a hermit and said to himself, "To become a religious has ever been praised by the wise and this shall be my refuge and the refuge of others and shall yield the fruit of life and immortality." [31] He then gave up his beautiful wife and newly born only son to start an existence of extreme asceticism for the next six years, until it was said that the pit of his stomach touched his backbone. Realizing his error when he found himself no longer able to think, he decided to live moderately, avoiding the extremes of either self-denial or self-indulgence, thus taking the Middle Way. Settling down under a Bodhi tree, he experienced ecstasy and attained supreme enlightenment.

Siddartha Gautama did not intend to be the founder of a new religion but merely to depart from the Hindu practice of idolatry, animal sacrifice, and the caste system. Soon he gathered about one hundred fifty followers. Upon returning home, his little son Rahula became a monk. This practice is still continued today where the initiation ceremony of boys repeats Gautama's renunciation of the world and its enjoyments to embrace a life of meditation, celibacy, and poverty. The youth is first presented to the assembled guests by his father who has clothed his son in costly garments. Then the boy's head is shaved and he is clothed in the yellow robe and handed a begging bowl. A monk is also permitted to have a razor, a needle, a strainer for his drinking water, and a string of beads on which he counts his meditations of the Great Enlightened One. Since Burma and

30. Albert Verwilghen, *op. cit.*, p. 94.
31. Jerrold Schecter, *The New Face of Buddha*, p. 5.

Thailand consider the religious life as the perfection of all earthly existence, most men of twenty spend a few months in monastic life as a part of their formal education.

Yasodhara, the wife of Gautama, also joined his order as a female mendicant. The community grew and after preaching for forty-five years, Buddha died with these words, "Decay is inherent in all compound things. Work out your own salvation with diligence." [32]

The foundation of Buddha's teaching consists in the Four Noble Truths concerning suffering:

a. Life is full of pain.
b. Unhappiness is caused by desires for earthly things which do not satisfy.
c. There is a way to eliminate these desires.
d. Selfish desires can be destroyed by the Eightfold Path.

Essential preliminaries constitute the first two steps of the Eightfold Path—Right View and Right Resolution. Right view of the problem of life makes us recognize that every individual must endure sadness, sickness, old age, and death. These things would not make us miserable "were it not for the blind demandingness in our nature which leads us to ask of the universe, for ourselves and those specially dear to us, more than it is ready or even able to give." [33] Then when we become frustrated we begin to act in ways that hurt others, and this must be brought under discipline. Now each person is responsible for bringing this factor under control "in order that he may be a source of true and dependable well being to himself and to others." [34] Nothing short of rooting out all selfishness will do, "for as long as any taint of it is left, it cannot help affecting our action and poisoning our mental state." [35]

Right Resolution is a firm determination to renounce our-

32. Edwin A. Burtt, *The Teachings of the Compassionate Buddha*, p. 22.

33. Edwin A. Burtt, *op. cit.*, p. 28.

34. *Ibid.*

35. *Ibid.*

selves, hold no resentments, and harm no living creature in order
to achieve a solution for the human condition. By the next three
steps—Right Speech, Right Conduct, and Right Livelihood—we
so structure our daily life as to build an impregnable moral
foundation which makes a decent virtuous life possible, that is,
peaceful, truthful, and pure. The last three steps—Right Effort,
Right Alertness, and Right Concentration—are necessary conditions for achieving progress toward the goal of Nirvana. We must
work strenuously to develop the good that is lacking and preserve
the good that already exists. Mental awareness of all our activities
in thought, word, and deed, brings self-mastery.

> What should be known, that I have known;
> What should developed be, I have developed;
> What should forsaken be, that I forsook.
> Hence, Brahmin, am I Buddha,—One Awake. (Sn 558)[36]

Finally, Supreme serenity is acquired by right concentration.
Silence, seclusion and the regularity of monastic life are the
milieu for accomplishing these last steps of the Eightfold Path.
And so the monk enters Nirvana—"a state marked by a sense
of liberation, inward peace and strength, insight into truth,
the joy of complete oneness with reality, and love toward all
creatures in the universe." [37]

Only after Buddha's death did his teachings develop into a
popular religion. The first Council that gathered together to carry
on Gautama's work accepted the Tripitaka: Discipline, Discourses,
and ultimate Doctrines. The second Great Council held in
338 B.C. caused a schism. The Theravada group remained orthodox according to the strict rules of the Theravadan Canon which
is the oldest record of the thought of the Enlightened One.
Ceylon, Indonesia, Cambodia, and Thailand have Theravada
Buddhism which stresses monastic asceticism.

Buddha had said that minor rules could be lightened to meet
the changing needs of society. This caused the liberals after the

36. Edward Conze, *Buddhist Meditation*, p. 46.
37. Edwin Burtt, *op. cit.*, p. 29.

second Council to spread Mahayana Buddhism which moved into China, Korea, Tibet, and South Vietnam.

American foreign policy has neglected the political role of Buddhism in Asia where church and state cannot be separated. Buddhism is a complete way of life for the Asians who are not only concerned with material, intellectual, and political needs, but also draw inspiration and strength from continuity with past tradition. The authority of the family, the local mandarin, or the prior of a Buddhist monastery is more important to the people than the orders of the central government. The rupture between the Buddhists and the Saigon officials has caused Thich Tri Quang to say that the President of the United States "only wants a doctrine of colonialism," and that the Saigon regime has been more concerned with taking advantage of anti-communism than with fighting the Communists. He remarked: "The Vietnamese people have been protected for centuries, first by the Chinese, then by the French. When you (the United States) come in it recalls the awful souvenirs of the past. The United States will fail with that protection." [38]

It might prove rather enlightening for American Christians to study the struggle of the Communists and the Buddhists in the East. Certainly, the destiny of the Orient is in their hands and will vitally affect us.

Mao-Tse-tung's China is restoring the monuments of Chinese Buddhism not as a center of worship but as shrines to the "cultural creativity of the Chinese people under the feudal empires of the past." [39] However, underneath the facade of a few showcase monasteries, the territories of the monks have been appropriated by the government and of the half a million Chinese monks existing twenty years ago, there are only a few thousand remaining. Ten Catholic priests are there at present amidst a population of over 700 million people.

Some China scholars suggest that the land reform in itself, without any physical coercion, changed the composition of monkhood and pressured a good many less than total be-

38. Jerrold Schecter, *op. cit.*, p. 26.
39. Schecter, *op. cit.*, p. XV.

lievers back to the temporal life. The upheaval of the Great Leap forward reduced the size of the monastery properties and the number of monks and nuns. Many Buddhists self-consciously left their monasteries and headed for the cities and work in industry. Many temples dispersed surplus premises to promote social and collective welfare undertakings. Writing on their study forum, four monks concluded that "the interests of socialism and production must be taken care of first, and all kinds of religious activity disadvantageous to national construction and production must be reformed. In religious activity, public interest must take precedence over private interest." [40]

However, we must not conclude that Communism will wipe out religion in China. The conquerors of this five-thousand-year old civilization have always been absorbed into the splendor of Chinese culture. The United States would like to support the Buddhists as a stabilizing factor in Asia, but Buddhist philosophy eschews our individualistic, materialistic society. The monks wish to protect their own sectarian interests even though they appreciate freedom and naively think that their spirituality can balance the Marxists.

Americans find it difficult to concentrate without tension and so rarely enjoy great religious experience. Yet, most would like to achieve eternal life, perpetual health, and not be subject to decay, as was the aim of Gautama. He considered the three signs of created being to be impermanence, suffering, and non-self. By impermanence was meant that the creature undergoes constant change, but that the Source of Life is immutable. That which changes can be destroyed, and so this physical universe is certainly not the ultimate reality. Man experiences suffering if he ascribes importance to earthly trivialities and is attached to these. A Buddhist poem reads:

> Heedless of body, heedless of goods, of the merit
> I gained and will gain still,
> I surrender my all to promote the welfare of others. [41]

40. *Op. cit.*, p. 44.
41. Edward Conze, *op. cit.*, p. 59.

9 The Spirit in Our Weakness: Religious Experience in Pauline Theology

PHEME PERKINS

Several years ago Bishop J.A.T. Robinson gave a lecture at Harvard in which he decried the gap between the experience of contemporary man and the theological formulations of the Christian churches. During the discussion period, a theologian in the audience suggested to the bishop that if he had the right theology, he would have the right experience. Such a statement points to the complex relationship between our cognitive and symbolic presuppositions and what we encounter as "reality." In approaching the problem of religious experience in Pauline theology, we should be extremely sensitive to this correlation. Paul's letters are not simply—indeed not even primarily—theological treatises. Rather they are directed to the specific religious situation in individual churches. Paul is not simply correcting their theology, but is also directing himself to the religious faith and experience correlated with it.

This essay is not, then, a theological sketch of Christian existence or experience according to Paul, such as Schnackenburg and Cerfaux have provided for us.[1] Nor do I intend to employ a method of writing New Testament theology, which collects all the texts in which Paul deals with a particular concept and then welds these into an impenetrable theological armour. Such a procedure all too often allows us to obtain

1. R. Schnackenburg, *Christian Existence in the New Testament*, tr. J. Blenkinsopp (Notre Dame: 1969), pp. 1-84; L. Cerfaux, *The Christian in the Theology of St. Paul*, tr. L. Soiron (New York: Herder & Herder, 1967).

answers from the New Testament authors to questions that have never really been of concern to them, as J. Munck has pointed out.[2] We must first of all remind ourselves that the religious "symbol system" of a group will in some sense define and limit what that group perceives as "real" or holds as true. F. Streng has demonstrated the importance of such a realization in dealing with certain "theological" concepts in Buddhism.[3] It is equally important to our understanding of the theological controversies in which Paul engages. P. Berger and T. Luckmann's work on sociology of knowledge has pointed out that many of our conceptions of what is objectively the case are socially derived and maintained.[4] We must be constantly aware that the theological options against which Paul writes are closely tied to the actual religious experience of the churches in question.

The second focus in our choice of procedure is the growing realization among students of Christian origins that early Christianity was an extremely diversified phenomenon theologically. What is true of a Christian community in one area may not be assumed to be the case in other churches in other areas. This insight, which W. Bauer had in the 1930's,[5] is rapidly becoming a major factor in the study of early Christianity. H. Koester has traced this diversification behind the New Testament writings to the multiplicity of the earliest Christian traditions and creedal formulations.[6] We must constantly take into account the given social and historical context to which an assertion is addressed.

2. Munck, J., "Pauline Research since Schweitzer," *The Bible and Modern Scholarship*, ed. P. Hyatt (Nashville: Abingdon Press, 1965), p. 175.

3. Streng, F., *Emptiness* (Nashville: Abingdon Press, 1967).

4. Cf. P. Berger & T. Luckmann, "Sociology of Religion and Sociology of Knowledge," *Sociology and Religion*, ed. N. Birnbaum & G. Lenzer (Englewood Cliffs: Prentice-Hall, 1969), pp. 410-18; idem, *The Social Construction of Reality* (New York: Doubleday, 1966).

5. Bauer, W., *Rechtglaeubigkeit und Ketzerei im aeltesten Christentum*[2] ed. G. Strecker (Tuebingen: 1964).

6. Cf. H. Koester, "One Jesus and Four Primitive Gospels" HTR 61 (1968), pp. 203-47; idem, "Gnomai Diaphoroi: the origin and nature of diversification in the history of early Christianity," HTR 58 (1965), pp. 279-318.

As J.M. Robinson has put it:

> Again we see that primitive Christian statements cannot be
> understood as doctrinal assertions in and of themselves, in
> isolation from the situation to which they spoke and hence
> apart from the way they cut. Orthodoxy and heresy have
> not only not yet separated into different ecclesiastical organ-
> izations, they have not even yet separated their theological
> conceptualizations.[7]

He goes on to emphasize that in Pauline studies we must discover the continuity involved in particular formulations addressed to specific situations and thus come to a more compre-
hensive and nuanced view of Pauline theology than has generally been the case.[8]

We cannot carry out such an investigation for all of the
Pauline corpus. But we can sketch out such an investigation by
focusing upon the problems that seem to have arisen in two
areas of the Pauline mission. In both Corinth and Galatia Paul
finds his churches adopting understandings of religious experience quite different from his own. His disputes with these
churches are not over minor points of theological doctrine, but
touch the foundation of Christian faith and experience. The
enormity of the problem Paul faced emerges from a sociological
perspective. If the positions which Paul opposes have the support of the majority of the religious community in question,
then they are likely to correlate with what any member of that
community would experience as objectively real or true. Not
just the theological opinion, but the religious experience of the
Church itself would support Paul's opposition. In time the individual's fundamental categories of experience, memory, and
communication would be affected. Thus E. Kaesemann is certainly correct in insisting that the New Testament reflects as
much variation in anthropology as it does in Christology.[9] But

7. J. M. Robinson, "Kerygma and History in the NT" *The Bible and
Modern Scholarship*, p. 143.

8. *Op. cit.*, p. 146.

9. E. Kaesemann, "Blind Alleys in the Jesus of History Controversy,"
New Testament Questions of Today, tr. W. J. Montague (Philadelphia:
Fortress Press, 1969), p. 38f.

his attempt to exalt the investigation of Pauline Christology at
the expense of anthropology, soteriology and ecclesiology is
surely questionable.[10] All of these questions are interrelated in
Paul's dealing with specific situations as we shall see in the case
of Galatians and Corinthians.

The Galatian Judaizers: Our weakness in the Spirit

For those of us who have, consciously or unconsciously, absorbed the view that Christianity's great achievement was doing
away with the Jewish Law, the Galatian church presents a
strange picture indeed. This Gentile church had from the beginning been free from the observance of the Law. Yet much of
Paul's argumentation in Galatians is intended to point out to
them that they are saved without becoming Jews or adopting
Jewish practices, for—*mirabile dictu*—this church seems to have
been eager to take on certain Jewish ritual practices and, even,
circumcision. They are not at all impressed with the glorious
Christian freedom which Paul has painfully won for his Gentile
churches. He reminds the Galatians of his own painful controversies over this issue (Gal 2:11-14). But more importantly
he sees the crucifixion as having won this freedom, since Christ
had thus brought the Law to an end by taking its curse upon
himself (Gal 3:13f.). Paul conducts his arguments on two fronts
in Galatians. Against the Galatian Christians who are enthusiastically adopting Jewish practices, Paul argues that to do so is to
abandon the promise which has come to them through the Spirit
as a result of Christ's death (Gal 2:15-21; 3:14, 22-29; 4:6f., 29-31;
5:4). Against those who are preaching such doctrine to the
Galatian community, Paul argues that they are following only
part of the Law. But the man who is circumcised is obliged
to keep the whole Law (Gal 5:3). They are demanding that
the Galatians be circumcised but do not themselves observe
the Law (Gal 6:12f.).

We might wonder—as Paul himself does—what had come over
the Galatians that they wished to keep any part of the Law

10. *Ibid.*, p. 60.

and more especially of the ritual Law. We must shed the mental picture of the Law as a series of duties to be fulfilled which make possible a "bank account" salvation if we are to see the Galatian situation in its true colors. It seems that the Galatians thought of the Law in cosmic terms. Paul heaps scorn on such a position by equating it with their former subservience to pagan gods:

> But when you did not know God, you were enslaved to those who really are not gods. Now that you do know God—or rather, are known by God—how is it that you are turning to the weak and miserable, elemental spirits and wish to serve them again? Are you keeping days, months, seasons and years? I'm afraid I have worked among you in vain.[11]

From other Jewish literature of the period, we can make a guess as to what was involved in the Galatians' understanding of the Law. We learn from Philo that the Law of Moses could also be seen as the Law of Nature. In his exposition of Gen 17:2-4, he comments that the covenant contains all the incorporeal principles, forms and measures for everything out of which this world was made.[12] D. Georgi's study of religious propaganda in this period has shown that this equation between the Covenant and the Law of Nature was a common feature of Jewish apologetics.[13] We also know of a widespread tendency in Judaism to allegorize elements in the ritual law. Elaborate allegories of the high priest's garments show that the ritual law was identical with that of the cosmos.[14] Thus the Law was frequently equated with that governing the world.

Keeping days, months, seasons and years easily fits into such a context. H. Schlier has pointed to the widespread interest in astrological and calendrical speculation in intertestamental Jew-

11. Gal 4:8-11. (Translations of NT texts are the author's).

12. Q. G. III 40-42.

13. D. Georgi, *Die Gegner des Paulus im 2. Korintherbrief*, (Neukirchen-Vluyn: Neukirchener, 1964), p. 142f.

14. Cf. Sap Sal 18:22-25; Josephus, Antiq 179-187; Philo, Vit Mos II, 117-75.

ish literature.[15] I Enoch 72-82 gives revelations of days, months, seasons and the various creatures associated with running the heavens. At Qumran knowledge of the true calendar was one of the mysteries of the Law. Knowing the correct calendar distinguished true Israel from the false.[16] Nor is Galatia the only place in which we have evidence of a Christian community that is concerned with such speculation. A similar problem seems to have arisen later in the church at Colossae.[17] Schlier suggests that the "days" meant in the list cannot refer to the Sabbath, but must refer to days for the celebration of ritual feasts in the context of such astronomical speculation.[18] But we should also remember that in Jewish apologetic the Sabbath itself was given a cosmic significance. Philo, for example, argues that since the Sabbath is the birthday of the world, all who follow the law of nature will keep the Sabbath, devoting themselves to the study of philosophy on that day.[19] Such cosmic interpretations of the Covenant and the ritual law provide the background for the Jewish-Christianity to which the Galatian church has turned. In this context circumcision was not seen as a burdensome, legalistic requirement but as the way of entering into this great cosmic covenant. Commenting on Gen 16:16, Philo remarks that Isaac is called "Joy" because he is the first of the race to be circumcised by Law and is a blessed nature.[20] Paul might agree that Isaac is blessed, but never because of his circumcision! Indeed he goes to some lengths to portray Isaac as the prototype of those who are to inherit the promise which came to Abraham apart from circumcision. However the particular details were worked out, the Gentile Christians of Galatia found the 'cosmic' dimension of their religion through their Judaizing. The Covenant and the ritual law brought them into harmony with the law of the universe.

15. H. Schlier, *Der Brief an die Galaeter* (Goettingen: Vandenhoeck & Ruprecht, 1962), pp. 204-206.

16. Cf. Jub 1-6; I QS I, 13ff; CD III, 12ff; CD XVI, 1ff.

17. Cf. Col 2:16-23.

18. *Op. cit.*, p. 206.

19. Vit Mos II, 209-12.

20. Q. G. III, 8.

Paul does not give us any hint as to how Christ was worked into the Galatians' cosmic scheme, but we know from Colossians that such an amalgamation was possible. Paul's comparison of the Galatians' present state with their former pagan practices may not be so wide of the mark, when we recall the intense fascination with astrology and fate in the ancient world.[21] The Galatians may have found the Judaizing, "cosmic" edition of Christianity more congenial to their understanding of religious reality than the version of Christian freedom which Paul had preached among them. Paul, on the other hand, will have none of such "cosmic interpretation." He insists that God's promise to Abraham, which the Christians now inherit, came apart from circumcision and 430 years before the Mosaic Law came into existence.[22] Now that Christ has fulfilled the curse of the Law it is over,[23] while the promise to Abraham remains and is received through the Spirit by Jews and Greeks alike. The Law, thus, is not the law of the universe, but an historically limited entity, which can in no way be the object of a cosmic religious interpretation. Paul makes it quite clear that he considers such a religious endeavor as a relapse into paganism and the abandonment of Christianity.

Just as Paul insists upon the historical interpretation of the Covenant, he also insists upon the historical, concrete responsibilities of the individual Christian as the focus of his religious existence. As H. Koester has put it:

> For Paul, Jesus did not enhance the religious greatness of the old covenant into new cosmic dimensions, but he brought it to an end by suffering its consequences, the curse.
>
> Thus, the Christian's task is not the reverence of powers beyond and above time and history through observance of their rules (Gal 4:10), but the human responsibility to an existing community: *agape* (Gal 5:6, 22; cf. 6:2ff.).[24]

21. Cf. R. MacMullen, *Enemies of the Roman Order* (Cambridge, Mass.: Harvard University Press, 1966), pp. 128-62.
22. Gal 3:6-18.
23. Gal 3:14.
24. "Gnomai Diaphoroi," p. 309.

According to Paul, the Christian shares the crucifixion of Christ through such a style of life:

> The fruit of the Spirit is love, joy, peace, patience, kindness, goodness, faithfulness, self-control. There is no law against these. Christians crucify the flesh with its passions and desires.[25]

We have to understand Paul's assertion that through the cross of Christ the world has been crucified to him (Gal 6:14) and perhaps even his reference to the marks of Jesus which he bears about (Gal 6:17) in such a context. From this perspective, E. Kaesemann's suggestion that Paul recognizes no bearer of the Spirit who does not also bear the marks of the Lord Jesus [26] [27] seems justified.

We may at least wonder, however, how the Galatian church would have responded to Paul's critique of their "cosmic" orientation toward religion and religious experience. Although Paul chastizes them for "returning to slavery," such a return may have been exactly what appealed to them. The cosmic interpretation of the Law offered by those who were then preaching to them and the religious experience which must have accompanied it, could easily have provided a welcome continuity with the type of religious experience and orientation to which they had been accustomed. At the same time they could have felt liberated from the tyranny of their former pseudo-gods through entry into this new cosmic covenant.

The Galatian position, then, would imply some continuity between their past religious experience and their present one. They could see their Christianity in religious categories and symbols which were familiar to them. Paul, on the other hand, pushes for a negative evaluation of all such previous religious experience whether it be theirs as Gentiles, or—which was a little better—his own as a Jew, who zealously pursued the traditions of his fathers and, as a corollary, the Christians. Paul puts his

25. Gal 5:22-24.

26-27. E. Kaesemann, *Jesus Means Freedom* (Philadelphia: Fortress Press, 1969), p. 71.

finger on the difference between his experience and that which
the Galatians seem to be enthused about when he comments:
"Neither circumcision nor uncircumcision is anything, but a new
creation is." [28]

The Corinthian Enthusiasts: Our greatness in Spirit

The Galatian church did not take the Spirit's new creation
seriously enough. Paul's Corinthian congregation, on the other
hand, seems to have understood it all too literally. The outpouring
of the Spirit practically carried this church into heaven itself.
R. Knox appropriately begins his classic on enthusiasm [29] with
a chapter on the Corinthians' theology. Before we turn to a consideration of their religious experience we might sketch briefly
the general characteristics of enthusiastic movements as Knox
finds them, which we see coming up on the Corinthian church.
He points out that the enthusiast expects and experiences evident
manifestations of God's grace. The exceptional case becomes
the standard of religious achievement. Man is so transported into
the future world that he possesses its perfection in the present.
He belongs to a new order of being; has a new set of faculties
proper to this state. He achieves a new religious status. He is
at last fully man. Such perfectionism has no place for weaker
brethren.[30] Knox goes on to point out that this mentality often
combines ethical rigorism and libertinism, for, if the group has
a legend of its own impeccability, it may come to assert that
what would bring damnation on an outsider is inculpable in the
children of light.[31] Knox also shows that such groups tend to
splinter into rival parties once the initial discipline is lost. Schism
begets schism.[32]

One of the crucial features in the enthusiast's understanding
of himself is his ability to experience his own "perfection" over
against the "outsiders." Berger and Luckmann have shown that
an individual, who has acquired a conception of himself as a

28. Gal 6:15.
29. R. Knox, *Enthusiasm* (Oxford: Oxford University Press, 1950).
30. *Op. cit.,* 1-3.
31. *Ibid.,* p. 2.
32. *Ibid.,* p. 1.

result of secondary socialization, which is not allowed social realization, tends to objectify this new identity in his consciousness as his "real self" over against his social role.[33] The religious sect will, of course, provide a social context for such an identity on the part of its members over against their position in society at large. They are able to understand themselves as "perfect," the "sons of light" over against the evil outsiders. Paul is quite opposed to such a change of roles in the religious sphere. He reminds the Corinthians of the status in which they were called and insists that Christians remain in their "calling" (I Cor 7:17-24).

The Corinthian community has also begun to fragment. Paul brings these manifestations of disunity against them as indications of the fact that their understanding of themselves as "perfect" must face evidence to the contrary. The exact interpretation of the divisions mentioned in I Cor 1:12 is much debated,[34] but, whatever we make of that specific text, it is clear that the claim of the different groups is based on allegiance to one apostle or another. Paul plays down his role in baptizing any of the Corinthians (I Cor 1:14-17),[35] though it is clear that he has baptized some of them, probably more than he would care to admit. This move suggests that the Corinthians saw the person who baptized them as a mystagogue. Berger and Luckmann have pointed out that in cases of re-socialization, such as conversion, the individual often establishes strong affective ties with those significant others who are seen as his guides to the new reality.[36] The Corinthians have carried this association to some extreme, it seems.

The most striking feature of the Corinthians' religious attitude is their strong emphasis upon ecstatic religious experience. As Knox's general characterization has pointed out, they saw the blessings of the future world as present in the spiritual phenomena manifest in the community. They worship among—and in the

33. *Social Construction,* p. 171.

34. Cf. H. Conzelmann, *Der erste Brief an die Korinther* (Goettingen: Vandenhoeck & Ruprecht, 1969), pp. 47-49.

35. Cf. Conzelmann, p. 50f.

36. *Op. cit.,* p. 157.

language of—the angels, a phenomenon known to us at Qumran as well.[37] Paul upbraids them for a number of ethical abberations of both a libertine and a rigorist flavour (I Cor 5-8), and their lack of tolerance for weaker brethren in the question of meat sacrificed to idols seems to have almost been a matter of pride (I Cor 8; 10:14-30).

The basis for their ecstatic experience was apparently the conviction that they had been possessed by divine Wisdom or the divine spirit. The view that there was a correspondence between the human and divine spirit was common enough.[38] Prophecy, speaking in tongues, and inspired interpretation of sacred scripture were all possible displays of religious power and experience.[39] Funk points out that this union with wisdom is seen by the Corinthians as making them so perfect that they fall outside the criticism of men and the judgment of God.[40] It gives them the lofty religious status of "perfect" men. And Paul cites disapprovingly the claims that they make about this new status, claims to true wealth, kingliness, power, perfection, etc. Such a list of claims is paralleled in philosophical literature of the period where it is used of the true state of the wise man.[41] The Corinthians seem to have employed a "vulgarization" of such philosophical tradition in understanding the status to which they had attained as a result of their possession by divine wisdom. Paul's degradation of wisdom is to be understood as directed against this specific concept of Wisdom, not philosophy.

Although we also know in the philosophical world the claim that the wise man is immortal,[42] I would agree with J. M. Robinson that what is at stake in the enthusiasts' denial of the resurrec-

37. Cf. J. Fitzmeyer, "A Feature of Qumran Angelology and the Angels of I Cor xi, 10" NTS 4 (1957/58), pp. 48-58; H. Ringgren, *The Faith of Qumran,* tr. E. Sander (Philadelphia: Fortress Press, 1963), pp. 85-87.

38. Cf. Sap Sal 7:22ff.

39. Cf. Philo, Migr 34f; Vit Con 12; Leg All III, 100-104; Plutarch, De Def Orac 40; and Test Job 48ff.

40. Funk, R., *Language, Hermeneutic and Word of God* (New York: Harper & Row, 1967), p. 291.

41. Cf. Philo, Quod Omn Prob 160; Agr 8f; Agr 157-62; Virt 187-227; Q. G. III, 22; Leg All III, 135; Pram 104.

42. Cf. Philo, Migr 37; Det 79-90; *Quod Deus* 148-51.

tion is not some form of Greek rationalism.[43] Robinson proposes that the Corinthians have misunderstood Pauline baptismal preaching to mean that we have now through baptism died and also risen with Christ, rather than seeing our resurrection as yet in the future as in Rom 6.[44] But I wonder if he has provided the best context for understanding this phenomenon when he cites the second century controversy over baptismal resurrection (cf. II Tim 2:18; Polycarp 7:1).[45] I would propose that the debate over the resurrection in I Cor is the result of their experience in living in a community which anticipates the blessings of the future life. Similarly the Qumran community shows no interest in theorizing about resurrection.[46] The connection with Adam, which Paul uses to argue that through Adam we all share in his death and will be made alive through Christ (I Cor 15:22), could have originally been used in the eschatological self-understanding of the Corinthians to indicate that eschatological salvation is now present in the community. We know from Qumran that the sons of light expected to possess "all the glory of Adam" in the last days.[47] For the Corinthians baptism is the entry rite to the community which now experiences such glory, and Paul objects that it is death, which our identification with Adam brings on us. The enthusiastic understanding of the Corinthians has no place for a resurrection theology.

The Corinthians' understanding has little place for the passion-resurrection creed, which Paul reminds them of in I Cor 15:3ff. We may even wonder if the Corinthians had any Christology whatever. If the resurrection is irrelevant, the passion seems as much so in their view. Koester has pointed out that they did not use a Wisdom Christology. Paul corrects them by insisting that the whole congregation is subject to Christ rather than Wisdom (I Cor 3:23).[48] Funk suggests that they subordinated both Christ and the apostles to divine Wisdom and by this sub-

43. "Kerygma and History," p. 124.
44. *Ibid.*, pp. 122-24.
45. *Ibid.*, p. 125f.
46. Cf. Ringgren, p. 148.
47. Cf. I QS IV, 12-14.
48. Gnomon 33 (1961), p. 591.

ordination created a theological situation which was entirely outside the confession of the crucified (and Risen) Christ.[49] He insists that the issue in Corinth is the basis of faith itself. Paul must insist that its foundation is the crucified Christ.[50] He opposes their designations of themselves as perfect, insisting that: they were not of high status when called (I Cor 2:26-29); they still are "babes" as Christians (I Cor 3:1). Further he opposes his own example as the world's "garbage" to their self-exaltation (I Cor 4:8-13). He insists that true wisdom allows one to see the Lord of Glory in the Crucified (I Cor 2:8).[51] Funk points out that in criticizing the Corinthians' charismata Paul claims that the wisdom of God is given to men so that they can discern among the gifts given by God.[52]

Part of the discernment applied to charismatic gifts, as well as to the Corinthians' claim to perfection, is the realization that we yet remain in the time of perishability. Bornkamm has pointed out that in I Cor 13 Paul pulls a reversal on the Corinthians. Rather than accepting the enthusiast position that the out-pouring of the Spirit was a sign that imperfection was ended, Paul asserts that only faith, hope and *agape* are imperishable. All these glorious gifts of the Spirit will perish![53] *Agape* is the bond which should unify the divided Corinthian community, a community divided even at the eucharist.[54] In Paul's understanding the building up of the community has priority, so he separates tongues and prophecy, which ordinarily would have been seen together as manifestations of the spirit in the community.[55] It may be that it is in a similar context of evaluation of moods of communication with the Lord that Paul appeals to sayings of the Lord as providing normative guidelines for the

49. *Op. cit.*, p. 290, n. 62.
50. *Ibid.*, pp. 280-84.
51. Cf. Funk, 291-97.
52. *Op. cit.*, p. 293.
53. G. Bornkamm, "On the Understanding of Worship," *Early Christian Experience,* tr. P. Hammer (New York: Harper & Row, 1970), p. 164f.
54. Cf. G. Bornkamm, "Lord's Supper and Church in Paul," *Early Christian Experience,* pp. 138-49.
55. Cf. G. Bornkamm, "Faith and Reason in Paul," *op. cit.*, p. 37f.

life of the community (I Cor 7:10-17; 9:14). No matter how intense its experience of the Spirit, no community can reject the earthly life Jesus lived or the death he died.

We do not have time to go into more details of Paul's handling of the complex situation at Corinth as we find it in I Cor. It is clear that the Pauline theology of cross-resurrection and his stress upon the edification of the community is opposed at every point to the enthusiastic religious experience of the Corinthians. For Paul, no religious experience can remove the Christian from his status in this world as weak and persecuted to a position of exalted and powerful dignity. As in the case of the Galatians, we may wonder if Paul was able to change the orientation of a community whose new Christian exaltation was so powerfully documented by the out-pouring of the Spirit. He has tried to point out to them that their quarrelsome, intolerant and even immoral behavior is equally empirical evidence of their "imperfection." Has he succeeded?

A brief look at II Cor reveals that the basic religious orientation of the Corinthian church remained enthusiastic. Certain problems are no longer mentioned, and Jewish Christian missionaries have given this orientation a slightly different frame of justification, but the basic understanding of religious experience at Corinth was not changed by I Cor. Georgi discusses the theology of this Jewish-Christian mission, which seems to have come into Corinth, at length.[56] It stands in a tradition of Jewish apologetic which views Abraham as the father of the true humanity. The spirit of God is manifested in powerful interpretation of scripture and the working of great miracles in imitation of those worked by Moses in Egypt. As Georgi suggests,[57] the "new" Jesus, whom Paul accuses them of preaching (II Cor 11:4), may be one whose earthly ministry is epitomized by comparing the glory of his miraculous deeds with that of Moses. These missionaries seem to have carried about with them letters of recommendation, which testified to the great deeds they had done elsewhere (II Cor 3:1). They were stirring preachers and apparently accused Paul of being unable to compete with them.

56. Georgi, *Die Gegner des Paulus*, pp. 31-82; 246-300.
57. *Op. cit.*, pp. 265-82.

Perhaps the Corinthians even demanded proof from Paul similar to that these missionaries were willing to give them (II Cor 13:3).

Paul's response to this challenge is in many respects similar to his argument in I Cor. He mocks their letters of recommendation with a paradoxical catalogue of his own sufferings (II Cor 11:16-12:10); compares himself to a prisoner of war being led in a triumphal procession by God (II Cor 2:14-17), and tells a ridiculous story of his escape from Damascus in a basket (2 Cor 11:32f.). Such examples give a vivid correlation between the experience of the apostle and his main point that Christ was crucified in weakness. The miracles that Jesus performed are not to be taken as the norm for religious experience. His weakness is. The pattern of the kerygma which Paul is using against his opponents is that of his assertion in II Cor 13:4: that Jesus was crucified in weakness but lives now through the power of God, as J. M. Robinson has pointed out.[58] It is to the crucifixion in weakness that the Christian must look for his model if he is later to share the glory of Christ (II Cor 4:7-18). It is in the bearing of—perhaps even the boasting in—this weakness that the power of God is manifest. This type of argumentation is an even more explicit spelling out of the implications of the passion-resurrection creed, which, we have seen in I Cor, was bypassed by the Corinthians in favor of enthusiastic manifestations of the presence of the Spirit. And in this fundamental orientation the Corinthians remained unchanged by I Cor. Against his opponents' claim that they stand in the glorious tradition of Israel, Paul is as insistent as he is in Galatians that with the coming of Christ the old covenant has passed away (II Cor 3:14).

In I Cor 1:12f. Paul remarks that the Greeks look for wisdom and the Jews seek signs. Neither can understand the preaching of Christ crucified. Under the guise of ecstatic possession by Wisdom, the Corinthians have found Wisdom at variance with Paul's theology of the cross. Their subsequent venture into prophecy understood as inspired interpretation of scripture, powerful preaching—not in tongues this time—and miraculous signs was equally ill fated. Paul's understanding of Christian

58. *Op. cit.*, p. 144.

experience as the manifestation of the power of God in the weakness of Christian life and the crucifixion of Christ did not, it seems, sell well on the Corinthian religious market. In our investigation of the Galatian situation, we suggested that a continuity with their previous modes of religious experience and understanding may have been possible in the "cosmic" orientation which Paul is opposing. The Corinthians persistently pursue another type of religious experience, and their persistence may indicate that it is more congenial to their modes of religious apprehension than the passion-resurrection creed as Paul has preached it. But, if we are to pursue our initial suggestion that the diversity of theology and religious experience in early Christianity must be correlated with the sociological diversity of cognitive and symbolic presuppositions in different areas of the church, then we have one question to ask yet: What appealed to Paul in the passion-resurrection creed? Why did it become the norm of Christian experience for him? The fact that this creed was to become *the* basic creedal formula of orthodox Christianity, and dominates the form of the canonical Gospels [59] should not blind us to the fact that at the time Paul writes all of these developments are in the future. Mark has not yet been written, and Paul's own preaching of the passion-resurrection creed may have been vital in its adoption.[60] The answer I would suggest to you—which will have to be elaborated in a further study of the question—is to be found in Paul's strong identification with the prophet Jeremiah. He appeals to him in his epistles (cf. I Cor 1:19,30), and in Gal 1:15 formulates his understanding of his call in language parallel to that associated with the call of Jeremiah (cf. Jer 1:5;41:9;49:1).[61] Nor is Paul the only one to make this association. The account of Paul's call in Acts 26:16ff makes the connection using different passages of Jer than Paul has in Gal 1 (cf. Jer 42:7-16). The importance of this identification in answering our question emerges when we remember Jeremiah's many complaints to Yahweh about the

59. Cf. H. Koester, "One Jesus," pp. 206-208.

60. Cf. W. Marxsen, *Mark the Evangelist,* tr. R. Harrisville (Nashville: Abingdon Press, 1969), pp. 130-38.

61. Cf. Schlier, p. 53, n. 1.

suffering and opposition that his prophetic ministry has entailed, the so-called "confessions of Jeremiah." [62] In Jer 20:7-18, for example, Jeremiah complains that preaching the word of Yahweh has meant mockery and derision and he will live out his days in toil and sorrow, but at the same time he sees the power of Yahweh as delivering him. I would suggest that Paul's identification with the prophet Jeremiah is at least one of the symbolic presuppositions, sustaining his understanding of Christian experience as the manifestation of God's power in weakness, mockery and suffering, and forming his theological understanding of Christ crucified. And Paul can claim that he comes not relying on his own power but the power of God (I Cor 2:3f.).

62. Cf. H. H. Rowley, "The Early Prophecies of Jeremiah," *Men of God* (London: Nelson, 1963), pp. 53-58.

Religious Experience in Nineteenth Century Protestant Thought: Friederich Schleiermacher

CARL F. STARKLOFF

The basis of Schleiermacher's entire apologetic lies in the individual's "total feeling." Consequently, we shall begin with the individual and follow his progress in religion as he moves toward fellowship and dialogue, to find ultimately that this is where his feeling first became active. Here I have chosen Schleiermacher's best known and perhaps most significant works. They are *On Religion: Speeches To Its Cultured Despisers* (or "critics" if one chooses a less violent but also less accurate translation), *The Christian Faith*, and *Christmas Eve: A Dialogue On The Incarnation*. All of these are parts of an effort by the great theologian and preacher to confront the scorn of the Enlightenment, of critics for whom the absolute ego was supreme and pure reason the true divinity.

In the *Lectures*, Schleiermacher introduces his audience and readership to the person it needs most, the "priest" or "mediator," the true man of piety, "a person in whom the higher feeling has mounted to an inspiration never more to be silenced and by whom the very pulsebeat of spiritual life is revealed in word and symbol." [1] He is one whose mission it is to awaken the slumbering seed of a better humanity, to proclaim the eternal amid the temporal. Like Kierkegaard some years later, Schleier-

---

1. Friederich Schleiermacher, *On Religion: Addresses in Response to its Cultured Critics*, trans. Terrence Tice, (Richmond, Va.: John Knox Press, 1969), p. 46. Cited henceforth as *Religion*.

macher always asserted the indispensable value of the person's initial and authentic religious experience.[2] Religion is such that whoever offers any expression of it must necessarily have had that experience, so that even a reading of the scriptures can only be a pittance or a stumbling block to one who has not experienced piety in himself.[3] Piety has its own province, or locus, within the human spirit, a province to which ministers of religion have paid precious little attention, and so have failed to understand the religious needs of their people, especially the young.[4]

To speak so strongly of religion is to lead up to an understanding of its "essence." In the unsystematic manner of the *Lectures*, given first in 1799 when the theologian was thirty-one, we read first about what religion is *not*—not science, not morality, not metaphysics.[5] Waiving all such claims, religion or faith (note here the equivalence!) is essentially contemplative: it is the state of having all the senses open to the life of the world, and more, to the eternal in the world. "Where this awareness is found," he writes, "religion is satisfied; where this awareness is hidden, religion experiences frustration and anguish, emptiness and death."[6] Man must see his existence in the totality of the world by uniting his senses with the infinite; through perspectivity and the feeling that is in him, he must be reconciled to the object world apart from himself.[7] Therefore the value of esthetics is very much emphasized here, especially art and music, which Schleiermacher found indispensable to religion. All things, in their essences (about which we know nothing), become objects for the impress of that inner existential awareness. This includes

2. *Ibid.*, p. 42.
3. *Ibid.*, p. 48.
4. *Ibid.*, p. 62.
5. It should be observed that fundamentally, whatever Schleiermacher's development, he does not seem to have changed in basic principles from his early to his late works. Cf. James K. Graby, "The Question of Development in Schleiermacher's Theology," *Canadian Journal of Theology*, Vol. X (1964), No. 2, pp. 75-87.
6. *Religion*, p. 79.
7. Cf. *Religion*, p. 358, footnotes by translator n. 93. Terrence Tice points out Schleiermacher's use of a Kantian method that we might relate to the later development of the "religious apriori."

as object the individual's very "outer self." Schleiermacher
writes that the sum total of religion is to feel all that moves us
in its supreme unity, which means that being and life are being
and life in and through God.[8] Important here is the evidence
that piety itself tends to retreat within to the realm of the Holy
rather than to break forth into deeds. This leads the author
to pass from the essence of religion to its *loci*, of which there
is an outer locus and an inner locus.

The outer locus is simply a sense for nature, perhaps for
mythology: "Religious reverence is the glorious feeling of our
relationship to the whole."[9] Then, in a bit of spatial terminology
that was to cause some misinterpretation by critics and followers
alike, Schleiermacher calls the inner locus "the inward recesses
of our own spirit."[10] But even the inward recesses in some way
manifest themselves, because Schleiermacher, unlike Kierkegaard, never divides person from community. He urges his
listeners to seek for religion in others, even as they seek for other
qualities, for in this search, the existence of the other becomes
a revelation for me.[11] "From the wanderings through the whole
area of humanity," he writes, "pious feelings return with a sharper, better informed sense of things to a man's own self."[12] From
this one sees the relation of religion to ethics—not as servant
but as necessary friend, removing man from the narrowness of
his own culture and one-sidedness, affecting him with the infinite
for which he thirsts, a religious instinct for the universe. It is a
typically Johannine observation of Schleiermacher that the function even of miracles is simply to bring forth this experience,
so that, for the truly religious person, *everything* is miraculous.
Revelation is likewise "every new and original communication
of the universe and its inmost life to man,"[13] and inspiration is

8. *Religion*, p. 94.
9. *Ibid.*, p. 115.
10. *Ibid.*, p. 120ff.
11. *Ibid.*, p. 122.
12. *Ibid.*, p. 128.
13. *Ibid.*, p. 141. It should be observed, however, that in his less
apologetic dogmatic work, Schleiermacher brings out the distinction between the "general revelation" of the *Addresses* and the "special revelation" occurring in Jesus Christ. Cf. *The Christian Faith*, ed. H. R. Mackin-

every feeling for true morality and freedom. Schleiermacher's words on the reading of scripture, later reflected in the work of liberal exegetes, are worth citing in full: "Not everyone who believes in some sacred scripture has religion, but only the man who has a direct and vital understanding of scripture and who could therefore most readily do without it, as such." [14]

The pious function as such is not some particular function (and this negates the former impression about spatiality), but rather our whole being existing in and encountering the world. The essence of religion is the totality of all of man's relations to the deity. We have in this totality of feeling an excellent view on the idea of immortality, which reflects again the Johannine bias permeating Schleiermacher's theology. Immortality is not outside and beyond time, but in its totality, in that which we already possess in this temporal life of ours, an aim to fulfill, a problem we shall always be seeking to solve. "In the midst of finitude to become one with the infinite, and to be eternal in every instant—that is the immortality of religion." [15]

Schleiermacher offers a more systematic exposition of what he calls the essence and locus of piety in his *Glaubenslehre—The Christian Faith*, where he discusses the touchstone of his method, the feeling of absolute dependence, which, in a note later appended to the above lecture, he calls not a feeling related to parts of the universe, but to it as a unity determining everything.[16] All piety is central to the human consciousness. He arrives at this by means of an elimination of all other human qualities as possible *loci* of religion. Of the consciousness triad of knowing, doing and feeling, knowledge cannot be *the* experience, because obviously holiness would then depend on the ability to theologize [17]—a kind of gnosis against which Schleiermacher struggled all his life. Nor is piety found in *doing*, because

tosh and J. S. Stewart, (Edinburgh: T. & T. Clark, 1956. Third English impression of the second German edition. N. 13, pp. 62-68. Cited henceforth as *CF*.

14. *Religion*, p. 144.
15. *Ibid.*, p. 157.
16. *Ibid.*, p. 162.
17. *CF*, p. 9.

one may *do* many abominable things under the guise of piety. It is not any kind of act, but rather motive that we must search out.[18] In other words, man finds piety, not in any "passage-beyond-self," but by abiding within the very self.

The pious consciousness arises from man's yearning to overcome separateness.[19] While one feels himself in possession of a self-caused element, he also experiences a non-self-caused element; he is "being" as well as a "having-by-some-means-come-to-be." In an attack on the proponents of the absolute ego, Schleiermacher asserts that the immediate self-consciousness is not only active but receptive, and one can do nothing to find within himself that which causes this. The common element, then, in all determinations of self-consciousness expressing a receptivity is a feeling of dependence.[20] Man's "being-in-the-world" shows him that he will never experience the exhilaration of pure freedom, because being-in-the-world is temporal. Further, man can exert no counter-influence on the most basic experience of this element, as he can upon all other creatures. He recognizes here the presence of a self-caused independent reality, entirely free and unconditioned, standing outside any moment in time. This is the God-consciousness, arrived at by a process of dialectic that seems regressive to Hegelians, even to Kierkegaard. There is a passage from a primitive unreflective animal consciousness, to a sense of reflective awareness of separateness, to the annulment of separateness in the relation with God—the feeling of *absolute* dependence.[21] Consequently, Schleiermacher advises the critics of religion that they actually have religion within themselves if (like the devout Hindu, I might add) they will but look, and growth in piety is growth in this basic feeling.

In the least systematic way, and that which Schleiermacher seems to have preferred above all others to convey his thought, his *Christmas Eve*, we find a life-portrait of a community's mu-

---

18. *Ibid.*, p. 10.

19. Cf. the fine collection of essays in William W. Meissner, *Foundations for a Psychology of Grace*, (Glen Rock, New Jersey: Paulist Press, 1966), especially the essay on Erich Fromm's theory of love as overcoming separateness, pp. 37ff.

20. *CF*, p. 13. As basis of his system, see pp. 131-141.

21. *Ibid.*, pp. 19, 5-26 especially.

tual endeavor to arouse and preserve religious emotion. The participants in the dialogue, through their own personal means of expression and narrative, sometimes accompanied by sacred music played on the piano, attempt to render one another receptive to religious movements. This is a rubric, of course, that Schleiermacher prescribes for the whole Church. Again, the contrast in the dialogue of the polarity in the masculine and feminine religious experience is stressed. In general, we have here a short work that commentators recommend to readers who want to understand the theologian's efforts to convey appreciation of religion, which is summed up by a young woman in the party, epitomizing Schleiermacher's ideal: "All radiant, serene joy is religion." [22]

Next, we can work backwards from *The Christian Faith*, with its more detailed and precise description of the movement from personal experience to association, which, as Joachim Wach wrote, is a necessary movement from religious experience.[23] The feeling of absolute dependence is present in a person in such a way that he will pass beyond himself to community; he must share his basic aspiration, and the context in which this sharing happens is the Church. Schleiermacher's understanding of the essence of preaching is significant (especially in light of the angry reaction it provokes from Karl Barth): "Such preaching must always take the form of testimony; testimony as to one's own experience, which shall arouse in others the desire to have the same experience." [24] Again, the best illustration of this phenomenon is taken from the *Christmas Eve* diologue on the Incarnation. Here the devout German family shares its Christmas with friends, each partaker in the evening's festivities contributing his or her own experience—from childlike wonder to hard rationalism to

22. Schleiermacher, *Christmas Eve: Dialogue on The Incarnation*, trans. Terrence N. Tice, (Richmond, Va.: John Knox Press, 1967), p. 63. Cited henceforth as *Christmas*.

23. Joachim Wach, *The Comparative Study of Religions*, ed. Joseph M. Kitagawa, (New York: Columbia University Press, 1966), pp. 121-143. This is a vast improvement over the moralistic theory of religion of William James in *Varieties of Religious Experience*, and reflects Schleiermacher quite emphatically.

24. *CF*, p. 69.

theological analysis to feminine mysticism to esthetic delight—
and all culminates in a sense of gratitude expressed in song.
Most typical perhaps is the account given by Ernestine, of her
encounter in church with a young mother and her child, distract-
ing her from a dull sermon and convincing her that *here* was the
true "holy place," manifested in the love between mother and
child.[25] In other words, there is a seeking here to experience the
Incarnation as a community in dialogue. As Eduard says toward
the close of the dialogue, the Church fellowship relates itself to
human life much as the individual's own consciousness relates
to what lacks consciousness in his, and everyone in whom the
new religious self-consciousness arises enters within the bounds
of the church.[26] In fact, wrote Schleiermacher in the *Glaubenslehre, the* one ground for belonging to the Christian Church is
to maintain absolute facility and constancy of religious emotions.[27]

Actually, I would say that Schleiermacher has said it best in
his lectures on religion, especially in those on the cultivation of
religion and on association. Here too, perhaps, lies his most
significant contribution to theology—a theology of community
not unlike and more detailed than that of Buber. Asking himself
how to cultivate piety in others, the author comes up with an
answer foreshadowing Kierkegaard's about the relationship between human discourse and faith, very likely stemming from
their mutual interest in the midwifery of Socrates. Schleiermacher points out that all one person can do for another is to
share his own conceptions with that person and thus enable him
to ground his own thinking. When the time is ripe, it is hoped
that these ideas will be remembered, and a personal experience
of religion will occur.[28] This theory of communication is especially valuable in conveying Schleiermacher's ideas about religious education, and has its basis in the assertion that religion
is fundamentally the same feeling even in the youngest of children, and must be cultivated as such, according to age and condition. Community is seen as a milieu in which the guardians of

25. *Christmas,* p. 58.
26. *Ibid.,* pp. 81-85.
27. *CF,* p. 68. See also the systematic discussion of association in
the same volume, pp. 44-93.
28. *Religion,* pp. 179-180.

religion can stimulate the young to surrender to the ever-present influences of the infinite. Ultimately, Schleiermacher sees this activity, when carried on among the mature, where one-directional communication ceases, as the very essence of Church dialogue,[29] building on an analogy of shared discovery. He decries the image of the Church as a mere purveyor of dogmas; [30] the truly religious person, in fact, would be forced by his own dynamics to abandon such an assembly. He advocates different kinds of ecclesial groups, especially for beginners, established in such a way as to develop the innate capacity. The teacher is central to such an effort, and his work will be facilitated in groups of persons whose sentiments are similar.

In examining Schleiermacher's order of worship, we see something of a pentecostal spirit. In the reading of the Bible, he is typically uninterested in the historical Old Testament books, and even indicates that the historical elements in the Passion are secondary. It is the idea, the impression, especially the words of Jesus during the Passion that are important—a reflection of Schleiermacher's Christ as the epitome of the human God-consciousness. Such communications are the vital and sublime elements to which the believer can link his own vital religious communication. Bible reading by the laity continues only for this reason, that there dwells in it a quickening spirit.[31] However, learned exposition is also important, demanding a skilled teacher or preacher, and preaching may even take the form of didache, or dogmatic exposition.[32] Schleiermacher is not a mere illuminatist, and demands sufficient church order to forestall the random reading of passages for inspiration, an action he considers frivolous.

In the long run, though, what really makes a community gathering is the religious spirit, and not "discussion of topics." Didactic efforts have value, but it is the experience that matters. The speaker's task is to help his audience become aware of some-

29. *Ibid.*, p. 241.
30. *Ibid.*, p. 140.
31. *Ibid.*, p. 244.
32. *Ibid.* In fact, preaching may even take the form of dogmatic teaching. Cf. *CF*, p. 79.

thing—something that he may indeed presuppose exists in them somehow, but which he does not suppose would have developed in this form all by itself.[33] Hence the high esteem for religious poetry, art and music—the less "intellectualized" forms of communication. Order there must be to avoid fanaticism, but always an order that is congenial to the assembly of the pious, never inhibiting the response of religion. The stress on the knowing of one's associates, even as one has to know an author, in their own contexts, is important for all of Schleiermacher's hemeneutics, because one must always find the point of contact for the communication of piety.[34] To this end, he writes in praise of small local communities, which should ultimately supersede the more established churches. "Religious associations," he cautions, "deserve the praise given only insofar as they disclose a rich productivity in religious communication." [35]

Schleiermacher has had his reactors, pro and con. He has been a watershed in Protestant thought, between the "liberal" and the "neo-orthodox." Judging from the present situation, he may well be every bit as applicable to the Roman Catholic search for community and genuine religion. A brief look at the positive and negative responses may teach us some wisdom in our own growth.

First, we might put some questions to Schleiermacher. With Soren Kierkegaard, we might leap *in medias res* and challenge the feeling of absolute dependence. Is it truly a personal response to the infinite, even when developed? Even if we choose not to follow the flippant judgment imputed to Hegel that "in that case my pet dog is the most religious of beings," we might well share Kierkegaard's criticism that,

What Schleiermacher calls "Religion" and the Hegelians "faith" is at bottom nothing but the first immediate condition

33. *Religion,* p. 246.
34. *Ibid.,* p. 250. The *"Anknüpfungspunkt,"* a great bone of contention with Barth, who will allow only that the Word of God creates such a point of contact, if faith is to follow. Cf. Karl Barth, *Church Dogmatics,* I, I, p. 221.
35. *Religion,* p. 251.

for everything—the vital fluidum—the spiritual atmosphere we breathe in—and which cannot therefore with justice be designated by these words.[36]

This critique is cogent on at least one point: If faith is so closely related to, perhaps identified with a state of feeling absolutely dependent, of satisfying one's spiritual need,[37] faith then seems to be more a vague sense of transcendence than a commitment. Even if we grant here that Schleiermacher is talking about the self prior to experience, we might still object that he has not allowed for faith as passage beyond self in the choice to respond to revelation, but seems more to promote a kind of oriental resting in the Self of transcendental meditation. The charge of pantheism is not out of place.

With Martin Buber, who is otherwise so congenial to Schleiermacher in thought, we have to caution the disciple of this great apologist that, if he wishes to regard a feeling of dependence as the real element in the relation with God, he may be misconceiving Judeo-Christian faith—an event occurring between *persons*. As essential as feeling may be, it still remains subject to the dynamics of the soul, where one feeling is outstripped, outdone and abolished by another.[38] There is more to a relation than even the most total of feelings. Likewise, Buber warns that to stress "experience" is to stress not a personal relationship, an I-Thou, but an I-It, a somewhat narcissistic dwelling on a thing, an experience, something *within* and not *between*.[39] Joachim Wach joins this rank of critics by reasserting the doctrine of the phenomenologists since Brentano that, in the religious act, we must not neglect the *intention* (in the scholastic sense), the going-out, in favor of an analysis of a psychological act or state.[40] Richard R. Niebuhr also admits that Schleiermacher seems to lose touch

36. Soren Kierkegaard, *The Journals of Soren Kierkegaard,* ed. Alexander Dru, (London: Oxford University Press, 1951), p. 30.

37. *CF,* p. 70.

38. Martin Buber, *I and Thou,* trans. Ronald Gregor Smith, (New York: Charles Scribner's Sons, 1958), p. 81.

39. *Ibid.,* p. 5.

40. Wach, *op. cit.,* p. 29.

with the sense of sin by tying it up with psychological categories and a kind of analysis of cyclical world-involvement.[41]

Passing by Dietrich Bonhoeffer's undeveloped anti-religion reflections, we can find the roots of his critique in his old master, the passionate critic, Karl Barth, who speaks so highly of Schleiermacher in places. Since Barth's entire method, from *Romans* even to his very mellow *The Humanity of God*, is a gigantic reaction against this man with whom he hoped to settle accounts in heaven, it is impossible to cite many individual cases of criticism. Perhaps we can turn to Barth's ace-in-the-hole against all of liberal theology, Ludwig Feuerbach, who admired the theologians of experience (including Luther![42]) for their talent in predicating human feelings and activities of the God-experience. To Feuerbach, of course, this God of experience was simply human self-alienation, proving to him conclusively that theology is really anthropology in the strictest sense of the word—a study of human states and activity. Barth calls Schleiermacher into Feuerbach's court to answer charges about the loss of faith in divine transcendence, about infidelity to proclaiming God's personal encounter with man, which is the goal of all preaching in the New Testament, about the place of Christ as a Redeemer in deed as well as teaching, about the very essence of the Church. Another vehement objection Barth had was to Schleiermacher's emphasis on culture and adaptation to it. No doubt, although I have not found it mentioned anywhere, Barth reacted strongly against Schleiermacher's embarrassing eulogy of the German soul as the ideal locus of the sense of the sacred.[43] Coupled with his adversary's failure, as he saw it, to take the New Testament seriously as the indispensable witness to faith, was the inevitable fate of liberal Protestantism—to be devoured by any culture that hungered to have it. In this case it was the

41. Richard R. Niebuhr, *Schleiermacher On Christ and Religion*, (New York: Charles Scribner's Sons, 1964), p. 200.

42. Cf. Ludwig Feuerbach, *The Essence of Christianity*, trans. George Eliot, (New York: Harper and Bros., 1957 Torchbook edition), pp. 44-49, p. 127.

43. Cf. *Religion*, p. 48. However, Schleiermacher's restriction of Church activity to the realm of piety (Cf. *CF*, p. 5) should forestall the consequences of this.

Aryan myth of National Socialism. In general, Barth's indictment of Schleiermacher is that this theologian of experience had let himself be pushed into a mystical-naturalistic corner where the historical in Christianity could only play a questionable role.[44] And I rather think that it is on this hermeneutical battlefield that the crisis of religion is being met today.

But there is no lack of activity in the Schleiermacher camp. First, there is Paul Tillich, who, while he criticizes Schleiermacher on grounds similar to those of Kierkegaard—the over-emphasis on consciousness,[45] has yet been one of the first to rescue him from some of his own admirers who had isolated the feeling of absolute dependence as simply one among other feelings.[46] This, as we have seen, is a false conception of that total relationship. Tillich, in company with Richard R. Niebuhr, points out Schleiermacher's important insight, running through his entire method, into the irrelevance of the cleavage between nature and supernature—a discovery made by Ripalda as a voice in the seventeenth century wilderness, and much later by Rahner, DeLubac and other Roman Catholics. Tillich is likewise intrigued by Schleiermacher's representation of Jesus as the basic image (*Urbild*) of the human God-consciousness.[47] Although fearing that this concept lacks any ontological element in soteriology, Tillich finds his own approach conditioned by the "spirit movement" of Schleiermacher and others like him.[48] And, finally, the doctrine of "ultimate concern" seems to be reductively the same as the feeling of absolute dependence, with a more outgoing emphasis implied.

The work of Richard R. Niebuhr defends Schleiermacher on most points (admitting his weakness as to the doctrine of divine transcendence),[49] especially in the area of experience. We

44. Karl Barth, *Theology And Church: Shorter Writings,* trans. Louis Pettibone Smith (New York: Harper and Row, Publishers, 1962), p. 198.

45. Paul Tillich, *Systematic Theology,* (Chicago: Chicago University Press, 1970 Harper and Row edition), Vol. I, p. 42. II, p. 215. III, p. 285.

46. *Ibid.,* I, p. 15, 153, 41-42.

47. *Ibid.,* II, p. 150.

48. *Ibid.,* III, p. 126.

49. Niebuhr, *op. cit.,* p. 191.

have seen how he attributes the supernatural-natural controversy to a false start on the part of all theologians, including the neo-orthodox. But more, he praises Schleiermacher for his sense of Christ as mediated through historical fellowship, the Logos made flesh in time and history. This integration he calls a "massive thrust" in theology.[50] Along with Schleiermacher's American translator and commentator, Terrence Tice,[51] he eulogizes the theologian for his appreciation of the man-woman relationship and polarity in religion.[52] There is a prevalent human empathy in all of Schleiermacher's hermeneutics, says Niebuhr, that introduces us to modern method in both literary criticism and human dynamics. Schleiermacher always emphasizes the need to understand what an author or partner in a dialogue is *really* saying, in that person's own historical context, and perhaps even to "(raise) to a conscious level what was unconscious in the author."[53] It is only this kind of dialogue that can incarnate the divine in human experience.

In summary, it can be said that we have in Schleiermacher a great forerunner of modern method, as well as the prime example of both the positive and negative aspects of making religion and especially the Incarnation "relevant," through the feeling of absolute dependence. On one side, there is the danger of evacuating the central Christian kerygma, on the other of losing touch with real experience. Certainly it seems evident that we must, if we believe in a personal God, beware of catering to a totally man-centered experience, and of making "faith" little more than an admiring gaze at someone else's experience. We may well be chary of playing down faith in an objective real Person, however historically problematic, and of losing the historical witness of Christ and the primitive Church. At that point we leave religion with breast bared, not only to "culture," but to Sartre and Camus, who can simply conclude from such experience that the life of man is ultimately absurd. While Schleiermacher would never tolerate the insinuation, I would ask his forgiveness for suggesting

50. *Ibid.*, p. 68.
51. Cf. Tice's introduction to *Christmas*, pp. 16-18.
52. Niebuhr, *op. cit.*, p. 50.
53. Cited in Niebuhr, *op. cit.*, p. 104.

that his method, in taking so little cognizance of the decision character of faith, is congenial atmosphere for the "tune in, drop out, turn on" approach of psychedelic experience, and ultimately for a denial of the Incarnation by a flight from personal and communal history.

Still, we have to turn to Schleiermacher for an appreciation of that which is given its meaning by the Incarnation—human life, feeling, dialogue, community, the "*a priori openness*" of man to the infinite. It is in this man's work that we find perhaps the most detailed phenomenology of religion in systematic form. Whatever objections I may have to Schleiermacher in theory, I find myself constantly returning to methods like his in classroom procedure, much as I would like to proclaim the vigorous "word theology" of Karl Barth. Certainly the psychology of religious education mentioned here before has only recently come into its own, at least in Catholic circles. The young must be met in their "now" history, "where it's at," where "natural" piety resides. The chief caveat here, I would say, is to teachers, who possess a mature attitude toward faith, that they also find ways to awaken students to the fact of divine transcendence and to as much objectivity in religion as can be appealed to. We must teach that an adult faith should transcend all "experience" if it is to be free. In our struggles with these problems, we do well to consider the strengths and weaknesses of the work of Friederich Schleiermacher.

11   Religious Experience and Atheism

JAMES CHERESO

The best treatment of religious experience I have come across is that of John E. Smith in his *Experience and God*.[1] I have adopted his philosophy of religious experience and have worked it into the first part of this chapter. In the second part I will offer several definitions of theism and atheism of William James, Julian Huxley, and Roger Garaudy. I will then offer some conclusions as to whether atheism as such can lay claim to an experience which can be properly called religious.

The appeal to experience as a basis for human feeling, judging and acting has been a constant one from the earliest times. And this appeal has been made by thinkers of the most divergent philosophical persuasions: Platonists, Aristotelians, Nominalists, Idealists, Materialists, Empiricists, Pragmatists, and Positivists. It should not be surprising that each appeal involves its own theory of what experience is and what it ought to contain and what its value is (or, if a variety of experiences is admitted, what the relative values of these are).[2] But is not experience one of those basic realities which defines itself and needs no other criterion or measure than itself? The history of ideas replies in the negative, for in every appeal to experience there is a principle of selection at work, that is, a principle by which one decides what can and cannot count for experience as the basis for human feeling, judging, and acting. The only resort is to state which

1. New York: Oxford University Press, 1968.
2. Cf. John E. Smith, *op. cit.*, p. 21. All references through fn. 22 will be to this work.

theory of experience one is using and then come to some assessment of its value in comparison with other theories.[3]

What has all this to do with religion and religious experience? Precisely this, that there are theories of experience which deny that there is any validity at all to any experience called "religious," and that there is any experiential foundation at all for religion. Such is the position of radical empiricism, logical positivism, and dogmatic scientism. This position is so narrow as to admit only sense data, and to exclude such data as relations, tendencies, and other dimensions which have traditionally founded aesthetics, morals, and religion.[4] And if such narrow theories show themselves to be tolerant of experiences other than those of the sense, they relegate such experiences to a realm of subjectivity which, they say, is inaccessible to verification. Some empiricists went so far as to conclude that, since the relationships between color, sounds, and odors are not objects of any senses, they are not matters of experience but products of the constructive activity of the mind.[5] What is needed then is a theory of experience which will give an accounting of, and acknowledge the validity of *all* the dimensions of experience which are the foundations of all the occasions and moments of human feeling, judging, and acting.

In seeking for an integral theory of experience we must avoid certain snares. One of them is to look at experience as a passive reception by a mere theoretical observer of what is externally given; experience would then be the mind as depository of brute data, exclusive of relationships, tendencies, and other dimensions, as has been noted. Another is to consider the linguistic expression of experience so essential to the experience that the content or whatness of experience can be discovered by an analysis of the language itself. This latter approach can become so refined as to restrict any experience worthy of the name to what can be discovered with the analytical tools of symbolic logic and mathematical physics. These are snares to an integral theory of experience because experience is either undermined as a base for

3. Cf. p. 22.
4. Cf. *ibid.*
5. Cf. pp. 26-27.

human feeling, judging, and acting, or is reduced to what language can express.[6]

How can we speak about experience in a way which will avoid these snares? First of all, we must see experience as a product of an interaction, of an interrelating between what is and the being who is able to become aware of, respond to, and relate with what is. And what is essentially neeeded, in addition, for experience *as experience*, is a being who is able to express and interpret all this in at least a kind of inner language (reflective feeling and thought)—if not in the external language of formal sounds and written words.[7]

It is vitally important to see experience as a product of the intersecting, interrelating, interacting of both the experienced and the experiencer. To stress one factor over the other is to be caught on the snare of the objective/subjective dichotomy. In such a case the external world is regarded as objective, that is, steadfast, reliable, and devoid of prejudice; while experience is entirely a thing of the mind, subjective, shaky, unreliable, and fraught with prejudice. Looking at experience as the product of intersection would avoid the self-defeating tendency to lock experience entirely within the consciousness of the experiencer.[8]

There is another reason why we must avoid identifying experience with only one of its factors. Both the thing experienced and the one experiencing have their own modes of being and acting which together constitute the reality we call experience. But while the thing experienced has its own modes of being which do not depend on its being distinguished from the experiencer, the experiencer must represent or reflect the experienced, doing full justice to all the modalities of being and acting of the thing experienced. There is an asymmetry in this situation, in other words. It lies in the fact that the thing experienced need reflect nothing of the experiencer; and here we have what is true about the doctrine of realism.

But idealism reminds us of something which realism often forgets, namely, that experience is more than a faithful repre-

6. Cf. p. 23.
7. Cf. *ibid.*
8. Cf. p. 24.

sentation or a reflecting of what we encounter. The experiencer is as much a part of reality as the thing experienced, and the experiencer is constituted as such and produces an experience by *refracting* the thing reflected through the prism of its cognitive and conative powers.[9]

How, again, does it come about that experience is regarded as a subjective event in contrast with other events which are considered objective? When experience is relegated to the region of sense or of emotions, as contrasted both with the region of abstract thought and physical nature. Restricting experience to sense results in locating experience in the individual mind or consciousness and hence in making experience uniquely individual and incommunicable.[10] How explain this tendency to making experience a subjective event? It certainly does not rest on any self-evidence that experience is only sense data immediately grasped by the mind as present to itself. In other words, whatever we may be immediately aware of, there is no immediate awareness that what we are immediately aware of is identical with our private sensations, feelings, and thoughts. This is an inference. It is a theory probably motivated by the belief that, if experience is considered to be only sensations, feelings, and thoughts, then the experiencer can be sure of *these*, whatever may be the situation of the realities which occasioned these subjective states.[11] How correct this tendency to making experience a subjective event? By refusing to admit any theory of experience which will decide beforehand what kind of thing experience *must* contain. Experience is not only of colors, sounds, and odors, but also of persons, places, things, relationships, tendencies, fears, hopes, disappointments, and everything that in any way presents itself to the reflective and refracting sensitivity and reactivity of conscious being. And while a theory of experience will be *general*, it will not generalize or reduce experience to one kind of content, for it will only generalize the *way* reality is approached, remembering that any *particular* experience is needful of special analysis.[12]

9. Cf. pp. 24-25.
10. Cf. p. 26.
11. Cf. pp. 28-29.
12. Cf. p. 27.

Another way of correcting the subjectivizing tendency is to insist on the social nature of experience. Experience is social not only because our social nature can consider as trustworthy only those experiences which we somehow test, modify, and enrich in sharing them with other selves; it is social also in regard to connections between repeated encounters, the connections cumulatively disclosing more and more of the thing encountered and affording us the occasion of critical comparisons and siftings. This latter meaning of the social or transindividual character of experience is manifested in our appeal to the man who "has experience." Such a man has experience in horseback riding or sail boating or curing backache, but not because he rode a horse or sailed a boat or cured a backache on just one occasion.[13]

Still another way of correcting the subjectivizing tendency is to form a theory of experience based on the way we become aware of selfhood. We do not *begin* with self-consciousness *and* an external world into which we move with caution. Rather, we have to *discover* that we are a self distinct from the world, and this discovery comes as a shock. It is when we become aware of our power to discriminate, judge, and select external things that we become aware of a self which is more than a faithful recorder of external things. And it is only with the emergence of this awareness of selfhood that the subject/object problem arises. The individual does not start out by immediate knowledge that his experiences are private and contained only in his consciousness. This is an inference, and, as we have seen, one based on the desire for certainty; for if we cannot be sure about what is "out there," we can at least be sure about what is "in here." If we maintain that the self is discovered *in* the experience of other things and is not something opposed to them, we shall avoid the error of making experience a subjective event confined to individual consciousness.[14] Even granted that we will always have the problem that the discovery of the self will awaken us to the possibility of error—that what we experience may indeed be completely solipsistic and not truly intersubjective there is the solidly based doctrine that experience is social in character and

13. Cf. pp. 30-31.
14. Cf. pp. 32-33.

that we do not begin with a private experience on the one hand and a public external world on the other.[15]

If we start out in private, we will finish in private. And if we fall prey to the seductive suggestion that this is precisely our embarrassment, that the external world is inaccessible to us because we are restricted to our internal world, we have only to ask how we come to this conclusion that our starting point is the private realm of our mind. The burden of proof has for too long been placed on the wrong side of the argument.[16]

The restrictive theory of experience we have been criticizing fails us in another important area: that of the dimensions of meanings or of the contexts in which the items or units of experience are immersed. The restrictive theory sees these items or units of experience as a collection of atomic phenomena, waiting to be assimilated and interpreted by an individual mind. And when this theory does acknowledge contexts or dimensions of meaning, these are considered to be the work of the mind rather than contexts or dimensions *of* experience.

A more realistic theory sees these contexts or dimensions of meaning as conditions in the things themselves, and, as the foundations for the experiences which can be designated political, moral, aesthetic, religious, and so on. For example, a diamond-studded tie clasp can be experienced in many different contexts or dimensions of meaning: besides being a union of sense qualities that fill up a space, it can be an item of exchange, an art object that delights the eye, a historical pointer to a past culture, and a peculiar instance of the capabilities inherent in material believed to be divinely created. Since experience is basically the product of interaction between the thing encountered and the encountering self, the dimensions of experience are likewise the resultant of these two factors, that is, of the reality encountered which has the ability to relate with several other realities in several different ways (the tie clasp *has* exchange value, it *has* aesthetic qualities, it *is* a historical marker), and of the experiencing self which has many goals and interests in encountering

15. Cf. pp. 33-34.
16. Cf. p. 35.

the external world—goals and interests which are expressed in its
assent to these capacities in the thing encountered.[17]

The restrictive theory speaks of experience as the realm of
"fact," and admits of dimensions of meaning only as mental constructs which come *after* the fact and which have no foundations
in the encountered thing. But not even empirical science can lay
claim to isolating such a bare fact. Empirical science, in its
hypothesizing and theorizing, decides first what will count for
fact, and then sets up experiments in order to discover or prove
that fact. The fact of experimental science is a highly abstract
reality which, though well founded, is not a disclosure of neutral
reality. The project of theoretical science can lay claim to lay
hold of *one* of many dimensions of experience. It cannot claim
to so lay hold of the irreducible nature of things that all other
dimensions of meaning are just so many subjective additions
which, though they cannot be disproved, cannot be proved.
Empirical theoretical science is the occasion of only one among
many dimensions of experience. Other dimensions, based on other
interests and goals, also enter into our experience of external
reality.

This assumption of scientism, that the really real is disclosed
only through the project of theoretical abstract investigation,
would be harmless enough left to itself, even though it is false.
It becomes harmful when the demand is made that all other
claims to an experience of reality must produce the same kind
of proof and verification as that of natural science. While this
demand is understandable in the light of the brilliant successes
of modern science, it must be denounced as contradicting the
fact that there are many and diverse goals behind the different
dimensions of experience and that there is no one privileged way
to represent reality, either in a *basic* dimension, or in all its
dimensions. The dimension of historicality gives one interpretation of the world and man; that of natural science gives another;
that of morality another; and that of religion still another.[18]

What of the modern trend toward linguistic analysis as *the*

17. Cf. pp. 37-38.
18. Cf. pp. 39-40.

critical philosophy? This trend has discredited experience. Experience, however, will never fail to transcend expression, so that experience will never be rightly judged by its verbal expression, but by a return to encounter; and it is by this return that the verbal expression itself will be subsequently corrected.[19]

As we shall see, attempts to give an empirical base to religion end up in what I consider to be failure when religion is identified with specific subjective states. Neither religious faith nor the object of that faith (transcendent being) ought to be identified with the religious dimension of experience. But neither is the proper *interpretation* of faith and its object in terms of religious experience, but of the *religious dimension of experience*. Divine being is encountered *in* a dimension of human experience called "religious." Divine being does not constitute, nor is it reducible to, that dimension. Divine being is affirmed when the necessity is seen to appeal to a divine disclosure from beyond human consciousness. The religious dimension is the product of man's encounter with the mystery of existence suggested in every other encounter with finite existences. While man is himself a finite existence, he bears the name "religious animal" because he questions existence itself and is supremely interested in it.[20]

The religious life which is founded in the religious dimension of experience is not a matter of so many special interventions of the divine into man's life. It is not a matter of atomic phenomena such as visions, or any other awareness of the presence of numinous forces. The religious life is based on the reflection and refraction that the holy and the profane are polar realities. The holy infuses the profane with purposiveness and poignancy, while the profane, by providing the holy with concrete being and historicality, makes the holy available to man as a dimension of his experience.

Now while religious life is not a matter of special divine interventions, there are special events in human life which give rise to the religious dimension of experience. Aside from the ordinary daily routine of getting up, eating, working, playing, and going to bed, there are times for being born, reaching pu-

19. Cf. pp. 43-45.
20. Cf. pp. 46-48, 55.

berty, entering into adulthood, choosing a profession, marrying, suffering, and dying. The holy enters into these times of life because it is then when the whole purpose of life as such becomes a poignant question; it is then that we become acutely aware that we are frail, finite, dependent creatures, needful of a supreme object of ultimate concern which can ground and direct our lives. There is the sense that, at least at these times, we are in the presence of a supremely worshipful power which controls our destiny; and it is this power, *fascinans et tremendum,* which moves us to communal religious celebration.[21]

The idea of communality is important. The crises of human life are disclosures of the holy only when authenticated by a "public" disclosure or revelation. This public revelation takes place through an *historical* medium. It occurs in special persons and events which bear and disclose the divine presence. This divine disclosure or revelation must not be divided against experience as the supernatural against the natural. Experience, after all, is the only means by which anything at all—even transcendent being—can be revealed to man. Revelation is the necessary fuller development of religious experience; it is religious experience which has attained to its social dimension. And it is precisely a social or public revelation which is the "authority" rightly looked for when the question is raised concerning the "objective truth" of the transcendent object of religious experience.[22]

According to James Collins, the most general meaning we can assign to atheism is: a denial of the prevailing conception of God or the divine. But since the conception of God changes from one age to another, the definition of atheism also changes. Even though there have been attempts in times past and in the present to work out an absolute atheism, that is, a discrediting of every possible notion of God, it always turns out that the absolute atheist is working from conceptions of God which happen to be prominent in his own time and within the ambit of his own investigations.[23] Jean Lacroix has said, "to be an atheist is to live

21. Cf. pp. 53-62.
22. Cf. pp. 66, 68-73, 158.
23. Cf. James Collins, *God in Modern Philosophy* (Chicago: Henry Regnery Company, 1959), p. 238.

fully in relation not to God but to others . . . atheism is a denial
of theology in favor of anthropology." [24] James Collins has also
observed that it is Ludwig Feuerbach's way of proposing the
question of mind and nature that atheism has become the defining characteristic of the humanisms and naturalisms of the last
one hundred years.

Feuerbach advances the historical thesis that the main
work of modern thought is to humanize God. Protestantism
concentrates upon God's significance for human salvation;
pantheism encloses God completely within nature; empiricism
judges God by the standard of human practicality; idealism
treats both God and nature as aspects of a single spiritual
whole. Hegel is the apex of this humanizing tendency, but,
unfortunately, he lacks the courage to spell out the inevitable
conclusion, which would consist in reducing everything super-
human to man and everything extranatural to nature. His
system falls short of this ultimate reduction by retaining absolute spirit. Feuerbach regards his own special vocation to be
the thorough humanization and naturalization of absolute
spirit. . . . Thus Feuerbach makes a twofold reduction: first,
of absolute idealism to theism; second, of theism to our subjective religious dispositions. His point is that speculation
about God or absolute spirit is not merely in harmony with
our subjective wishes but is nothing more than a hypostisi-
zation of them. [25]

We shall now apply what we have said about religious experience and atheism to three specific atheisms: the empiricism,
of William James, the naturalism of Julian Huxley, and the
Marxism of Roger Garaudy. Admittedly, the application of the
atheistic label to any man or system is arguable; nevertheless,
the broad definition of atheism we have offered would seem
to warrant such an application (even when, as in the case of
James, the religious thought ends up sounding very much like
theism). William James defines religion as

24. *The Meaning of Modern Atheism* (New York: The Macmillan
Company, 1966), p. 44.
25. *Op. cit.*, pp. 240-241.

"... the feelings, acts, and experiences of individual men in their solitude, so far as they apprehend themselves to stand in relation to whatever they may consider divine. Since the relation may be either moral, physical, or ritual, it is evident that out of religion in the sense in which we take it, theologies, philosophies, and ecclesiastical organizations may secondarily grow. In these lectures ... we shall hardly consider theology or ecclesiasticism at all." [26]

William James uses the pragmatic criterion for the "truth" of a religion. "The best fruits of religious experience are the best things that history has to show ... the highest flights of charity ... patience, bravery, to which the wings of human nature have spread themselves have been flown for religious ideals."[27] The collective name for the fruits of religion is "saintliness," and its psychology is comprised of "a feeling of being in a wider life than that of this world's selfish interests ... a shifting of the emotional center towards loving and harmonious affections." [28]

James does not fail to raise the crucial question. "So far as this analysis goes, the experiences are only psychological phenomena ... including 'the more than me with which I desire union and from which I hope to receive fulfillment'.... What is the objective 'truth' of their content?" [29] James then hypothesizes that this "more," whatever it may be on its *farther* side, is on its *hither* side the subconscious continuation of our conscious life. Although James insists that the power beyond us which we see as controlling us is the higher faculties of our own hidden mind, he still says that "the sense of union with the power beyond us is a sense of something, not merely apparently, but literally true ... disregarding the over-beliefs and confining ourselves to what is common and generic we have in *the fact that the conscious person is continuous with a wider self through which saving experiences come,* a positive content of religious experience

26. *The Varieties of Religious Experience* (New York: Collier Books), p. 42.
27. *Ibid.,* p. 211.
28. *Ibid.,* pp. 220-221.
29. *Ibid.,* pp. 393-394.

which, it seems to me, *is literally and objectively true as far as it goes.*" [30]

All the proposed explanations of what the "more" is on its farther side are "over-beliefs." Pantheism, theism, polytheism, Buddhism, rationalism, reincarnationalism, and mysticism are over-beliefs. William James has his own over-belief: "God is the natural appellation, for us Christians at least, for the supreme reality.... We and God have business with each other ... the universe takes a turn genuinely for the worse or for the better in proportion as each one of us fulfills or evades God's demands." [31]

James accords literal and objective truth to religious experience "as far as it goes." But we must note that this doesn't really go very far, inasmuch as he identifies religion with the religious experience itself. He identifies the experience of religion as its object with certain kinds of feelings and mental states. The basis for this is that he has adopted the scientific model for the nature of experience. [32] This leads to his considering feeling as the deeper source of religion, and to considering philosophic and theological formulations as secondary products, "like translations of a text into another tongue." [33] He states that "the attempt to demonstrate by purely intellectual processes the truth of the deliverances of direct religious experience is absolutely hopeless." [34] James is guilty here, I think, of the fallacy of injecting a *consequent* inference into the primal substance of experience. Just as identifying sense experience with one's mental states is an inference and not the experience itself, so the identification of the disclosure of a religious object with the religious experience is an inference, and not the revelational experience itself. Men have believed that certain persons and events have revealed God long before they began talking about revelation as a way of knowing distinct from the way of knowing other things.

James asks whether the sense of divine presence is a sense of anything objectively true. He observes that mysticism involves

30. *Ibid.,* pp. 396-398 (italics as in the text).
31. *Ibid.,* pp. 399-400.
32. *Ibid.,* p. 396.
33. *Ibid.,* p. 337.
34. *Ibid.,* p. 355.

an intense and heightened sense of the divine, and yet cannot claim a universal authority because it is "too private in its utterances." [35] This observation is typical of a lack in the whole of James' work on religious experience: the lack of seeing a social dimension which completes and fills out the religious experience: the lack of seeing a social dimension which completes and fills out the religious experience of the private individual. Connected with his failure to see a social dimension to religious experience is James' acceptance of an absolute distinction between immediate experience of God and rational inference of God. Since religion is for James too intimate to be a matter of rationalistic inference, the only alternative is the *immediate* data of experience. But there is a middle between, which is also a beyond of, these two extremes: history and historical persons and events. These are media of divine disclosures. God is not immediately revealed (as in the claim of mysticism), nor indirectly (as in the rational proofs), but directly in a medium. [36]

Julian Huxley's main thesis is evident from the title of the work we will examine: *Religion Without Revelation.* [37] He has a conception of religion and its object which is intolerant of any appeal to transcendence whatsoever—not even in the form of James' over-belief which has truth and objectivity because of definite results. For Huxley, the supernatural, supernatural beings and all religious truth are creations of the human mind based on a feeling of reverence toward what is considered sacred in reality. The religious life is neither more nor less the work of man than are science, art, and politics. [38]

The chief tool in Huxley's analysis is the method of experimental science as applied by the disciplines of comparative religion and psychology. There is no truly religious experience in Huxley's world view, if only because he crowds all of man's normally religious aspirations into the dimension of man's scientific experience of reality. Huxley's is a narrow theory of experience which equates religion and its object with subjective

35. *Ibid.,* p. 337.
36. Smith, *op. cit.,* p. 81.
37. New York: The New American Library (Mentor), 1957.
38. Huxley, *op. cit.,* pp. 20-25, 27-28, 31-32, 157, 161.

states because religion and its object are not empirically verifiable. But this is unacceptable not only for reasons we have already seen, but also for the following. Just because something enters into our experience does not mean that it must be transmuted into a mere psychological reality. There is no more reason for interpreting revelation and God into mere psychological realities than there is for so interpreting a tree that we see with our eyes. Experience is always an encounter, and the thing encountered, while it truly enters into the substance of experience, still transcends the experiencer. And religious encounter leads at once to the idea of divine disclosure or revelation. The philosopher does not produce religious experience. His work is to interpret it. He is not faithful to his task when, faced with a religious situation, he assumes the impossibility of revelation at the very outset.[39]

The general thesis we have proposed is confirmed in the cases of both James and Huxley: the divergence between naturalism and theism arises from their respective philosophical analysis of human experience, not simply from the scientific methods and findings as such.

We have now to see what there is of religious sentiment in Marxism. Our spokesman for this system of life and thought is Roger Garaudy. A theist might begin by asking Garaudy how man acquires the dimension of infinity; whether its meaning is exhausted by the indefinite dialectical process of man's surpassing of himself on the level and within the limits of his own history; and whether this awareness of incompleteness might be the mark of man's openness to a transcendent ontological future. Garaudy admits that Marxism needs to incorporate into its vision of the world the dimensions of subjectivity and transcendence which Christianity has brought into it,[40] but this assertion is amply modified by him.

"Marxist criticism rejects illusory answers, but it does not reject the authentic inspiration which aroused them. Beyond

39. Smith, *op. cit.*, pp. 48-51.
40. Cf. Roger Garaudy, *From Anathema to Dialogue* (New York: Herder and Herder, 1966), pp. 19-20.

the myths about the origin, and meaning of life, beyond the alienated notions of transcendence and death, there exists the concrete dialectic of finite and infinite, and this remains a living reality as long as we remain aware *that it is not in the order of answers but in the order of questions.* "Marxism asks the same questions as the Christian does, is influenced by the same exigency, lives under the same tension towards the future. The crucial factor is that Marxism does not consider itself entitled—because it is critical rather than a dogmatic philosophy—to transform its question into an answer, its exigency into a presence. . . . Marxism, by reason of its Faustian and Fichtean inspiration, does not succumb to the temptation to affirm, behind the activity, a being who is its source. My thirst does not prove the existence of the spring. For the Marxist, the infinite is absence and exigency, while for the Christian it is promise and presence. . . .

"There is thus indicated an indisputable divergence between the Promethean conception of freedom as creation, and the Christian conception of freedom as grace and assent.

"For a Christian, transcendence is the act of God who comes toward him and summons him. For a Marxist, it is a dimension of man's activity which goes out beyond itself towards its far-off being.

"This far-off being, on the horizon of all our projects is, in Father Rahner's terms, absolute future. Only for us it is a human future, and as such it is not a set future . . . of necessity limited by the alienation of our present projects . . . but a future always moving and expanding, a future which grows in direct proportion to our progress." [41]

A theist asks Garaudy if Marxism impoverishes man, and he answers, "in the measure that Marxism believes that the earth can be enough for him, yes, it impoverishes him." [42] For the Marxist, the transformation of the earth means more than new economic and political institutions among men; it is also a pro-

41. *Ibid.,* pp. 89, 92-93 (italics as in the text).
42. *Ibid.,* p. 93.

found spiritual metamorphosis of man, an increase in hominization. A future open on the infinite is the only transcendence known to the Marxist atheist. If he were asked to give it a name, he would not call it God, for it is impossible for him to conceive of a God who is always in process of making himself, in process of being born. The most beautiful name the Marxist can give to the never-satisfied exigency of totality and absoluteness is the name of man. And the theory that defines atheism is the reducing of the religious fact to the human fact: it is man who creates God.[43]

It is strongly suggested that if the religious dimension in the atheistic experience is genuine, atheism is a passageway to a purified theism. Marx certainly *began* with the presupposition of atheism in order to free man to take himself, as he concretely is, as a starting point.[44] But there are several reasons for believing that atheism is only a starting point. The Marxist-Christian dialogue of the past decade has revealed that, not only Christianity, but also Marxism (if it is to remain true to its high appreciation of the historical process) must be aware of the need of a theory of doctrinal development.[45] Marx himself seems to have given the nod to the inevitability of development when he said, "All I know is I'm not a Marxist." Engels explained that Marx intended by this that his studies should serve as a *guideline* for *future* studies.[46]

Garaudy speaks approvingly of John Robinson's assertion that it is no longer "God *or* the world," but "God *and* the world." "Seen in this perspective," he comments, "transcendence is no longer an attribute of God, but a dimension of man, a dimension of our experience and our acts."[47] Garaudy also speaks approvingly of Teilhard de Chardin's program for uniting both science and religion, and Marxism and Christianity. Garaudy quotes Teilhard in regard to the latter. "The synthesis of the [Christian] God of the Above and the [Marxist] God of the Ahead: this is

43. *Ibid.*, pp. 94-95, 109.
44. Cf. Lacroix, *op. cit.*, p. 36.
45. Cf. Leslie Dewart in his introduction to Roger Garaudy, *op. cit.*, p. 17.
46. Garaudy, *op. cit.*, p. 18.
47. *Ibid.*, p. 46.

the only God whom" we shall in the future be able to adore in spirit and in truth." [48]

It is in regard to this God of the Ahead that Rahner challenges the atheism of Marxism. He has stated to Garaudy that if Marxism is to be an integral humanism, it requires the experience of God, for an authentically human history and true human progress are possible only because of the transcendent existence of an absolute plenitude. The absolute future is present for everyone, Rahner says, and it is itself the very possibility of atheism; for the failure to recognize God results from man's confusion of the absolute future with one of his own (inevitably limited) projects for a fixed time in the future.[49] Garaudy is aware that Rahner's challenge tends to show that the future itself contains, though the Marxist may not be aware of it, the question which God asks us and which Christianity answers. Following Rahner, the theist insists that Marxism simply cannot evade the theistic question, for at the very heart of a humanism which strives to be integral, the question of the future of man gives birth to the question of the future of God.[50]

The time has come for some concluding observations, and we begin by asking whether there is religious experience in naturalistic religion. There is, but it is truncated and unauthenticated when it remains without the capstone of public historical revelation concretized in a definite historical community of believers. Naturalistic religion has had no identifiable religious community (although one must acknowledge small sects, here and there, professing a "religion of humanity" or an "ethical faith"). The patrimony of naturalistic religion is comprised of the revelation of God in nature and of the common religious truths philosophically distilled from the historical religions of mankind. But while this patrimony is universally accessible to all men, it does not constitute a community of faith. Some naturalistic believers, feeling this lack of community, grafted their universal religion onto one or another Christian church and thereby formed a deistic brand of Christian community. But a concrete community of faith is possible only when you have

48. *Ibid.*, p. 54.
49. *Ibid.*, p. 58.
50. Cf. *ibid.*, p. 61.

a historical situation where the divine disclosure in particular persons and events is acknowledged, accepted, and acted upon by a particular group of people who find, in the public revelation, an authentication and completion of their own individual religious experiences.

We would conclude with a brief nod to a possible conclusion that could result from further investigations along the lines we have pursued. If religious experience is a constant of human history, then practical atheism is impossible. By this I mean that an atheist is someone who has *theorized* his religious experience into a category of the natural by assuming, at the beginning of his inquiry, the impossibility of a transcendent object of religious experience, that is, an object which transcends every natural and human condition. Paul Tillich comments more radically that it is possible to be an atheist only if one remains indifferent and unconcerned about the question of the meaning of existence.[51] Karl Rahner makes a similar comment: "If atheism really understands itself and comprehends what is meant by God, it denies that the whole question of being, and of the personal subject as such who is propounding that question, can or may be raised at all. But such a question arises anew as a condition of its very denial. To the extent, therefore, that atheism understands its own nature, it suppresses itself."[52] It can also be argued theologically that radical orientation towards God is so much a part of the essence of man that there cannot be any real atheists, but only those who think they are; unless, of course, we can find a man whose life is completely devoid of the religious dimension of experience.

51. Cf. *Dynamics of Faith* (New York: Harper Torchbook, 1958), p. 45.

52. *Sacramentum Mundi* (New York: Herder and Herder), Vol. I, p. 117, col. 2.

12   Religious Experience in Atheism

JOHN CARROLL WHITE

If there is such a thing, in fact, as religious experience *in* atheism, there ought to be some evidence for it in the language of the atheist, for language is the way in which man reflects his experiences. One pattern of language which seems to be common to most men regardless of how they would identify themselves in terms of theism or atheism, is the pattern of symbolism. In the use of symbolic language the atheist permits us to discover an experience of his life which can be called religious experience. The experience gives rise to a concern on the part of the atheist to identify that experience, and the fact that he presents us with a language of symbols about the experience, and not a language which reflects the experience in terms of empirical events, enables us to conclude that the experience was meta-empirical, that certain events have arisen in his life which lie beyond the scope of empirical descriptive language to enumerate. The atheist is *not* telling us in his symbolic language that meta-empirical realities *exist*. He is trying, however, to come to grips, even if feebly, with certain events of his life which are unquestionably meta-empirical. For the theist, symbolic language is able to say something about the existence of God, at the very least; there is a truth-value to the affirmation of existence which the symbolic language makes, in this case. For the atheist, his symbolic language can have no such function; the appearance of a descriptive language within symbolic language are precisely that—appearances. And yet, even though the atheist differs from the theist in this important matter, he uses his symbolic language with much of the same concern that the theist has toward symbolism.

The language unquestionably reflects matters important to the atheist's life, yet they are matters which lie mysteriously outside the sphere of his empirical science.

The difference between symbolic language in theism and symbolic language in atheism seems to rest chiefly upon the matter of the truth-value of the statement, "There is a God." Of course, there are many contemporary theists who would challenge the way in which that statement has been used in the history of theology, but their difficulties with the use of the statement would hardly lead them to conclude that God's existence could not therefore be affirmed. J. B. Phillips, for example, argues against the God of traditional theism, what he calls the Sunday-school God, and concludes that the God about whom most theists are taught is really "too small." [1] John A. T. Robinson challenges the conception of God in classical Western theism, and makes the assertion that such a God is not, in fact, the God of the bible.[2] Paul Tillich, explaining his "Protestant Principle," denies the absoluteness of any statements about the Ultimate, but at the same time shows that such statements point toward a real Absolute, which for him certainly exists.[3] Outside of the Western tradition of theism, moreover, Hinduism and Buddhism do not deny an Absolute. Despite Heinrich Zimmer's assertions to the contrary,[4] Vedanta Hinduism takes Ultimate Reality very seriously and therefore cannot be called "atheism." [5] In addition, there is a

1. J. B. Phillips, *Your God is Too Small* (New York: Macmillan, 1961), p. 8.

2. John A. T. Robinson, *Honest to God* (London: S. C. M. Press, 1963), p. 44.

3. Paul Tillich, *The Dynamics of Faith* (New York: Harper Torchbooks, 1958), p. 29.

4. Heinrich Zimmer, *The Philosophies of India* (New York: Pantheon Books, 1951), p. 13. Zimmer writes: "[Vedanta identification of the Atman-Brahman is] precisely the non-theistic anthropocentric position that we ourselves are on the point of reaching today in the West, if indeed we are not already there."

5. On the impersonal, infinite, quality-less Absolute of the Vedanta system of Shankara as an example of Hindu affirmation of an Absolute, cf. S. Vernon McCasland, *et al.*, *Religions of the World* (New York: Random House, 1969), chapter 16, "Hinduism," p. 417.

serious question about whether the Buddha was in fact an atheist. The chapter on "The Foundations of Buddhism" in Vernon McCasland's *Religions of the World* asserts that Buddha was an atheist,[6] but Nancy Wilson Ross, in *Three Ways of Asian Wisdom*, writes the following:

> It is hardly fair to accuse of atheism a teacher who could state about an inconceivable power well beyond human imagination and speculation: "There is an unborn, an unoriginated, an unmade, an uncompounded; were there not, O mendicants, there would be no escape from the world of the born, the originated, the made and the compounded."[7]

Such men, and the religious experience in their lives which gave rise to their various languages, lie within theism, not atheism. To use Paul Tillich's fortunate expression, these are all men of ultimate concern; so by Tillich's definition, men of faith.[8] The atheist is not such a man. In his refusal to affirm an Absolute, an Ultimate, his concern must remain on the level of the less-than-ultimate. But he has concern, to be sure. His concern, like the concern of the theist, leads him on occasion to make use of a language of symbols which arises for him, as it does for the theist, out of a certain experience of life. The experience is one which he shares with the theist, to a degree: at least it is an experience of the meta-empirical in his life, even if he refuses to admit the existence of the Absolute. It is an experience which, like the experience in theism, leads to its being interpreted through symbolic language patterns, although in the case of the theist the content differs in that the theist affirms the existence

6. *Ibid.*, chapter 20, "The Foundations of Buddhism," p. 546: "Buddha wanted to eliminate the metaphysics and sacerdotalism of Vedism . . . . He refused to admit a metaphysical Being beyond the changeable process. His religion was neither monistic nor theistic; instead, he confined himself to a program of personal enlightenment."

7. Nancy Wilson Ross, *Three Ways of Asian Wisdom: Hinduism, Buddhism, Zen, and their Significance for the West* (New York: Simon and Schuster, 1966), p. 94.

8. Tillich, *op. cit.*, p. 1.

of the Absolute whereas the atheist does not. Such an experience in the atheist's life is what we may call religious experience in atheism.

Religious experience in atheism necessitates attempts on the part of the atheist to interpret his experience. The necessity is felt, to a certain extent, because the experience forms part of the raw material of the totality of the life of the atheist, a life which must be identified as much as possible, just as must be the life of the theist. Being aware that one has had a religious experience, or perhaps more accurately in the case of the atheist, being aware that one has experienced something in one's life which lies beyond the ability of empirical descriptive language to comprise is to respond to a need to interpret experience even before actually becoming conscious of that need. Religious experience in the life of the atheist at once demands some conceptualization of what he has experienced, and at the same time partly fulfills its own demands simply by having happened.

One may conclude that there is both something in the religious experience itself within the life of the atheist, apart from any interpretation he may give to it, and at the same time the necessity on his part to bring some interpretation to the experience. What is the cause of the experience, for example? The theist might reply that the cause was God, that the experience was in fact a means of contact with God, but the atheist cannot make this answer. God did not cause the experience, for the atheist, since for him cause is that which operates *within* the universe, and not upon it or upon anything within it from the outside.[9] For the atheist, the experience is his own, the feeling is within him, although it may arise in response to what is outside, such as natural phenomena, or communication with other people. The experience defies precise interpretation with respect to its origins and its nature, but the atheist is concerned with making some statement in order to interpret it, from his general concern to identify the totality of his life as he is able to apprehend it. He is

9. Ronald W. Hepburn, *Christianity and Paradox: Critical Studies in Twentieth-Century Theology* (London: Watts, 1958), chapter 9, "God and Cosmos (1)," esp. pp. 160-170.

no more able than the theist to remain satisfied with an interpretation of only those parts of his life which lie within the sphere of his empirical knowledge. His need, therefore, arises from within him, as an unwillingness to leave some part of his life uninvestigated.

In the process of making an interpretation of a religious experience, the atheist discovers that he must resort to unscientific thought models, just as the theist must. He is dealing, in the case of his experience, with life events which resist the attempts of empirical science to interpret them, with the result that any use of scientific thought categories is condemned in advance to imprecision. An atheist, for example, may be heard as frequently as any other man to speak of his sense of beauty, and his sense of love. Reflection upon these phrases, however, forces upon the atheist the conclusion that what he calls senses are not, in fact, *senses* at all, in the scientific meaning of the word, which is properly applied to sight, hearing, taste, touch, and smell. Rather, he is using the word imprecisely, unscientifically, since he must, in the case of such mysterious matters as love and beauty, interpret his experience symbolically. Thus it is with any experience of the numinous. As Ronald Hepburn writes, in *Christianity and Paradox*:

> Sense of the numinous does not bring with it its own interpretation. This is the product of reflection about the experience and of what thought-model will distort it least. To call it ultimately irrational is to confess that no thought-model seems to contain it really neatly.[10]

Where the theist and the atheist differ in interpretation of the religious experience is not in their use of imprecise language, therefore, but in their conclusions about whether or not the existence of some being may be deduced from the experience. Most importantly, they differ on whether one may affirm the existence of God, of course, but the difference goes further than

10. *Ibid.*, chapter 11, "Skepticism and the Naturally Religious Mind," p. 206.

that. The atheist would admit that in the symbolic language that results from his religious experience he is attempting to interpret episodes of his life which lie outside of his science. Such episodes are therefore meta-empirical. But the sense of the numinous, which the atheist shares with the theist, does not allow the atheist to draw conclusions about the *existence* of an Absolute, nor of anything else, for that matter. To quote Ronald Hepburn again:

> The sense of the "numinous" or holy [may be shared by both the theist and the skeptic]. This is the characteristic tone of claimed encounters with deity; the awe of Moses at the burning bush, the Israelites' terror on Mount Sinai; the dread and fascination felt before certain phenomena of nature: it even appears in some of the Romantic poets' response to mountain crag and chasm. The common element in these most varied experiences is what [Rudolf] Otto memorably described as the "numinous," a stunning but not horrifying experience, a blend of wonder, ecstasy, and fear at what is too great to be coped with intellectually. It is none of these feelings *exactly*: beyond them all is some element of quite inexpressible strangeness. . . . There is something irrational, ultimately non-intellectual about the experience. It does not yield us any clear concept that entitles us to claim we have learned something about God: at least not in the way a visit to a zoo can teach us what a tiger or racoon is like. I should want to go further and ask whether numinous awe need necessarily be interpreted as cognitive experience *of* any being at all.[11]

The refusal of the atheist to affirm the existence of God has its intellectual basis in the principle of empiricism that if the existence of anything is to be affirmed, its existence must be verifiable. For the atheist, the existence of an Absolute is not verifiable. This conclusion on the part of the atheist seems at first to destroy any receptivity he might have toward the meta-empirical episode, but it need not do so. He affirms the existence of that which he can verify. The experience exists, for him as for

11. *Ibid.*, pp. 205-6.

the theist, in which he is confronted with the mystery of his total identity and of his meaning in the world, but a statement which affirms God's existence must nevertheless be rejected as without truth-value. Truth-value lies in verifiable statements, not statements arising from the religious experience. Their meaning must be sought elsewhere.

Why does the atheist reject the truth-value of the statement, "There is a God"? First of all, he compares it with an apparently similar statement, but one in which the truth-value can be checked out, for example: "There is a tree outside my bedroom window." Unlike the latter statement, the statement, "There is a God," does not permit a man to go somewhere to check and see whether or not the statement is true. From the standpoint of empirically observable realities, then, the statement of the existence of an Absolute is non-verifiable, and therefore without truth value. Of course, there are empirically real things which resist such an easy verification of their existence, as for example sub-atomic particles. Here the trained observer begins with a hypothesis that a particular sub-atomic particle exists. Could not the same statement be made with respect to God's existence? Thus it would happen that the statement, "There is a God," is held as a hypothesis, and consequently data may be brought forth in support of the hypothesis, and a proof emerge.

The statement, "There is a God," cannot have truth-value as a hypothesis to be proved, however, since the atheist demands that if there are data which serve to prove the hypothesis, there must also be the possibility of data which would disprove it. Although the theist is ready with a great deal of data which serves to prove for him the hypothesis of God's existence, the atheist discovers that there is no data which, for the theist, would lead him to abandon the hypothesis. If the statement *cannot* be falsified by data, then of course neither can it be verified by data, and thus would have no truth-value as a hypothesis.[12]

12. *Ibid.*, chapter 1, "Contemporary Philosophy and Christian Apologetics," pp. 11-12, especially the citing of A. Flew, *New Essays in Philosophical Theology* (London: S. C. M. Press, 1955), pp. 96ff.

Neither can the statement, "There is a God," have truth-value for the atheist as a statement of mathematical or logical necessity. R. B. Braithwaite, in an important article entitled, "An Empiricist's View of Religious Belief," shows how this third attempt to give the statement some verifiability is no more successful than the previous two attempts:

> The view that the statements of natural theology resemble the propositions of logic and mathematics in being logically necessary would have as a consequence that they make no assertion of existence. . . . $2 + 3 = 5$ makes no assertion about there being any things in the world; what it says is that *if* there is a class of five things in the world, *then* this class is the union of two mutually exclusive sub-classes one comprising two and the other comprising three things.[13]

The theist would hardly be willing to have his statement, "There is a God," make no assertion about the existence of any being, which Braithwaite argues it must if it is assigned a mathematical or logical truth. The atheist, in fact, might grant the logical truth, such as that developed in the ontological argument of Anselm, for example, but continue to maintain that God did not exist in reality.

The intellectual life of the atheist forms a part of his total identity, too, of course, and it is his total identity which he seeks to maintain in his adherence to his conviction about the truth-value of God-language at the same time that he meets other requirements of his life through religious experience. The consistency of what he is trying to do may not always be apparent, even to him; but he is conscious of the numinous experience as undeniably present, and at the same time, as important as it surely is, he is willing to renounce any truth-value to statements he might make about that experience. It is a part of him that remains basically unknown, in this instance, consigned to the

13. R. B. Braithwaite, "An Empiricist's View of the Nature of Religious Belief," in *Christian Ethics and Contemporary Philosophy*, edited by Ian Ramsey (London: S. C. M. Press, 1966), p. 57.

language of imprecision, the language of symbols. But this is the only language available, and the only likely to be available. For if the atheist is truly such, then he renounces *all* absolutes, including the god of science, and does not put his faith in the ability of science to one day be able to answer all the presently unanswerable questions. He has *no* God, not a *false* God. This means that he will be a mystery to himself so long as he lives. The numinous experience, part of his experience as it is the experience of others, gives him no facts on which to decide about that part of his life which seems at times to be the most important part of all (although not *ultimate,* surely) and which nevertheless lies beyond his empirical science.

Closely related to the identity of his life, which his religious experience mysteriously and ambiguously communicates to him, is the relationship of that life to its surroundings. Here, as before, the totality of life is involved. Here, as before, the most important questions do not have answers. Science cannot tell him whether it is in the nature of the universe to offer to man hostility or friendship. Science cannot tell him what it is really all about that one man is able to communicate with another. And life is in motion, or at least it so appears to him. What is the future of man? The atheist asks this question as do other men, and his answers, arising from his personal experience of the numinous, are shaped in symbolic, imprecise language. Because there is the numinous, there is the evidence of the meta-empirical episode. For the atheist, this meta-empirical episode means that he can look toward the future with a certain confidence. He can project his destiny forward, and not only his own destiny, but the common destiny of mankind. He can hope. Hope is the common note of life which both the theist and the atheist hear through their experience of the numinous.

Has the atheist an eschatology, then? No, not in the sense that if tomorrow were to bring about the fulfillment of what he was hoping, he would know and recognize that tomorrow. But in another sense, the atheist, like the theist, has an eschatology. For he believes that the tomorrow will come, the tomorrow for which all men hope, even though he insists that we have no guarantee that we will recognize it when it arrives.

His language of the tomorrow, as his language of himself, is a symbolic language, somehow fulfilling without informing.

Religious experience in atheism does continue to be reflected in the language patterns of the atheist, language patterns of symbolic complexity which express for him some meaning to his life now and his life in the future, his identity and his eschatology. In his very admission of their scientific imprecision, moreover, the symbols become free from the criticism of his science. They need not be precise; they are not expected to inform him about the existence of meta-empirical forces and realities, and therefore they can function in another way, to express his life's meaning, and his hopes for the common destiny of mankind in a way that science cannot do.

In his choice of a language of symbols, finally, the atheist will probably be less likely than the theist to adopt traditional symbolic language as that language has historically reflected religious experience. It may be that he will respond much more in terms of what we would identify as poetry and music rather than myth and liturgy. But in the life of the atheist, a life in which the experience of the numinous is not absent, nor the concern over his identification of self, of relationships, and of hopes, the function of the myth and the liturgy of the theist. In both cases, the language serves to reflect a religious experience; in both cases, mysterious parts of the life of man, alone and with others, in the present and in the future, and man's place in the universe of whatever things there are somehow find their way into the experience. The experience is seen as having a value in both theism and atheism; in atheism, religious experience has value even apart from the affirmation of the existence of God. Ronald Hepburn writes about this common value:

If we regard the ultimate nightmare (from which religion seeks to deliver us) as the failure of all efforts toward "humanizing" the context of life, a nightmare in which other people are seen only as threats to our own existence, and nature as utterly foreign to us, then we shall still wish to accord a place of importance to the numinous and similar experiences, whatever their origin or whatever the mechanism by which they occur. . . . It is still a matter for wonderment that nature should "take" our projections, and (from sometimes uncompromising material!) make something so rich and strange out of them. This is a fact of importance about nature itself, one of the many reasons against thinking of it as destructive of, or at least hostile to, all value.[14]

14. Hepburn, *op. cit.*, chapter 11, "Skepticism and the Naturally Religious Mind," pp. 207-8.

III **The Self-Experience of the Catholic Community of Faith**

13 The Infallibility of the Roman Pontiff: Problems in Understanding

JOHN P. DOYLE

How far have we progressed since 1870 in our understanding of papal infallibility? In many ways, not far at all! We do not understand the meaning of "teaching on a matter of faith and morals," nor do we understand the relation of faith to morals. One reason for this is the emphasis we have had in Catholic teaching on assent rather than truly critical understanding. Another is the false notion faith will be secure as long as systematically stated teachings are preserved. Serious reflection on Gordon Allport's book, *The Individual and His Religion,* will help us to understand the fallacy of such an approach. Early in the book, Allport states:

> It follows that subjective religion ... must be viewed as an indistinguishable blend of emotion and reason, of feeling and meaning. When we study it we are dealing with neither rationality nor irrationality, but rather with a posture of the mind in which emotion and logical thinking fuse.[1]

The term that Allport uses to designate this cognitive-affective fusion is "sentiment." He defines the mature religious sentiment as:

> a disposition, built up through experience, to respond favorably, and in certain habitual ways, to conceptual objects and principles that the individual regards as of ultimate impor-

1. Gordon W. Allport, *The Individual and His Religion* (New York: Macmillan, 1960), p. 18.

tance in his own life, and as having to do with what he regards as permanent or central in the nature of things.[2]

Obviously, what Allport is attempting to establish is the role of religion for the whole person. Consider now this statement:

in probably no region of personality do we find so many residues of childhood as in the religious attitudes of adults.[3]

Many adults have taken over the ancestral religion much as they take over the family jewels because, lacking outside pressure, they find a certain comforting value in the essentially juvenile formulation of their childhood religion. By contrast,

in a mature personality a mature religious sentiment ... has a heavy duty to perform. ... The mature religious sentiment lays itself open to all facts, all values, and disvalues, and claims to have the clue to their theoretical and practical inclusion in a frame of life. With such a task to perform, it is impossible for this sentiment in a mature stage of development to remain disconnected from the mainstream of experience, relegated to a corner of the fantasy life, where it provides an escape clause in one's contact with reality.[4]

In an address given at Villanova in June, 1969, Harvey Cox, speaking on "Secular Holiness" observed that the person himself must decide what the quest for a life style must be. Cox insisted that this style is a total way of living in the world; one that is consciously arrived at; one that is original, not derived or appropriated. Schubert Ogden, speaking at Montreal, August of the same year, expressed similar thoughts. Ogden suggested that we consider Augustine's classic statement on faith, "Unless you believe, you cannot understand," in a very broad and general sense. In this broad sense, faith would be a necessity because man exists. In other words, man must "lead a life," not merely "live."

2. *Ibid.*, p. 64.
3. *Ibid.*, p. 59.
4. *Ibid.*, p. 61.

Man must consent to his existence and direct his understanding to analyze reality. In this view, faith is existential and cognitive. What Christianity does is to *re-present* man's true humanity. Christianity presents itself as the bearer and restorer of this humanity through the grace of God.

What I hope is becoming obvious in these remarks so far is something that we all accept, but, which I am afraid we do not take seriously enough—if faith is to be really meaningful in our lives, then it must embrace far more than assent to teachings. Mere acceptance of teachings, especially as these proliferate, does not contribute to mature development.

In describing the role of the mature religious sentiment, Allport uses six categories. Let me refer to two: the *integral* nature of the mature religious sentiment, and its heuristic character. With reference to the first Allport writes:

> (the mature individual insists) that his religious sentiment compose a homogeneous pattern . . . its design must be harmonious. . . . To fashion an integral pattern is the task of a lifetime—and more.[5]
>
> . . . To be truly integral a religious sentiment must admit the disturbing fact that human conduct, to a large degree, is determined. . . . Yet an adroit mind will readily perceive that the degree and type of freedom a man has depends in part on what he believes. If he thinks he is hopelessly bound, he will not exert himself. . . . A well differentiated religious sentiment engenders freedom simply because the possessor of such a sentiment finds that obdurate though nature and habit may be, still there are regions where aspiration, effort and prayer are efficacious. A person believing he is free uses what equipment he has more flexibly and successfully than does the person who is convinced he dwells in chains.[6]

With reference to the heuristic character of the mature religious sentiment, Allport says:

> An heuristic belief is one that is held tentatively until it can

5. *Ibid.*, p. 79.
6. *Ibid.*, p. 80.

be confirmed or until it helps us discover a more valid belief.... Perhaps the person accepts the authority of some
revelation. If so, he does it not because he can demonstrate
its final validity by events occurring in time and space, but
because that which he accepts helps him find out better and
fuller answers to the questions that perplex him. His faith
is his working hypothesis.[7]

What Allport is stressing here is the fact that the mature person
can act without absolute certainty; that faith is a risk; that all
accomplishment results from taking risks in advance of certainties.

When speaking again of the role of integration, Allport men-
tions the importance of humor:

Religion takes up where humor leaves off. Having decided
that there is something beyond laughter, a core of life that
is "solemn, serious, tender," there yet remains plenty of clear
room for jesting. For to the religious person, as well as for
the irreligious, the design of the universe is by no means
apparent at all times, and its *non sequiturs,* its "mechanical
elasticity," are fair game for laughter—so long as the ultimate
direction of one's life intention is fixed. Humor helps to integrate personality by disposing of all conflicts that do not
really matter.[8]

I am personally convinced that in general we Roman Catholics have taken ourselves far too seriously. This is perhaps one
of the chief reasons why change has been so difficult in some
areas and on some levels of the Church. This is why, perhaps,
we hear some expressing concern lest the "simple faithful" be
upset by too many and too rapid changes, without even raising
the questions: who are the "simple faithful," and, is it not
perhaps time that this group was upset?

We are recognizing more and more today that there is a
direct proportion between alienation, de-personalization and the
lack of appreciation of the symbolic. Nathan Scott, in a book

7. *Ibid.,* p. 81.
8. *Ibid.,* p. 105.

entitled, *The Broken Center,* refers to and quotes Romano Guardini:

> In Romano Guardini's famous little book, *The Spirit of the Liturgy,* there is a chapter in which we are asked to think of the Church's liturgy as a kind of play.... Msgr. Guardini is, of course, aware that this is a perspective that will be offensive to those grave and earnest rationalists in the Church for whom every aspect of its life must have a moral purpose: ... they will want to insist that the Church's liturgical actions are channels of grace and serve the indispensable purpose of the soul's renewal and edification.... Msgr. Guardini denies that the liturgy is informed by "the austere guidance of the sense of purpose." The prayers, the gestures, the garments, the colors, the holy vessels ... are all, he asserts, simply "incomprehensible ... when measured by the objective standard of strict suitability for a purpose." For the liturgy, in quite the same way as a child's play, has no purpose. "The child, when it plays, does not aim at anything. It has no purpose. It does not want to do anything but to exercise its youthful powers, (to) pour forth its life in an aimless series of movements, words, and actions...."
>
> "That is what play means; it is life pouring itself forth without an aim." And, similarly, the liturgy ... is a pouring forth of "the sacred, God-given life of the soul."
>
> The liturgy, in short ... is a form of art. For whenever the human spirit, in a deep and radical way, apprehends through the configuration of things and events a threshold beyond which is a Something More, the taproot ... of everything that has reality—whenever the human spirit is granted such a moment of contact with the unplumbed Mystery from which everything is sprung—its most primitive impulse, in Jonathan Edwards' phrase, is simply "to consent to being." [9]

It is precisely in relation to man's cognitive-affective reaction and response to this confrontation with mystery, the ultimate

9. Nathan A. Scott, *The Broken Center* (New Haven: Yale University Press, 1966), pp. 212-213.

mystery of life in Christ, that our traditional understanding of "teaching on faith and morals" has failed. We have had to explain everything. We have had to insure that every one, as it were, had his own "road map" with the route carefully marked out. Karl Rahner once stated that theology must show man's radical orientation to mystery. Then, this mystery will not be overly systematized. That this mystery has been over-systematized is a legitimate criticism that Eastern Orthodoxy makes of Western Christianity. Listen to Fr. Schmemann: Recover the meaning of the symbol. The deep inner, or central meaning is "mystical." The language of the great statements of the Church Councils is to be understood symbolically—positive affirmation is not exhaustive definition. Tradition is not an accumulation of texts. It is man's development in all its aspects.

In the light of our failure to develop a truly critical understanding of "teaching on a matter of faith and morals," we can better appreciate why there has been such great difficulty in working out the relation of the pope to the bishops, and of the pope and the bishops to the rest of the Church. I feel strongly that this is also the reason why we do not have any concept of loyal dissent. What hope is there that progress and new understanding will occur? Great hope!

First of all, the *Constitution on Divine Revelation* from Vatican II re-emphasizes historical theology. Consider these highly significant words:

> This tradition which comes from Apostles develops in the Church with the help of the Holy Spirit. For there is a growth in the understanding of the realities and the words which have been handed down.... This happens through the contemplation and study made by believers, who treasure these things in their hearts, through the intimate understanding of spiritual things they experience, and through the preaching of those who have received through episcopal succession the sure gift of truth. For, as the centuries succeed one another, the Church constantly moves forward toward the fullness of divine truth.... [10]

10. Walter M. Abbott, ed., *The Documents of Vatican II* (New York: Guild Press, 1966), "The Constitution on Divine Revelation," p. 116.

Statements such as this, together with the whole pastoral thrust of Vatican II, make it no longer possible to equate the teachings of the Catholic Church with eternal truth. How is it that such an equation ever developed in the first place? Why should the relation of Catholic teaching and Catholic truth have been a problem? At the risk of oversimplifying, my immediate answer is because Catholics on every level have presumed in a most uncritical fashion that the teachings of the *magisterium* and Catholic truth are one and the same thing. In fact, the two are not the same at all. To understand this, it is necessary to examine the relation of Scripture and Tradition as these apply to Catholic truth.

The most important thing to recognize about the early centuries of Christianity is the fact that scripture and the teachings of the Church co-inhere. It is interesting to study Irenaeus when he writes concerning apostolic succession. For him, episcopal succession is a channel through which scripture is transmitted. The succession of the bishops, with the pope, does not exist separately from scripture. The bishops are not merely interpreters of scripture; they are witnesses to the truth contained in scripture. This witness is dynamic: the Church responds according to the time and the situation. It is useful and instructive to observe that the Church in the struggle against Gnosticism always insists that the scriptures are *not* a source of new, hidden truths. Both Tertullian and Cyprian, for example, defend what they consider true tradition against those who would add human customs to holy scripture. In this brief reference to early Christianity, one thing is to be noted carefully—tradition is not merely handing down truths from the Apostles to their successors. Real tradition, the living witness to Catholic truth, demands the co-inherence of the Church and scripture.

Basil the Great in the East and Augustine in the West both speak of equal respect for scripture and tradition. Observe that this new emphasis occurs only when Gnosticism ceases to be a threat. It is not certain to what extent Basil really held this equal respect, or whether others used Basil's authority. In the Middle Ages, for example, Ivo of Chartres quotes Basil's words: "equal respect for the written (scripture) and the unwritten," and this is incorporated by Gratian in his *Decretals* which were so important for Canon Law. From the thirteenth century on, Canon Law understands two sources of Catholic truth. All papal decrees in the late Middle Ages have two sources—Canon Law, as embodying Church teaching, and scripture. This is the reason for the great tension between the canon lawyers and the doctors of theology.

Augustine is firm in the authority of scripture. Scripture is the source of authority for Catholic truth. He deviates only on the point of infant baptism. Augustine feels that Church authority is necessary here because of the difficulty of establishing a sound scriptural base for infant baptism. A well known statement of Augustine is important here:

> Ego evangelio non crederem, nisi catholicae ecclesiae auctoritas me *commoverit*.[11] (I would not believe the gospel unless the authority of the Catholic Church moved me.)

The word *commoverit* is especially significant because, as Augustine uses it with reference to Church authority, he understands the Church as an instrument of instruction. By the Middle Ages, not only is this understanding changed, but, the word *commoverit* is actually changed to *compelleret* in citing the words of Augustine. Note the antithesis: *compelleret* has the force of legal authority that binds exteriorly; the internal, instructional aspect (*commoverit*) that brings true internal consent, disappears. Thus, during the Middle Ages, the theologians (*doctores*), in general, are pledged to the authority of scripture with the Church as an instrument that instructs, and hence moves one to accept Catholic truth. The canon lawyers, however, view the Church as that which compels assent. By the time of the Avignon period and the Great Schism, the issues become, more and more, legal issues. As the bishops align themselves with the canon lawyers, Church leaders become more secular, and the gulf between the theologians and the bishops becomes wider and wider. The bishops tend to identify more and more with the two sources of Catholic truth as understood by canon lawyers. What has ultimately resulted from this is: the Protestant position, since the

11. *Contra Epist. Manichaei,* 5, 6.

sixteenth century, gives a most important place to the theologians —the *successio doctorum;* the Roman Catholic position, on the other hand, gives real importance only to the teachings of the pope and the bishops, the *magisterium.* In other words, the Roman Catholic position places the pope and the bishops *over* scripture rather than with scripture.

A common interpretation of the Protestant Reformation presents the dispute as a struggle between scripture (*sola scriptura*) and Tradition (Church teachings). This is a seriously oversimplified view. What really took place was a confrontation between two approaches to Catholic truth. The first, which we can call tradition I, is the position held generally by the doctors of theology in the late Middle Ages. In this view, the Church, by bearing witness to the truth contained in the sacred writings, is the instrument of scripture. By instructing the faithful, the Church establishes a living exegetical tradition that moves them (Augustine's *commoverit*) to accept Catholic truth by internal consent. The second, tradition II,[12] emphasizes the Church as the authoritative receptacle of teachings. In this view the Canon Law view, and the position generally held by the hierarchy, the authority of the *magisterium* compels acceptance. In this view, the exterior force of law is paramount. Tradition II insists that many Church teachings are "implicit in scripture"—infant baptism, the Immaculate Conception, for example. By the fourteenth century, *implicit in scripture* became "scripture is silent." In practice this meant that as long as scripture did not oppose a doctrine, it could possibly be held.

By the time of the Council of Trent, the lines had been clearly drawn. Luther had launched his attack and the Church had to respond. The response of Trent was that Catholic truth is contained both in scripture *and* tradition. In practice this came to be understood as opting for tradition II. The Roman catechism of 1566, for example, explains that Catholic truth is contained partly in scripture and partly in Tradition (Catholic teachings). Robert Bellarmine and Peter Canisius, in their cate-

---

12. For further treatment of tradition I and II, see the essays of Heiko Oberman, to be found in Elmer O'Brien, ed., *The Convergence of Traditions* (New York: 1967).

chisms, likewise emphasize the tradition II concept. Vatican Council I implies that Trent taught two parallel sources of Revelation (Catholic truth). Vatican II does not solve this problem. *The Constitution on Divine Revelation,* however, in its final form does not speak of two sources of Catholic truth.[13] It does strongly emphasize that scripture is transmitted in a living community which bears witness to the meaning of scripture according to the needs of the time. Recall the citation that I made earlier:

> For there is a growth in the understanding of the realities and the words which have been handed down ... the Church constantly moves forward toward the fullness of divine truth....[14]

This document states that scripture, tradition and the *magisterium* must interplay. This document makes it quite clear that biblical faith is far more than intellectual assent to propositions.

Before proceeding, a few considerations of the Vatican I debate on the definition of Papal Infallibility are in order.[15] Before the question was moved up on the agenda, it was well known that a majority of the Council Fathers were in favor of such a definition. In the debate that took place, the minority position centered on the problem of the communion between the pope and the bishops. The minority refused to be satisfied unless the role of the bishops in relation to the pope was publicly spelled out. The minority feared that the *schema* of papal power that was presented at the Council was vulnerable to having the pope isolated as a separate power over the Church. The minority could not swallow the notion of a part as supreme over the whole. This is the reason why sixty-six of the minority bishops left Rome before the final vote rather than declare *non placet.*

13. "The Constitution on Divine Revelation," #10, in Abbott, *ibid.,* p. 117.

14. *Ibid.;* cf. #10, above.

15. For an excellent treatment of the Vatican I discussion of papal infallibility, see Dom Cuthbert Butler, ed., *The Vatican Council 1869-1870* (Westminster, Md.: Newman Press, 1962).

I am not now suggesting that, in theory, the pope has become isolated as a separate power over the Church as a whole. I am suggesting that, in practice, this has happened. This is why there was such great discussion at Vatican II on chapter III of the *Constitution on the Church* which deals especially with the episcopate. This is why the famous *nota explitiva* was necessary to satisfy the minority bishops.[16] I am suggesting that our approach to papal infallibility has been very much influenced by the tradition II concept of Catholic self understanding. In the minds of many, papal infallibility is another truth added to the receptacle of truths that constitute Catholic teachings. The uncritical defense of papal authority has obscured the real issue —the positive role the whole Church, the communion of Pope, Bishops and Faithful has. This is to bear witness to Gospel truth. The definition of Papal Infallibility at Vatican I was a compromise statement that did not please the most ardent infallibilists and was completely unacceptable to three-fourths of the minority. Yet, between Vatican I and Vatican II, this definition has been understood, in practice, in terms that would have pleased the most ardent infallibilist of Vatican I.

This is why the *Constitution on Divine Revelation* is so important, and such a great source of hope for the future. I have already cited paragraph eight. Please recall the words: ". . . the Church constantly moves forward toward the fullness of divine truth. . . ." Note especially the singular *veritatis* (truth). This is a totality given from the beginning. It is full. Yet, we have not grasped it in its totality. Thus, movement and progress are essential. What is truly significant about this paragraph is the fact that this movement and progress is the task of the whole Church. In the first draft of this constitution, only the *magisterium* could progress. Recall also the words: "For there is a growth in the understanding of the realities and the words which have been handed down. This happens through the contemplation and study made by believers. . . ." Note that the word contemplation comes before study. Note also that to contemplate,

16. For a discussion and explanation of this, see Herbert Vorgrimler, ed., *Commentary on the Documents of Vatican II* (New York: Herder & Herder, 1967), Vol. 1, especially pp. 135-137 and 198-200.

one must listen. The mystery·must really be appreciated before
study and instruction is possible. This is a far cry from the
tradition II approach. We read in paragraph 10:

> Sacred tradition and sacred scripture form one sacred deposit
> of the word of God, which is committed to the Church.
> Holding fast to this deposit, the entire holy people united
> with their shepherd remain always steadfast in the teaching
> of the Apostles, in the common life, in the breaking of the
> bread, and in prayers, so that in holding to, practicing, and
> professing the heritage of the faith, there results on the part
> of the bishops and faithful a remarkable common effort.[17]

The text proceeds to speak of the teaching office of the Church:
"This teaching office is not above the word of God, but serves
it." [18] The relation of these two paragraphs, numbers 8 and 10,
is our problem today. Because of our tradition II orientation,
we, the faithful, have failed to educate the *magisterium* that
they must listen to us: before one can contemplate, one must
listen. This is the great challenge the Church faces today. The
direction, the mandate, if you wish, has been given. This is our
hope. It is especially our responsibility as teachers to act. To
those who say that the *magisterium* refuses to listen, I say, perhaps we have not really presented our case. This is why I say to
my students: right now it is more fun to stay in the Church
and agitate in the best sense of the word.

A second source of hope that we will progress in our understanding of "teaching on a matter of faith and morals," and
thereby better appreciate the meaning of papal infallibility is the
Constitution on the Church of Vatican II. In paragraph 10,
we read:

> The baptized, by regeneration and anointing by the Holy
> Spirit, are consecrated into a spiritual house and a holy
> priesthood. . . .
>
> Though they differ from one another in essence and not only

17. "The Constitution on Divine Revelation," in Abbott, *ibid.,* #13.
18. *Ibid.,* p. 118.

in degree, the common priesthood of the faithful and the ministerial or hierarchical priesthood are nonetheless inter-related. Each of them in its own special way is a participation in the one priesthood of Christ.[19]

What is clearly emphasized here is the concept of the Church as a priestly community. Paragraph 11 goes on to state that the total sacrament, that is the Church, is explicated in the celebration of the individual sacraments. The summit of this celebration is, of course, the Eucharist. Here is manifested as nowhere else, "the will to fellowship with the person and destiny and life of Christ." [20] Here we see emphasized the true notion of *communio ecclesiarum* which is basic for the future of the Church.[21] The next paragraph is really the key. Here I quote Aloys Grillmeier:

> This article, in fact, like the whole of Chapter II, is concerned with basing the infallibility of the Church, like that of the *magisterium*, on the people of God as a whole. In the mind of the faithful, as in that of the *magisterium*, the gift of infallibility has been too one-sidedly concentrated on the office, and even on a papal primacy which was considered in isolation from the episcopate as a whole.[22]

Developing these remarks, Grillmeier continues:

> The people of Christ, as a whole, including the holders of office, is infallible *in credendo*, which, however, is not to be taken in a passive sense....[23]

> The holders of office are infallible ... also *in docendo*, by virtue of the charism given to them, which embraces their teaching.[24]

Here is Grillmeier's crucial observation:

19. "The Constitution on the Church," #10, in Abbott, *op. cit.*, p. 27.
20. Vorgrimler, *op. cit.*, p. 159.
21. *Ibid.*, p. 162.
22. *Ibid.*, pp. 164-165.
23. *Ibid.*, p. 165.
24. *Ibid.*

The instinct of faith in the people as a whole and the infallible *magisterium* of the Church stand in the same relation to each other as the common priesthood of all the faithful to the consecrated priesthood, into which is absorbed the priesthood of all the baptized.[25]

Reflection on paragraphs 10 to 12 of this Constitution together with Grillmeier's commentary, makes it quite clear that we must no longer regard the Church's tradition as a receptacle of truths dispensed for our belief. In this regard, I am reminded of the Council of Florence where so many problems were resolved by the hierarchy. The faithful in Byzantium, however, refused to accept these solutions. In our own day, illustrations of the same are far too numerous. Once again, I feel that teachers have a very special task to help our students understand the mutuality of the relationship between the hierarchy and the faithful. We should not fear whatever tension may arise here. Where there is tension, there is life.

A third source of hope for progress is the Synod of Bishops which seems to be developing a real concept of collegiality. A very thorough treatment of the recent Synod can be found in *Herder Correspondence,* December 1969. Before the Synod opened, there was a general attitude of pessimism because the schema that had been prepared by the Doctrinal Congregation gave the impression that the hierarchy was the most important aspect of the Church. When the bishops had assembled, however, and heard Cardinal Seper's *relatio,* there was a marked change of attitude. The *relatio* started by mentioning the attention that had been focused on collegiality since Vatican II and went on to talk of the growing demand for coresponsibility. In this way, the *relatio* followed the direction of the *Constitution on the Church* of Vatican II by recognizing that the Church is a community before it is a hierarchy. That the assembled bishops recognized this was obvious the following week when they voted to accept the *relatio* rather than the schema as the basis for further study. Of great significance in this regard was the consensus of the bishops that the international commission of the-

25. *Ibid.*

ologians should take up the question of the meaning of collegiality. While the issue was not formally remitted to this group, I consider the fact that many bishops suggested this a real step forward in re-establishing the status of theologians in the Roman Catholic Church. Theologians, since the Reformation period, have been second class citizens. This, more than any other reason, in my opinion, is the cause of Rome's being so tradition II conscious; so concerned with the Church as a receptacle of truth. In this regard, it is interesting to note that one of the French-speaking bishops' groups at the recent Synod suggested that the staff of the Roman Congregation should not consist exclusively of canon lawyers.

The main reason why the Synod is such a great cause of hope is revealed by the voting. Thirteen propositions were voted on under three general headings: the principle of subsidiarity; ways of promoting communication between the Apostolic See and the bishops' groups of the Eastern and Western Churches; the structure of the Synod itself. All of the propositions are distinctly of the *communio ecclesiarum* spirit that I referred to earlier. What is exciting is the fact that each proposition gained at least a two-thirds majority. Considering the fact that, under the procedural rules, *placet juxta modum* votes indicated approval in principle, it can be stated that the propositions expressed virtually the unanimous opinion of the Synod. Pope Paul's response to the deliberations and votes of the bishops was immediate. He accepted them in principle, while warning that he must be careful to maintain the necessary unity in the universal Church. This, of course, indicates where the tensions and difficulties will arise. At the same time, I am convinced that what we are witnessing is the recognition that the chief problem in the Church has not been papal infallibility as such; nor has it been the *ex sese* clause of the Vatican I definition: "such definitions of the Roman Pontiff are irreformable of themselves and not from the consent of the Church." The recent Synod of Bishops has reaffirmed their consciousness of what the true role of a bishop is. As the bishops become more aware of their responsibility as pastors and leaders in the sense of *communio ecclesiarum,* so will all come to understand that the true role of the pope can *not* be adequately expressed only in juridical terms. A statement in *Herder Correspondence* is quite blunt on this:

> Quite probably, in fact, like authority of the best type, the primacy is something that should not have to be used at all in an explicit fashion. It could indeed be the case that the whole point of defining the primacy was simply to show where . . . authority finally existed in the Church, and that, once having got this clear . . . we could in practice forget about it and carry on with the business of Christian living.[26]

It would seem that Paul VI is also deeply aware of this. The same issue of *Herder Correspondence* summarizes the Pope's closing speech. One part reads:

> This synod, he continued, was not meant to breed rivalry over power . . . but to put into practice the mutual tendency of Pope and bishops towards closer communion and collaboration. . . . This did not mean abdication on his part from the duties and responsibilities of his own primacy, but this he expressed in terms of charity, suggesting that the Pope should be compared to the heart of the universal Church with the job of ensuring that the blood-stream of charity flowed through the veins of the body of Christ.[27]

I consider this address of Paul as of the very highest importance because of the circumstances in which it was given. In the past, such words would have been accepted with a pious nod. Today, because of Vatican II, especially the Constitutions on the Church and revelation, we can take these words with the seriousness that they deserve. I spoke earlier of Karl Rahner's statement that the theologian must show man's radical orientation to mystery. I also stated that the current loss of appreciation of the symbolic is a direct result of our Western penchant to over-systematize. A prime illustration of this is the tradition II approach to Catholic truth that I have referred to so often. This

---

26. *Herder Correspondence* (December, 1969), p. 357.
27. *Ibid.*, p. 382.

is why "teaching on faith and morals" is such a problem for so many today. Let us really reflect on these words of Paul in the depth of their symbolic meaning, and in relation to the constitutions of Vatican II that I have mentioned so often. Perhaps we will then begin to understand how much of a problematic Christian faith is. Perhaps then we will really begin to appreciate that the primary purpose of "teaching on faith and morals" is not to offer systematic explanation, but to make us more aware of the mystery of Christian life. Then we can grasp Allport's words in a new light when he says that accomplishment results from taking risks in advance of certainties; that faith is a risk.

I have tried to show that our chief problem with papal infallibility is our concern for expressing our "teachings on faith and morals" in concise, juridical terms, the tradition II approach. This has led to our "safe and secure" attitudes as Catholics—spell out everything so that everyone will know what to do. In this framework, the pope is, in a sense, the final arbiter. The result of all this is that faith is stifled. It becomes essentially a cognitive expression rather than the cognitive-affective expression that I spoke of at the start. I feel that it is precisely this which makes it so difficult for Western Catholics to appreciate the true nature of the symbolic especially as this unfolds the basic mystery of God-in-Christ. I feel that only when we really take the cognitive-affective nature of faith seriously will we be able to make the Christian challenge meaningful. I have indicated what I consider the real sources for hope that this attitude can change and is changing. What is at stake if this hope is not realized?

First of all, the future of the Church is at stake. There is the real possibility that the essential role of the Church—bearing witness to the Truth of the Gospel—will be lost. I do not have to remind you that there is a credibility gap right now between the *magisterium* and the Church at large. Consider, for example, *Humanae Vitae* and *Populorum Progressio*. It was necessary for the bishops' conferences of the various countries to take a stand and interpret *Humanae Vitae* to their people. Nothing of this nature was thought necessary for *Populorum Progressio*. There is also a gap in communication. A good illustration was the investigation of Fr. Schillebeeckx. I had the opportunity to ask Cardinal Alfrink about this. He made two things clear: first, Fr. Schillebeeckx is a most able and reliable theologian; second, that if he, as Primate of Holland, had been consulted first, most of the notoriety could have been avoided.

The role of the pope cannot, of course, be separated from the role of the Church. The pope enjoys a moral prestige that is totally unique. We do not have to be reminded of the impact that John XXIII made on the world. I, for one, was proud when Paul VI addressed the United Nations. I really wonder if many Catholics truly appreciate how the pope can speak for the moral conscience of the world. Is this something that should be allowed to die out? I am greatly concerned that this can happen by default.

What is the role of college teachers? First of all, I want to emphasize our uniqueness at the present time. We enjoy a day to day relationship with the generation that is the future of the Church in America. I consider this a position of incredible responsibility. What is our task? I would describe it as doing all that we can to dispel the traditionally passive role of the laity. This is what I meant before when I said it is more fun to stay in the Church and agitate. To dispel this passivity we must explain and illustrate the real meaning of the *sensus fidelium,* as developed in the Vatican II documents that I have referred to. If the spirit of these documents can be implemented in America at Detroit, and in Holland, it can happen elsewhere also. Our task is to exploit and direct the creative energies of college students. We must insure that they see, in historical perspective, why the laity has no voice in the Church. We must emphasize that this need not continue. Our students must become aware that there is a battle to be waged, and that success will not come overnight. This is precisely why it is so important to understand that faith is a risk.

All of this means, of course, that we must do everything possible to avoid the trap of making theology or religious studies courses optional. Requiring such courses is neither paternalistic nor defensive. The purpose of such courses is to enable the students to develop a true awareness of our Christian heritage. Only if such an awareness is developed, can they view religion, "teaching on faith and morals," with a genuinely mature and critical sense. Only then will they have the opportunity to make faith the cognitive-affective response that it must be. Such a response can be the basis for a mature recognition of what is the task of the pope and the bishops as leaders. One of the primary tasks of both is to break the "security syndrome" that has afflicted us as Catholics. If the pope and the bishops are to do this, they must have assistance. The help of a well informed and critically mature laity is crucial.

If we have not and, perhaps, do not really understand the primacy and infallibility of the pope, especially in its practical application, this means that we have not taken the Vatican II documents with the seriousness that they deserve. Have we been threatened by the current turmoil within the Church without making a critical examination of the true cause? "Teaching on a matter of faith and morals" can be truly liberating if our response is genuinely cognitive-affective.

To conclude I will quote a brief selection from Nikos Kazantzakis, in his fictionalized autobiography, *Report to Greco*:

Three kinds of souls, three prayers:
1) I am a bow in your hands, Lord. Draw me lest I rot.
2) Do not overdraw me Lord. I shall break.
3) Overdraw me Lord, and, who cares if I break! [28]

28. Nikos Kazantzakis, *Report to Greco* (New York: Bantam Books, 1966), p. 11.

14 Understanding Papal Infallibility: 1870 to 1970

JEREMY MILLER

The critical issue in the classic debate between Charles Davis and John L. McKenzie over the relevancy of the Catholic Church had to do with dogma, not structure. Davis not only felt that the institutional structures of the Church were obsolete and corrupt, impeding the Christian life of its members, and therefore should be opposed as such; what complicated the matter for him was that this social reality of the Church rested, since 1870, on doctrinal definitions. His opposition, accordingly, took the form of his leaving the Catholic Church.

In a process going back over centuries, but reaching a point regarded as irrevocable only in the First Vatican Council, the Roman Church formulated the theology implicit in its existing social reality in doctrinal statements. The social structure I regard as obsolete and corrupt therefore now rests upon a doctrinal legitimation that declares as a dogma its key features—papal primacy in episcopal jurisdiction and papal infallibility—declares these features to be permanently normative of the institution of Christ. I wanted to maintain as a conviction of conscience that the dogmatic statements of the First Vatican Council, together with much that they imply about the nature of the Church, were wrong. I am convinced they are erroneous statements. I could not with intellectual integrity, content myself with speaking of "development" or "reinterpretation." The appeal to development in this instance seems to me to be an ideological evasion.

No one, so far, has given me even an inkling how the development many desire can prove compatible with the retention of the First Vatican declaration as true.[1]

McKenzie's response was based on his faith in the development of the social structure. "I believe that the Church is able to break its structures—I didn't say transform them, I said break them." It has happened. Davis' problem, however, with the doctrinal legitimations of Vatican I was not being met. He asked McKenzie to focus on this. McKenzie remarked:

I think Charles gives these definitions of Vatican I a terminal value which no other dogmatic declaration has ever had in the history of dogma. Like him I feel they are unfortunate. . . . They certainly are open to re-statement. . . . As statements they will not endure because they are not final. They need correction.

Some people see in the definitions of Vatican I a triumphal assertion of papal powers. In a true sense the dogmas were a curtailment. An excessive "papalism" existed in the years just prior to the Council. Men like W.G. Ward, the influential editor of the *Dublin Review*, considered the doctrinal parts of all encyclicals and allocutions to be *eo ipso* infallible. The Bull *Quanta Cura* of 1864 was called the "word of God."[2] Veuillot revised the hymn of None so that it applied to Pio Nono instead of God. Granted, these were extreme tendencies within the "infallibilist" party at Vatican I, but they constituted a dangerous line of thinking.

On the other hand, a number of council fathers were opposed to defining the dogma, and not because it was *inopportune*. Among the American bishops, Hughes, England and Purcell denied publicly it had to be believed. It is often mentioned that only two bishops opposed the dogma in the final voting.

1. Excerpts from the debate can be found in *Readings in the Theology of the Church*, pp. 105-115 (Englewood Cliffs, N. J.: Prentice-Hall, 1970). The remainder is from my own notes of the debate.

2. H. Küng, *Structures of the Church* (Univ. of Notre Dame Press, 1968), footnote, p. 327.

This is true; 433 to 2. But a test vote five days earlier came out: 451 in favor, 88 opposed, with 62 conciliars voting *secundum modum*. At least 166 conciliars absented themselves from the final vote. As interesting as this numerical break-down might be, the fact remains that papal infallibility was defined and became in the words of Karl Rahner "a datum of consciousness" *as* revealed.[3] To ask how the dogma was understood in 1870 it is not enough merely to repeat verbal formulations from *Pastor Aeternus*—I will, however, make use of Bishop Gasser's explanatory report later. The real question is how *Pastor Aeternus* was understood by people at that time. How did they paraphrase its teaching, for instance? I shall make use, in some detail, of an 1874 Pastoral Letter of the Archbishop of Westminster, Henry Edward Manning, purporting to explain the conciliar decree.[4] I will grant that one man's views are not a scientific cross-section of an epoch, and I will further grant that Manning was a strong papalist at the Council. But he was influential at the Council and privy to its stratagems.

Manning sees six ideas included in the definition of 1870.

1. Infallibility is limited to acts *ex cathedra*, viz., the acts of a Supreme Pastor. If the Pope acts as a private person, or private teacher, or local bishop, or as a political sovereign, there is no infallibility.

2. The scope of infallibility is limited to matters of *faith and morals*. Manning understands this phrase broadly. Faith and morals include "things pertaining to piety, things of religion, controversies of religion, things pertaining to natural and divine law, things pertaining to the good estate of the Church."[5] He becomes more specific. He quotes Bellarmine to the effect that a Pope cannot err in moral precepts enjoined on the whole church; *Humanae Vitae*, for Manning, would be infallible teaching.

3. K. Rahner, *Theological Investigations* IV (Baltimore: Helicon, 1966), p. 27.

4. H. E. Manning, *The Vatican Council and its Definitions* (New York: P. J. Kenedy, 1900).

5. *Ibid.*, p. 71.

Furthermore, "the Church, having a divine office to condemn errors in faith and morals, has therefore an infallible assistance in discerning and in proscribing false philosophies and false science."[6] "The doctrinal authority of the Church is infallible in all matters and truths which are necessary to the custody of the Depositum. This extends to certain truths of natural science, as, for example, the existence of substance, and to truths of the natural reason, such as that the soul is immaterial."[7] Nor does Manning think the Church errs in judging censures such as temerity, scandal, offensive to pious ears. "All Catholic theologians, without exception, so far as I know, teach that the Church is infallible in all such censures."[8]

> In every censure the Church proposes to us some truth relating to faith or morals; and whether the matter of such truths be revealed or not revealed, it nevertheless so pertains to faith and morals that the deposit could not be guarded if the Church in such judgments were liable to error.
> The Apostle declares that "the Church is the pillar and ground of the Truth." On what authority these words can be restricted to revealed truth alone, I do not know.[9]

3. The papal definition rests on Christ's promise to Peter and hence, indirectly, to his successors.

4. Only an explicit act of defining enjoys infallibility. Other types of papal utterances are excluded. Manning, however, has a wide notion of solemn papal definitions. Included are the condemnations of the Synod of Pistoia, the approbation of Augustine's writings on grace, and all censures of whatever gravity.

> In a word, the whole *magisterium* or doctrinal authority of the Pontiff as the supreme Doctor of all Christians is included in this definition of his infallibility. And also all legis-

6. *Ibid.*, p. 73.
7. *Ibid.*, pp. 73-74.
8. *Ibid.*, p. 80.
9. *Ibid.*, p. 82.

lative or judicial acts, so far as they are inseparably connected with his doctrinal authority; as, for instance, all judgments, sentences, and decisions, which contain the motives
of such acts as derived from faith and morals. Under this
will come laws of discipline, canonization of Saints, approbation of religious Orders, of devotions, and the like; all of
which intrinsically contain the truths and principles of faith,
morals, and piety.[10]

5. Papal infallibility is personal. It is not the result of his
union with the episcopate. "The definition does not decide the
question whether the infallibility of the Church is derived from
him or through him. But it does decide that his infallibility
is not derived from the Church, nor through the Church." [11]
It would not be unfair to Manning to say that the Pope, apart
from the Church is infallible.[12]

6. A papal definition is infallible of itself and not because
the Church or bishops accept it.

Manning's six ideas indicate that he gave broad scope to
papal infallibility. Did he faithfully reflect the Council document? I would say he clearly extended it. Whereas Manning
puts practically the whole papal magisterium within the scope
of infallibility, Bishop Gasser, the official Relator of the Schema,
was more cautious. Asked if "faith and morals" meant only
formally revealed truths or could it include truths connected
to revelation, Gasser replied, "the Commission thought this
ought not be defined but left in its present state." [13]

Secondly, Manning so stressed the underived personal character of infallibility that he, in effect, separated Pope from

10. *Ibid.*, p. 95.
11. *Ibid.*, p. 96.
12. Manning quotes with approval the Dominican theologian of that
day, F. Gatti: "indefectibility is promised to Peter apart from (*seorsum*)
the Church, or from the Apostles; it is not promised to the Apostles, or to
the Church, apart from (*seorsum*) the head, or with the head .... Therefore Peter, even apart from (*seorsum*) the Church, is infallible." *Ibid.*,
p. 97. Not surprisingly, the title of Gatti's book is *Institutiones Apologetico-
Polemicae.*
13. Collectio Lacensis VII: 475.

Church. Bishop Gasser again: "We do not exclude this cooperation with the Church because infallibility is given to the Roman Pontiff not by way of inspiration or revelation but by way of divine assistance. Hence the Pope must take the right means . . . to find the truth." [14] There is no *absolute* necessity to consult the Church, but there might be a *"relative* necessity or opportuneness which is left entirely to the judgment of the Roman Pontiff to weigh." [15] Whatever the merits of Manning's extrapolation, his broadened view keynoted a mentality which has existed, at least on the popular level, until recently, and no doubt for some Catholics still does.

The Manualists make a convenient bridge between Vatican I and Vatican II. What was their conception of papal infallibility? Again I will use one man, Fr. Joseph Mors, S.J., as indicative. [16] His tractatus synthesizes the more important manualists, and I am fairly familiar with his material. Mors has two preoccupations. What truths are susceptible of infallible definition—the question of *objecta?* What levels of assent to magisterium are possible? Mors breaks no new ground. "Primary objects" are those truths *formally and per se* revealed, viz., directly revealed by God as opposed to a deduced theological conclusion. The Pope can define primary objects infallibly, and one assents to those on divine faith. "Secondary objects" are not revealed truths but are necessary to guard and expound God's revelation. These, too, can be defined infallibly. The reason is that these truths are so intimately connected wth revelation that error regarding them would imperil revelation itself. [17]

Four types of connections are envisioned: (a) as *presupposition,* e.g., the existence of God, the possibility of Revelation. (b) as *concomitant,* viz., truths needed to propose revelation aptly, e.g., the concept of person. (c) as *conclusion* drawn from

14. Mansi, *Sacrorum Conciliorum Nova et Amplissima Collectio,* 52: 1213.

15. Mansi, 52:1215.

16. Josephus Mors, *Theologia Fundamentalis* (Bonis Auris: ex typis Euditorial Guadalupe).

17. Cf. Journet, *Church of the Word Incarnate,* Vol. 1 (New York: Sheed and Ward, 1955), pp. 342-43.

revelation, e.g., limbo. (d) as *instrumental,* viz., required for obtaining the purpose of revelation (salvation), e.g., liturgical and disciplinary laws. Mors teaches that secondary objects can be taught infallibly, hence, are irreformable. For example, dogmatic facts (such-and-such a council is ecumenical or that Jansen's *Augustinus* is heretical), disciplinary decrees (clerical celibacy), canonizations, approbations of religious orders. Would one accept papal definitions in these areas with divine faith? Because faith is only of God's revelation, Mors would say no. Hence, the whole question of so-called "ecclesiastical faith." [18]

Charles Journet—not really a manualist—adds another distinction. He speaks of truths which are neither revealed nor capable of irrevocable proposal but which can be taught by the magisterium with a *prudential authority.*[19] "It is prudent to adhere interiorly to such and such a teaching and rash to refuse to do so. . . . Nevertheless the speculation content of this teaching remains reformable." [20]

The manualists added a precision to the discussion. Like Manning they held that infallibility extends further than the deposit of revelation; unlike Manning they did not infallibilize the whole papal magisterium.[21] They raised the questions of reformable teachings, of popes being in heresy, and of the possibility of dissent to non-infallible teaching.[22] Regarding the latter,

18. *Ibid.,* p. 344ff. Journet rejects *fides ecclesiastica* and argues for *fides divina.*

19. *Ibid.,* p. 350. Journet follows Marin-Sola.

20. *Ibid.,* p. 352.

21. Vatican I had a canon before it which proposed to define this as an article of faith. The canon read: "S.Q.D. that the infallibility of the Church is restricted simply to what is contained in the divine revelation and does not extend to other truths necessarily required to ensure the integrity of the revealed deposit, A. S." The Council did not adopt this canon. Cf. *Collectio Lacensis* VII: 577.

22. Some bishops at Vatican II asked the Theological Commission what if one could not give internal assent to papal magisterium. The response was to "consult the approved authors." For the implications of this response, cf. Joseph Komonchak, "Ordinary Papal Magisterium and Religious Assent," *Contraception: Authority and Dissent* (New York: Herder and Herder, 1969).

however, the most they speak of is "keeping a respectful silence." [23]

Vatican II reaffirms the teaching of Vatican I but did not clarify matters fully. Any ambiguity in paragraph 25 of *Lumen Gentium* must be understood in the light of controverted problems of manualistic Fundamental Theology, a complexity not due to the manualists but to the nature of human knowledge and the historical nature of revelation.[24]

Let me make two observations from my own reading of the text. First, I am confused why the Council describes the response of the faithful to infallible ordinary magisterium,[25] in paragraph 25, as *tamquam definitive tenenda* and to infallible conciliar teaching as "with the submission of faith." If one says, with Rahner,[26] it is because the former envisions infallible and irreformable teaching on truths not strictly revealed (i.e, secondary objects), would not conciliar teaching concern this also? Why the abrupt change from *definitive tenenda* to *credenda?* Or is the phrase meant as *the cue* to when one has ordinary magisterium? As McKenzie has put it, "to ascertain whether a proposition has always been presented as an article of faith in the ordinary magisterium of the Roman Church can be a research problem of some magnitude."[27]

Secondly, when the Church defines on faith and morals, the scope of infallibility extends as far as the deposit of revelation (§25). Is this a restriction to primary objects? Admittedly, the text adds immediately that revelation must be "religiously

---

23. *Humani Generis* overshadowed this discussion. It taught that once the Pope had spoken on a hitherto controversial subject, it was no longer free for debate among theologians (DS 3885). The original schema of *Lumen Gentium* incorporated this, but it did not find its way into the final draft. Cf. Komonchak, *op. cit.*, p. 102.

24. Cf. Rahner, *Commentary on the Documents of Vatican II* (Herder and Herder: 1967), Vol. 1, p. 209.

25. The distinction between ordinary and extraordinary magisterium dates from the mid-nineteenth century, just when encyclicals were coming into vogue. Post-tridentines distinguished Pope as *doctor privatus* and as *caput ecclesiae*.

26. Rahner, *Commentary*, p. 210.

27. J. L. McKenzie, *The Roman Catholic Church* (New York: Holt, Rinehart and Winston, 1969), p. 207.

guarded and faithfully expounded"—the classical catchwords for secondary objects. But further in the paragraph one reads that "revelation, which, as written or preserved by tradition" is what is pronounced on, and that "revelation is thus religiously preserved and faithfully expounded in the Church." I propose one can make a case that *faith and morals,* very broadly understood by Manning, tightened and precised somewhat by the manualists, is here further restricted to only what has been revealed.

Rahner takes a rather cautious position on this, but he does not rule out my proposal.

> The words "to be inviolably preserved" imply that the object of infallible authority includes truths which form a safeguard for the deposit of revelation strictly speaking, even though these truths are not formally revealed (implicitly or explicitly)—that is, if there are such truths.[28]

The hundred years since *Pastor Aeternus* also have seen development in the role of a defining Pope *vis-a-vis* the Church. The anti-Gallican teaching of Vatican I was that papal definition needs no approbation from the Church. Manning in consequence practically separated Pope from Church. Gasser denied an absolute necessity to consult the belief of the Church but spoke of relative necessity. Vatican II, however, reasserted the prophetic role of the faithful to witness to the faith *it* possesses and suggested that the *teaching* church is also a *listening* church (§37). Vatican I's strictures against the Gallican idea of *consensus ecclesiae* are complemented by Vatican II's encouragement of *sensus ecclesiae.*

Another way of posing this would be to ask if the Pope can define something which is not already believed by the faithful. Rahner gives an interesting slant to this.

> It may be affirmed *a posteriori* that up to this a papal definition has never been given where the object of the definition was not already in fact believed by the Church as a truth of faith. We will not now go into the question of whether

28. Rahner, *Commentary,* p. 212.

that must be so on principle. The *"ex se infallibilis"* of the doctrinal authority of the Pope has not yet settled the matter definitively. For this doctrine only means that the papal decision does not need the subsequent assent of the Church for its validity.... If then one were to say: the Pope defines on principle only what is already believed *as* a revealed truth in the Church, one would not offend, given the distinctions just made, against the doctrine in question.[29]

I am proposing that revelation is the infallible possession of the entire Church, and that periodically the Spirit makes use of particular organs within the community, such as papal definition, to assure the infallible proclamation of the Word. What is proclaimed is of revelation and reflects the community's consciousness of itself and its mystery. I would say, in principle, a *sensus ecclesiae*. Are not the infallible scriptures but the primal archives of the self-consciousness of the Apostolic Church?

The Protestant criticism of the Roman position is that revelation seems to be continually happening. It is not only scripture and tradition; it is also, in Barth's words, the "church of the present time" from which revelation seems to issue forth. Given a Church which is identical with revelation, the pope and the bishops then take on the authority of the Word of God.[30] Might anything in our teaching have justified this criticism?

If one extends infallibility and irreformable assent to secondary objects, is this not excessive? The Church is subject to the Word and proclaims infallibly what that Word is. This is not Barthian; this is Vatican II. "This teaching office is not above the Word of God, but serves it, teaching only what has been handed on.... It draws from this one deposit of faith everything which it presents for belief as divinely revealed" (*Dei Verbum*, §10). This is suggesting that it is only revelation that the Church, or the Pope, proclaims infallibly. I am suggesting this is only what it can do.

McKenzie had spoken of the need for "re-statement," "correction" of Vatican I's formulations. I conclude with a few remarks

29. Rahner, *Theological Investigations* IV, p. 31.
30. Küng, *op. cit.*, p. 318ff.

on conceptualization, suggested by Avery Dulles' important article on dogma.[31] The development of dogma is more than just a case of words. Culture influences our conceptualizations to the extent that one cannot simply undress the culture from the revealed truth. This would deny man's fundamental historicity. The definitions of Vatican I, despite Bishop Gasser's qualifications, could in fact be interpreted in terms of despotic absolutism, and Hans Küng offers different post-conciliar examples to this effect.[32] Dogmas stand in need of "correction" in this sense, because they are deficient.

Furthermore, given this conceptualization factor, is it possible that some opposing affirmations are rooted in irreducibly diverse forms of thought? Dulles thinks so.[33] If I read him correctly, opposing affirmations about the same reality can be unharmonizable without being strictly contradictory. They would be logically irreducible. There is something of truth here. Have you ever tried to explain to your college students how grace does not destroy freedom? Take one approach, and develop man's freedom to act. Take another approach, and develop that all is done through grace. I live with these truths. I do not think they are contradictory. But are they really harmonizable? Is man a sinner, or is he cleansed? I wager that many Catholic sermons this past Lent were Lutheran.

If you follow this line of thought—I do not think one can dismiss it out of hand—in what sense then is agreement on verbal formulae a measure of unity in faith? I don't know. But it is something we all have to think about. Dulles's position is this:

We never receive the revealed truth except in fragile human vessels. Thus even the most current dogmatic utterances must be questioned. The true test of orthodoxy is not whether a man accepts the official statements at their face value, but whether he has sufficient confidence in the tradition to accept its formulations, in spite of all their human

31. "Dogma as an Ecumenical Problem," *Theological Studies,* Vol. XXIX (1968), No. 3, pp. 397-416.

32. H. Küng, *The Church* (New York: Sheed and Ward, 1967), p. 450.

33. Dulles, "Dogma as an Ecumenical Problem," p. 213.

deficiency, as vehicles of a divine truth that lies beyond all formulation.[34]

I have been examining the terminal value of Vatican I's dogma on papal infallibility. Recall that here was where McKenzie faulted Davis. I tried to show that the original formulation has been corrected and modified by new viewpoints. Irreformability does not mean that a dogma is necessarily opportune, or that it fits the demands of a given mentality, or that it cannot be replaced by a better formulation. I concluded by introducing the problem of unharmonizable affirmations about the same reality. The reality is the Church of the Word. On the one hand, there is the teaching Church, and certain affirmations such as papal infallibility can be made about it; on the other hand, there is the believing Church, possessing the Word within it and living by its inner demands. Protestant ecclesiology operates here. Perhaps that itself will figure in a development of dogma leading to a Third Vatican Council.

34. *Ibid.*, p. 216.

15   Cardinal Newman: Consensus of the Faithful and the Magisterium

WEBSTER T. PATTERSON

Cardinal Newman's thought on this subject runs throughout a long list of published works, not to mention many other of his writings either not yet published or in the process of publication. Even to treat the subject very inadequately one is forced to concentrate on one aspect—one which in this case might be called the "dynamic aspect" of consensus. For the sake of clarity it might be well to set forth three statements. The first two will be touched upon rather briefly in order to concentrate more in detail on the third which seems in greatest need of clarification. The three statements are:

1. Newman's conversion was due to a change from a static to a dynamic concept of consensus in the Church.
2. A dynamic concept of consensus dominated Newman's thinking as a Catholic.
3. Newman held that the hierarchical magisterium is a norm for faith and morals in so far as it reflects a true and living consensus of the faithful.[1]

As regards the first statement, Newman's conversion essentially was due to a change from St. Vincent of Lerin's norm of faith *quod semper, ubique, quod ab omnibus* (what is believed always, everywhere, by all) to St. Augustine's living norm

---

1. The statement is not meant to infer that the hierarchical magisterium is a mere mouthpiece or reflection of the consensus of the faithful. Nor is it denied that the episcopal office exercises its own unique judgment based upon that consensus.

securus judicat orbis terrarum (the whole world judges secure-ly.[2] In his *Apologia Pro Vita Sua* Newman eloquently describes the impact which Augustine's words made upon him at the time: "For a mere sentence, the words of Augustine struck me with a power which I never had felt from any words before. . . . By these great words of the ancient Father . . . the theory of the *Via Media* was absolutely pulverized. I became excited at the view thus opened upon me."[3]

The view Augustine's words opened up was that "the deliber-ate judgment in which the whole Church at length rests and acquiesces, is an infallible prescription and a final sentence against such portions of it as protest and secede." Here was a surer, simpler, and more vital norm of faith than that of St. Vincent of Lerin's rule of Antiquity. "Nay," says Newman, "St. Augustine was one of the prime oracles of Antiquity; here then was Anti-quity deciding against itself. What a light was hereby thrown upon every controversy in the Church!"[4]

This, briefly, in his own words, is the fundamental break-through which led to Newman's conversion. Basically, it was an insight into the dynamic element in the Church, an insight into that living consensus of the Church as a whole as a norm of faith; in Newman's words, an insight into "the deliberate judg-ment in which the whole Church at length rests and acquiesces." Eventually, this basic insight was to lead him to write *An Essay on the Development of Christian Doctrine* and to such Catholic works as his article "On Consulting the Faithful in Matters of Doctrine."[5]

What, then, is this living consensus which was practically the inspiration of Newman's entire life-time? Essentially it can be described as that communal and experiential dimension of the *sensus fidei* (sense of faith) which is implanted and sustained

2. *Apologia Pro Vita Sua* (London: Longmans, Green & Co., 1889), 117.

3. *Ibid.*

4. *Ibid.*

5. *The Rambler*, I (New Series), July, 1859. John Coulson, (ed.) *On Consulting the Faithful in Matters of Doctrine* (London: Sheed & Ward, 1961).

by the indwelling of the Holy Spirit.[6] It is a sense of faith which implies *discernment, judgment* (as implied in Augustine's saying, *securus judicat,*—the whole world *judges* securely). It is a sense of faith which implies a particular kind of judgment best qualified by the word "experiential."[7] For Newman the discernment exercised by faith is not by learning merely or only, but through a certain connaturality acquired through experience.[8] He is best judge in a practical matter, says Aristotle, who has experience in that matter. And for Newman, lived faith is both practical and essentially experiential, a matter of the heart and emotions, not

---

6. *Sensus fidelium,* literally, "sense of the faithful," but better described as an instinct or power of discernment whereby one who has the faith is able to distinguish between what is true and what is false, what is compatible with his faith and what is not. See Webster T. Patterson, *Newman: Pioneer for the Layman* (Washington, D.C.: Corpus Publications, 1968), chapter 6, "The Foundation of Newman's Meaning," II, "The Deposit of Faith and the Sensus Fidelium." In Newman's thought the term *consensus fidelium* adds a collective dimension to *sensus fidelium.* Newman himself describes the consensus of the faithful thus: "1. as a testimony to the fact of the apostolic dogma; 2. as a sort of instinct, or *phronema,* deep in the bosom of the mystical body of Christ; 3. as a direction of the Holy Ghost; 4. as an answer to its prayer; 5. as a jealousy of error, which it at once feels as a scandal," Coulson, *op. cit.,* 73.

7. Newman's famous distinction between "real assent" and "notional assent" comes in here. In "real assent" the whole man is involved (not just the intellect), including the experiential element. See Newman's *An Essay in Aid of a Grammar of Assent* (London: Longmans, Green & Co., 1887), 133. Also, see Patterson, *op. cit.,* "The Devotional Principle," 130-140.

8. This is especially true in regard to the consensus of the faithful, or what Newman regarded as the social dimension of truth. According to Newman, the universal Church has a life, a spirit, a genius of its own which is a test of true doctrine. Principles and doctrines incompatible with its life will be rejected by the Catholic community, even though the members of that community be unlearned, a practical busy people with no keen analytical view of the principles which govern them. Nevertheless, such people will be attracted or repelled by doctrines which are consistent or incompatible with a faith which is not merely a matter of intellectual apprehension but which is their life. See Patterson, *op. cit.,* "The Social Principle," 119-130.

of the intellect only.[9] Not only is it experiential, but it is communal. Truth, according to Newman, has an essential social dimension; it is the concatenation of many minds working together, a principle he developed at length in his *Essay on the Development of Christian Doctrine*.[10]

In Newman's concept of consensus, therefore, certain elements would seem to be essential: experience (in the concrete), interaction and confrontation within the community, time and deliberation, and, above all, the activity of the Holy Spirit in the *whole* Church, not just in the hierarchical magisterium. The hierarchy, in Newman's view, is the *focus*, rather than the exclusive *locus* of the Holy Spirit's activity.[11] This last point bears

9. So it is that the *lex orandi* is the *lex credendi* — the norm of prayer is the norm of belief. As an example Newman gives the Athanasian Creed: "It is not a mere collection of notions, however momentous; it is a psalm or hymn of praise, of confession, and of profound, self-prostrating homage .... It appeals to the imagination quite as much as to the intellect. It is a war-song of faith, with which we warn first ourselves, then each other and then all those who are within its hearing, and the hearing of Truth, who our God is, and how we must worship Him, and how vast our responsibility will be, if we know what to believe, and yet believe not," *Grammar of Assent*, 133.

10. In his book *An Essay on the Development of Christian Doctrine* (London: Longmans, Green & Co., 1897), 50, Newman points out that Truth is not the heritage of any individual, but of mankind itself and that all men ought to seek and profess it in common. In an early sermon at Oxford on the "Connection Between Personal and Public Improvement," he stresses the necessity of seeking God's truth through, not apart from the community of Christians. See *Sermons Bearing on Subjects of the Day* (London: Longmans, Green & Co., 1898), 130. For Newman, the Church as a society is not merely a collection of individuals, but a collection *made one*. All the members who compose it exhibit the same common features, so that the society as a whole exhibits marked characteristics which distinguish it from all other societies. That is why one cannot fit the political institutions of one people upon those of another who are of different spirit and customs. See *Historical Sketches*, I, 180.

11. "I think I am right in saying that the tradition of the Apostles, committed to the whole Church in its various constituents and functions *per modum unius*, manifests itself variously at various times: sometimes by the mouth of the episcopacy, sometimes by the doctors, sometimes by the people .... One man will lay more stress on one aspect of doctrine, another on another; for myself, I am accustomed to lay great stress on the *consensus fidelium* ..." *On Consulting the Faithful*, 63.

upon the third proposition stated above, the one which stands most in need of clarification, viz.: Newman held that the hierarchical magisterium is a norm of faith and morals in so far as it reflects a true and living consensus of the faithful. The remainder of this essay will be an attempt to set forth the reasons and support for this statement more clearly.

In spite of the fact that Newman had the greatest possible respect for ecclesiastical authority; [12] and also, in spite of the fact that to the best of my knowledge Newman himself never formulated the matter in these precise words, nevertheless the proposition can be defended, it seems to me, as being perfectly consonant with the over-all view Newman took of the Church as a whole and of the function of the magisterium within the Church in particular, and this for several reasons.[13]

The first reason and the place to begin is with the following quotation from his work *Certain Difficulties Felt by Anglicans in Catholic Teaching*:

It is a common saying that political power is founded on opinion; this is true, if the word "opinion" be understood in the widest sense of which it is capable. A State depends and rests, not simply on force of arms, not on logic, not on anything short of the sentiment and will of those who are governed. This doctrine does not imply instability and change

12. For Newman's attitude toward authority see *Apologia*, 251.

13. While supporting the principle of authority, Newman reacted against exaggerated claims for authority held, for instance, by Cardinal Manning, W. G. Ward, and the Ultramontanists at the time of the definition of Papal Infallibility in Vatican I. To an Anglican friend, Alfred Plummer, Newman wrote: "Looking at early history, it would seem as if the Church moved on to the perfect truth by various successive declarations, alternately in contrary directions, and thus perfecting, completing, and supplying each other. Let us have a little faith in her, I say. Pius is not the last of the popes. The fourth Council modified the third, and the fifth the fourth .... The late definition does not so much need to be undone as to be completed. It needs *safeguards* as to the pope's possible acts — explanations; but there is a limit to the triumph of the tyrannical. Let us be patient, let us have faith, and a new pope and a reassembled Council may trim the boat." Quoted in *Concilium*, Vol. 37, 95.

as inherent characteristics of a body politic. Since none can put off his opinions in a moment, or by willing it, since those opinions may be instincts, principles, beliefs, convictions, since they may be self-evident, since they may be religious truths, it may be easily understood how a national polity, as being the creation and development of a multitude of men having all the same opinions, may stand of itself, and be most firmly established, and may be practically secure against reverse. And thus it is that countries become settled, with a definite form of social union, and an ascendency of law and order, not as if that particular settlement, union, form, order, and law were self-sanctioned and self-supported, but because it is founded in the national mind, and maintained by the force of a living tradition.[14]

From this quotation it is clear that Newman is using the term "public opinion" (and therefore *consensus*) in a much broader and deeper sense than ordinarily used. He is using it in the same way one might say that the Declaration of Independence, or the Constitution of the United States is based upon "public opinion" when they set forth such aims as "life, liberty, and the pursuit of happiness." The framers of such documents were not basing their formulations upon temporary judgments of a number of individuals dominated by private interests peculiar to entirely unique social and cultural circumstances. They consulted men in the sense of reaching down into the very essence of human nature itself. They were making explicit what is inherently buried deep within the human heart much in the same way as the Ten Commandments did long ago at Sinai. There was no question of taking a Gallup poll on the fleeting and ill-considered opinions and views of men—often contradicting one another—which all have upon the endless problems and circumstances of life.[15]

14. *Certain Difficulties Felt by Anglicans in Catholic Teaching,* II, (London: Longmans, Green & Co., 1898), 317.

15. See *Newman: Pioneer for the Layman,* 87-104, for Newman's views on the limited value of public opinion in general and popular religious opinion in particular.

The matter was much deeper than that. And that is why, by analogy, Newman regarded the hierarchical magisterium as having a serious obligation and profound need of giving advertence to that unique society, the whole body of the faithful, in which and through which the Holy Spirit is ever present and ever operating. In both cases, that of the nation and that of the Church, Newman saw an absolute necessity for profound communication between the framers of the law and the community to be affected and directed by that law. Since no human community, whether civil or ecclesiastical, is ever static, but constantly changing due to new developments in human knowledge and human relations, this regard for the whole community which Newman at one time summarized under the word "consult" and at another under the word "public opinion" is a factor that must be perennially present in all decision making on matters which affect the natural and supernatural life of man.[16]

As history progresses, so does the communal experiential knowledge of man. In the passage of time, men inter-acting together arrive at certain deeply felt, if not clearly expressed, conclusions. These conclusions must be more explicit according to time and occasion as history and human circumstances require. Advertence to the living communal experience of the Christian community is more needed at some times than at others; the occasions and times vary, as Newman pointed out in his article "On Consulting the Faithful in Matters of Doctrine." [17] Perhaps the most prominent recent occasion has been Vatican II. John XXIII in convoking the council seemed to indicate this when he said that "if we turn our attention to the Church, we see that it has not remained a lifeless spectator in the face of these events, but has followed step by step the evolution of peoples, scientific progress, and social revolution." [18] In noting that as history moves on, not only the world is profoundly changed but the Christian community "is also in great part trans-

16. On Newman's meaning and use of the word "consult," see *Newman: Pioneer for the Layman,* 56-65, 79-81.

17. See page 63ff.

18. Walter M. Abbott, S.J., ed., *The Documents of Vatican II,* New York: Guild Press, 1966) 704.

formed and renewed," Pope John pointed out that it is by this means that the Christian community is re-invigorated intellectually, interiorly purified, and thus made ready for trial.[19] The trial of which Pope John spoke is that which Newman indicated one hundred years before: the whole community of faithful must be subjected to the pains of growth and development, the chief characteristic of any truly vital body.

Newman's emphasis was on the *whole* Church of which the magisterium is a part, not separate and independent, but nevertheless a distinct part. What then is the relation between the part and the whole, between the hierarchical magisterium and the body of the faithful? It is true that in the flurry of controversy which followed publication of his article "On Consulting the Faithful" Newman rather unhappily took up the image coined by the chief Roman theologian of the day, Father Giovanni Perrone, S.J.,—the image of the seal and the wax.[20] The analogy is unhappy because, although Newman used it for want of a better image at the time it does not really express Newman's own view of the matter. The seal is the Church teaching, the magisterium; the wax is the Church taught, the faithful. The wax, the body of the Church, has only that impression which the seal, the magisterium, gives it. But the question is: whence does the seal derive its impression? Directly from God? According to Dr. Daniel Maguire of Catholic University, Pope Paul VI at least implied this on one occasion. Paul said that "the magisterium 'could preserve and teach the faith . . . without the help of theology.' It would not be easy, the Pontiff concedes, since it would be done without revelation and inspiration and 'only with the assistance of the Holy Spirit.' " [21] One might be tempted

19. *Ibid.*, 705.

20. Discussing whether infallibility lies in the Church teaching or the Church taught Newman says: "I understand Fr. Perrone to say, on the contrary, that it resides *per modum unius* in both, as a figure is contained both on the seal and on the wax and primarily in the mind of the engraver." Letter of Newman to Dr. John Gillow, May 16, 1859, Birmingham Archives. See Patterson, *op. cit.*, 59.

21. Daniel Maguire, "Holy Spirit and Church Authority," *Commonweal*, Nov. 8, 1968, 218.

with Maguire to consider that the image of magisterial activity without human means sounds dangerously close to magic, but there is a grain of truth in it, and I think Newman saw it. The grain of truth is—to use Newman's analogy—that the mind is greater than any of the instruments it uses; it does not depend absolutely on any of them. Unlike the seal and the wax, the metaphor this time is Newman's own image, one which he develops at some length in a second and lesser known essay on the development of doctrine which Newman wrote as a Catholic toward the end of his life.[22]

In this essay, Newman is trying to answer the question: what is the deposit of faith, and where actually does it lie, if it is neither a list of propositions nor can be identified either with any single Church Father nor with all of them put together? The answer he gives is that the deposit of faith is the same as the mind of the Church. Just as an Aristotelian philosopher is not one who has everything Aristotle said in all its applications explicitly before him, so the Church does not have Christ's revelation in all of its applications explicitly either. But given a specific problem, a true Aristotelian philosopher, given time, can answer the question as Aristotle would have, the reason being that he thinks like Aristotle; he has the Aristotelian *habitus*. For Newman, faith is a *habitus*; and given time, and a specific problem, the living apostolic mind which is the Church as a whole can recollect itself as it were, and address itself to the concrete problem or application of the faith in the same way that an apostle would have. The allusion to recollection which Newman uses is taken from another example, that of an apparent

22. *Unpublished Essay on the Development of Doctrine,* Birmingham Archives. Newman wrote this essay as a Catholic toward the end of his life in 1861 to answer some difficulties which he felt were not sufficiently treated in his noted book on the same subject. Actually, the so-called unpublished essay has been published three times. See Romuald Dibble, *John H. Newman, The Concept of Infallible Authority* (Washington: Catholic University Press, 1955), 287-293; C. Stephen Dessain, *Journal of Theological Studies,* 9 (1958), 324-335; and Hugo de Achaval, "An Unpublished Paper by Cardinal Newman on the Development of Doctrine," *Gregorianum,* XXXIX (No. 3, 1961), 585-591.

non-listening, in-attentive school boy who, when called upon by the teacher, mentally gathers himself together and often comes forth with a surprising answer.[23]

But is the mind of the Church to be identified with that special department within the Church known as the hierarchical magisterium? Or is it rather that the magisterium itself is an instrument, though granted, a superior instrument (but none the less an instrument)—which the mind of the Church collectively speaking uses? With Vatican II, it seems to me that the case is the latter. If Vatican II stresses anything, it emphasizes the truth that the Holy Spirit operates in the Church as a *whole* and not exclusively through one part only, as is seen from the following quotation from *Lumen Gentium,* the "Dogmatic Constitution on the Church:"

> The holy People of God shares also in Christ's prophetic office.... The body of the faithful as a whole, anointed as they are by the Holy One (cf. Jn 2:20, 27), cannot err in matters of belief. Thanks to a supernatural sense of the faith which characterizes the People as a whole, it manifests this unerring quality when "from the bishops down to the last member of the laity" it shows universal agreement in matters of faith and morals.[24]

It is true that the Council adds that "all this it does under the lead of a sacred teaching authority to which it loyally defers." [25] But this is a long way from the image of the seal and the wax. In the view of the second Vatican Council the hierarchical magisterium is seen as the *focus* of the Holy Spirit, not exclusively as the *locus;* as *within* the Church, not on top and apart from it; as *evocative,* not coercive; as an instrument of God's revelation, not as its source; as firstly having the obligation *to listen* (not "to extinguish the spirit"), and secondly, to teach.

All of this is clearly implied if not explicitly stated in the

23. de Achaval, *op. cit.,* 594.
24. Abbott, ed., *op. cit.,* 29.
25. *Ibid.,* 30.

Council's doctrine on the sense of faith which is in all the members of the Church (not only in the hierarchy), a sense of faith which enables the People of God to penetrate His word "more deeply by accurate insights, and apply it more thoroughly to life since He distributes special graces among the faithful of every rank." [26] The same view was expressed by Newman when he insisted that the sense of faith belonged to all the faithful, not merely to the so-called Church teaching.[27]

All of this may be well and good, someone might say, but should not the proposition be stated in reverse, not only for the sake of theological accuracy, but also to avoid the danger of at least appearing to tone down the importance of authority, a principle both so traditionally Catholic and so necessary, especially for these troubled times. So inverted the proposition would read thus: Newman held that a true and living consensus of the faithful is a norm for faith and morals in so far as it reflects the hierarchical magisterium.

To be sure, this way of formulating it would be better calculated to please many in the hierarchy today; and to some, it might seem more in line with the traditional Catholic way of thinking. But I submit that 1) this was definitely not the mind of Newman, and 2) in the circumstances of the present day I especially do not think he would consider this the desirable way to formulate the matter.

That this was not the mind of Newman can be seen clearly by anyone who reads his article "On Consulting the Faithful in Matters of Doctrine." Among other things he points out that such a way of formulating the proposition would simply not hold up when looked at historically.[28] He points out that at the time of the Arian heresy in the fourth century, there was a period when the majority of the bishops in the world were Arian, not Catholic; and he speaks of this period as a time when "the body

---

26. *Ibid.*
27. ". . . the body of the faithful is one of the witnesses to the fact of the tradition of revealed doctrine, and . . . their *consensus* through Christendom is the voice of the infallible Church," says Newman. See Coulson, *op. cit.*, 63ff.
28. Coulson, *op. cit.*, 75ff.

of bishops failed" and there was a "suspense of the Church teaching." [29] At this critical time the only thing that saved the day was the consensus of the faithful, the fact that the majority of the faithful, for the most part unlearned, simply held on to the faith and did not follow their bishops. Here was one case at least when a true and living consensus of the faithful proved to be a better norm for faith than the guidance of ecclesiastical authority. And we could cite other examples, as does Newman.

But besides the fact that this reverse way of formulating the proposition is clearly not the mind of Newman, I submit that if he were alive today he would consider this latter formulation especially undesirable in view of the twentieth century historical situation. I submit this on the same grounds Karl Rahner presents in his *Free Speech in the Church*.[30] In an age when totalitarian governments crush basic human rights and freedoms, the Church not only has an obligation, but a special obligation, not even to give the appearance that it is something of the same nature. Actually the Church is not something of the same nature, the difference being that in the suppression of basic human rights and freedoms totalitarian governments are acting in perfect accord with their fundamental principles; but when the Church appears to be doing the same thing, it is not acting in accordance with its basic principles.

Can it honestly be said that the Church has not often given the appearance, at least, of acting like a totalitarian government? And does not this appearance seem almost, at times at least, to be an integrated part of the hierarchical magisterium's own self-image? Perhaps it is not a true self-image, but is there not a basis for concern here lest such be the real case? At least Karl Rahner thinks so; and it is difficult to see how Newman

29. Patterson, *op. cit.*, 71-77, on "suspense of the *ecclesia docens*" and "the body of bishops failed."

30. Karl Rahner, S.J., *Free Speech in the Church* (New York: Sheed & Ward, 1959), 17. Rahner says: "In an age of totalitarian states, when individuality is suppressed and 'ideology' supplied, the Church has to delimit her position more clearly, to prevent her own character and nature from being confused with those of a totalitarian state. She will now have to come down more firmly on the side of the individual's responsibility and freedom both in his secular and his religious life."

would differ from Rahner, especially in the light of his article "On Consulting the Faithful in Matters of Doctrine."

To come to a definite conclusion, I should like to draw an analogy by choosing a specific example, even though the example chosen has the disadvantage of being considered by some as still controversial. But I do not think that the conclusion drawn (nor the analogy) rest on the example chosen, but rather upon the mind of Newman regarding the true and living consensus of the faithful. To be specific, I would formulate the conclusion as follows.

Today there is a genuine concern lest the same mistake made by the hierarchical magisterium regarding birth control also may be made regarding its own self-image. Regarding birth control, the mistake was essentially one of following an outmoded, biological-deterministic, a-historical view of human nature characterized by the ignoring of new dimensions given to human nature through the contributions of modern science,— physiology, psychology, sociology, and the like behavioral sciences. The attempt to see "built-in" laws of morality along thought lines akin to Aristotle's *Physics* was at one time in history based on a consensus of the faithful.

But contemporary consensus is certainly not this, but rather a consensus which sees nature not as something to *conform to* (understandable in an age close to nature and agriculture) so much as something which is an on-going creation in which God has left man a real function—a function which implies more conscious responsibility to modify, manipulate, change his own being as reason best dictates, considering the whole complex of factors which make up his contextual situation.

Regarding the hierarchical magisterium's self-image, the case seems similar. The picture of the hierarchical magisterium as the all-knowing school master, paternalistic and coercive, indoctrinal and non-dialogic, an *ecclesia docens* separate and independent from an ignorant *ecclesia discens*,—all this was an image understandable and fitting, perhaps, in an age when all structures of any kind were monarchical and the gap between the "knowing" and the "unknowing" was enormous. For such an age, the autocratic self-image rested on a real consensus. But such an image certainly does not rest on contemporary consensus. which is more socially and democratically self-conscious. As evidenced by Vatican II, this self-consciousness of the Church today manifests itself in greater stress on the action of the Holy Spirit in the *whole* Church (not just in one department), in stress on collegiality (not on autocracy) on human values and personalism (not on legalism).

In each case (the prohibition against birth control and the autocratic self-image), the teaching rested on consensus proper, or at least understandable, in a certain age. But also in each case, contextual consensus has shifted due to historical influences. The question at issue today is: will the norm for present-day hierarchical self-image be a static concept of consensus tied to the past, or a dynamic concept of consensus related to the present and to the future?

In the case of Cardinal Newman, his conversion came about through a change from a static concept of consensus to a dynamic concept—from the *quod semper, quod ubique, quod ab omnibus* of St. Vincent of Lerins to the *securus judicat orbis terrarum* of St. Augustine. "Signs of the times"—the present turmoil in the Church—indicate that a similar change of concept in consensus is taking place today in the Church as a whole, which should not be surprising. In the words of Newman: "In a higher world it is otherwise, but in this world to live is to change, and to be perfect is to have changed often."

16   Newman and Theological Pluralism

PAUL MISNER

At the Newman conference held at Oxford in 1966 there were several papers delivered on the influence of Newman's theological thought in various countries of Western Europe, some of a very high order of scholarship.[1] Reading them, one can easily get the impression that Newman was in the forefront of several decisive theological developments which have given the Second Vatican Council its specific contours, especially in comparison with Vatican I. One need not be a Newman expert by profession to make a list of prominent themes of Vatican II which Newman in his way anticipated. A more intimate acquaintance with Newman and his works allows one to bring out even more profound resemblances, as Bishop B. C. Butler does in his concluding paper of the Oxford Symposium on "Newman and the Second Vatican Council." One recalls Cardinal Gracias' remark to the effect that this was Newman's Council. It comes then as something of a shock to read Bishop Butler's conclusion or surmise as to the actual influence exercised by Newman's example or thought on the Second Vatican: "My impression is, that such influence cannot be found to have been deep or determinative."[2] In other words, the same issues would have been discussed in much the same way even if there had been no Newman!

Let me first state my thesis broadly and in an unguarded

1. Gathered in *The Rediscovery of Newman: An Oxford Symposium* (hereafter cited as *OS;* eds. John Coulson and A. M. Allchin, London: Sheed and Ward/SPCK, 1967).
2. B. C. Butler, "Newman and the Second Vatican Council," *OS* 245.

fashion; then, in the following explanation, nuances will show up. I would hold that Newman's thought was not in fact seminal, but only, in several instances, anticipatory; so that generally what happened was not that other theologians absorbed Newman's lessons and then went on to develop them further, but that when the same or similar territory had been covered due to influences quite apart from Newman, they recognized on looking back that Newman had said something on the subject previously. Have we not come across instances of this process in our own experience?

Why the lack of direct influence? Many reasons could be adduced. First of all, Newman as a nineteenth-century Englishman was on the other side of a formidable cultural barrier from the mainstream of ongoing Roman Catholic theology. Secondly, he was by nature an idiosyncratic thinker, displaying a surprising independence from contemporary trends of thought.[3] Nevertheless, he was inspired by a great desire to do a work for the Church, and a third reason why his efforts bore so little fruit in theology is that his superiors constantly undercut his attempted activities.[4] This deprived him in large measure of the chance to work his ideas out in the give-and-take of the theological forum or to raise up a generation of disciples, some of whom might have carried his influence into the theological schools.

Of course, a basic source of resistance to the utilization of Newman in theology stemmed from the idea that theology should be highly uniform, making use of a uniform *philosophia perennis* as its handmaiden, whereas Newman was obviously non-scholastic. But the question is, why were even the non-scholastic theologians in the age of neo-scholasticism who appealed so often to Newman's memory so little influenced by his thought? I think it is hard to avoid the conclusion that Newman commended himself to many hard-pressed theologians of a later generation less because of the content of his potential contri-

3. See the recent work on Newman's *Grammar of Assent* by David A. Pailin, *The Way to Faith* (London: Epworth Press, 1969), 91.
4. Wilfred Ward, *The Life of John Henry Cardinal Newman* (London: Longmans, Green and Co., 1912), I, 582-85 *et passim*.

butions to theology than because of his cardinalatial dignity which vindicates his impugned loyalty and orthodoxy. The spokesman of uniformity had to admit, once Leo XIII made the aged Newman a cardinal, that other approaches than the scholastic could be used sometimes to good effect.

This is the same as saying that Newman was *an example of theological pluralism* in the Church during the period when the officially encouraged neo-scholasticism would not admit its necessity (from *Aeterni Patris* of Leo XIII [1879] through *Humani Generis* of Pius XII [1950]). It is this aspect of Newman, I am convinced, more than any other, which led Newman's name and ideas to be introduced into the theological arena, there to be invoked by one side, then the other, until, out of the deeper study of their own traditions in history, the scholastics themselves advanced beyond unhistorical orthodoxy and the Second Vatican Council underscored their insights by a cautious acceptance of philosophical and theological pluralism in ecclesiastical studies.[5]

By "theological pluralism," I understand the situation which Karl Rahner has been describing and alluding to often in the recent past.[6] Two theologians try to enter into a dialogue, but find the undertaking fruitless because they do not "possess a common framework of mutual understanding, within which they start a debate over specific theses." They have different starting-points and different ways of treating the subject, so they part without ever really grasping one another's thought, without either agreeing or disagreeing. The time when one could hope to overcome all such cases by higher syntheses is over.

5. Gottlieb Söhngen, "Neuscholastik," *Lexikon für Theologie und Kirche* VII, 923-26. Cf. Vatican II's Decree on Priestly Formation, art. 15-16.

6. Karl Rahner, "Pluralism in Theology and the Oneness of the Church's Profession of Faith," *The Development of Fundamental Theology*, ed. J. B. Metz (*Concilium* vol. 46, June 1969), 103-23. Cf. *idem, Sacramentum Mundi* V, 20-24; *LThK* VIII, 566-67 and IX, 509-12; and *The Church after the Council* (New York: Herder & Herder, 1966); also "Kirchliches Lehramt und Theologie nach dem Konzil," *Schriften zur Theologie* VIII, 111-32. See also Heinrich Fries, "Theological Reflections on the Problem of Pluralism," *Theological Studies* 28 (1967), 3-26.

To support the generalization that Newman's influence *qua* theologian on Vatican II was so peripheral as to be negligible and at the same time to keep this contribution within proper limits, I propose to sketch a few vignettes illustrative of the course of Newmanian ideas in the Church of his manhood and old age.[7] I pass over what can be said about Newman's attitude to signs of theological narrowness and ultra-orthodoxy in his day.[8] And I must presume some familiarity with the course of the Thomistic revival in philosophy, in particular how Pope

7. Ironically Newman's influence on theology and the church order in the Anglican communion is more marked than in the Roman one.

8. The final chapter of the *Apologia pro Vita Sua* (1864) contains a discussion of the relationships that (should) obtain between the authoritative magisterium and churchly scholars, especially theologians. This was a very topical theme because of the Roman reaction to the Munich Congress of Catholic scholars organized by Ignaz Döllinger the year before. In *Tuas libenter,* the so-called "Munich Brief" of 21 Dec. 1863, Pius IX had called on theologians to comply with the decisions of the Roman Congregations and to stick to the accepted conclusions of the traditional school of theology (D 1680). In the *Apologia* Newman recommended moderation to both parties to the dispute in a veiled manner. On the one hand Newman sympathized with Rome's conservative attitude as regards scholastic theology: Catholic thought had been formed by great minds like Augustine and Thomas Aquinas, he said, and "I feel no temptation at all to break in pieces the great legacy of thought thus committed to us for these latter days" (*Apologia,* ed. David DeLaura, New York: Norton, 1968, 193; cf. Wilfred Ward, *William George Ward and the Catholic Revival,* London: Macmillan, 1893, 207; it was in this spirit that Newman received gratefully the encyclical of Leo XIII calling for the promotion of Thomistic philosophy, *Aeterni Patris,* cf. W. Ward, *Life of Newman,* II, 501-2).

But on the other hand Newman had a much greater appreciation of the need for freedom in scholarly work than did the Roman authorities, and so he also wrote eloquently about the vigor of intellectual debate in the medieval universities and about how slow Rome was to intervene authoritatively (*Apologia,* 204f; cf. Hugh A. McDougall, *The Acton-Newman Relations,* New York: Fordham U. Press, 1962, 89-92). In reality he was hinting as delicately as he could that Rome was getting too anxious, and that perhaps there was something to Döllinger's contention that "the decrees of the Apostolic See and of the Roman Congregations (were) hampering the free advance of scholarship" (D 1712, twelfth proposition censured in the Syllabus of Errors). Also in this connection occur the severe words for the "violent ultra party" grouped around the

Leo XIII and his successors decreed Thomism to be *the* philosophy which theologians should use,[9] thus insisting on a uniformity in theology which proved to be untenable. The thesis deals after all with the use or misuse of Newman in the process which led from Vatican I to Vatican II; and it is on his fate at the hands of later theologians that we shall have to concentrate.

The first illustration whose main lines I would like to draw concerns the still young church historian Louis Duchesne of the Institut Catholique in Paris and the theologian-cardinal, Johannes Baptist Franzelin. It took place in 1880, when Newman was still alive and had just been made a cardinal the previous year. Abbé Duchesne had been propounding Newman's theory of dogmatic development in his lectures and had been the object of some criticism. To be on the safe side, his rector, Msgr. d'Hulst, wrote to Franzelin, who had drawn up the schemata on faith and revelation for Vatican I, hinting that he could say a word to clear Newman's teaching of any suspicion that seemed to attach to it in some quarters. Franzelin's *sic et non* reply is symptomatic of the wary approach of theologians for some time afterwards to distinctively Newmanian ideas.[10] There was no

Holy See "which exalts opinions into dogmas, and has it principally at heart to destroy every school of thought but its own" (*Apologia*, 199). This is an allusion to the Neo-Ultramontanes who were making life so difficult for Catholic intellectuals of a conciliatory or liberal bent. It is doubtful whether Newman would have considered it opportune to publish even these guarded remonstrances a few months later, after the Syllabus of Errors had been published (8 December 1864). Also germane to the topic of pluralism is the passage where he speaks of the particular contributions the different nations should make to church life (*Apologia*, 206).

The Letter to the Duke of Norfolk is an exercise in reclaiming a broad freedom of opinion on the question of what Vatican I had defined about the Pope's powers, necessary because Manning had been giving out a papalist line as the authentic interpretation and the only allowable one. The Preface to the Third Edition of *Via Media* (1877) considers the priestly, prophetical and kingly functions of the Church as being in a necessary tension (cf. John Coulson in *OS* 136), as I have set forth more fully in an unpublished doctoral dissertation.

9. Cf. Yves Congar, *La foi et la théologie* (Tournai: Desclée, 1962) 155-56, and O. H. Pesch, "Thomismus," *LThK* X, 160-66.

10. Text from A. Baudrillart's *Vie de Mgr. d'Hulst* cited in Edgar

reason to suspect the orthodoxy of his fellow cardinal, Franzelin wrote, but Newman's treatment of the problem of development was a highly individual one, not to be confused with Franzelin's own theory, and indeed "not to be taken as a model, and certainly not to be brought into our lectures (*certe non in nostras scholas transferendae*)."[11]

The root cause of this extreme caution seems to be the helplessness which the dogmatic theologian of the time felt in the presence of history, history pursued for its own sake and according to its own rules.[12] This incomprehension of the theologian for the historians was to be demonstrated to the point of tragedy during the Modernist controversies. Thus Abbé Duchesne's own excellent history of the early church was put on the index in 1906. The effect this had on Newman's influence should be obvious. He had framed the hypothesis of development precisely in order to deal with certain serious difficulties arising out of historical studies (the late introduction of the dogma of purgatory, for instance, or of the supreme jurisdiction of the Pope). But the dominant neo-scholastic mentality of the period thought it a needless concession to difficulties which it could not even appreciate, owing to its unhistorical approach to doctrine.

But of course, in the 1880s the future was still open to other paths than that which history actually took. One could still have looked upon the whole incident as positive witness to the initial influence of Newman's theory of development, which could not but exercise an increasingly beneficial effect on the Catholic theological world through the expert mediation of Duchesne and his colleagues in France. But the fact is that Franzelin was the last representative of the "Roman School," which pursued positive dogmatic theology by preference.[13] Pope

---

Hocedez, *Histoire de la théologie au XIXe siècle* (Paris: Desclée de Brouwer, 1947) III, 163; cf. B.-D. Dupuy, "Newman's Influence in France," *OS* 151.

11. Hocedez, *loc. cit.*
12. Compare Owen Chadwick, *From Bossuet to Newman* (Cambridge: University Press, 1957) 182-84.
13. Cf. W. Kasper, *Die Lehre von der Tradition in der Römischen Schule* (Freiburg: Herder, 1962) 1-26.

Leo saw to it that those who followed him were of a more speculative, more Thomist bent.[14] Leo certainly was not aware that his other measures to encourage *historical scholarship* [15] would necessarily lead one day to the shipwreck of the thoroughly unhistorical, normative neo-scholasticism which he established, but such was the case. The dominant Roman theology after Franzelin displayed less, rather than more, appreciation of historical factors in theology, and thus a collision between history and dogma became all but inevitable.

My second scene is set in that time of confrontation around the turn of the century, and is crowded with the figures of Loisy, Brémond, de Grandmaison, Wilfrid Ward, W. J. Williams, George Tyrrell, and the shadowy forms of the authors of the Roman documents condemning Modernism (Billot?). Loisy looked into Newman at the urging of Fredrich von Hügel, of course *after* he had come to his own conclusions on the subject of development of doctrine, and wrote a "discerning article" about Newman's views, which he found useful for introducing the historical problems with which he was concerned to clerical readers, in 1898.[16] After that, however, attention turned more and more to another contribution of Newman's, his "psychology of faith," as his indefatigable popularizer, Henri Brémond, called it.[17] This is Newman's teaching in the *Oxford University Sermons* and in the *Grammar of Assent* about the moral conditions or predispositions required for the intellect to make an act of faith;

14. Cf. Eduardo Soderini, *Il pontificato de Leone XIII* (Milan: A. Mondadori, 1932-33) I, 280-83 (E. T.: *The Pontificate of Leo XIII*, London: Burns, Oates and Washbourne, 1934, 128). Leo followed up his encyclical *Aeterni Patris* with a Letter of November 15, 1879 which outlined measures to be taken to further neo-scholasticism in practice, especially in Rome.

15. Soderini, I, 287-97 (E. T. 130-35). Leo is famous for having opened the Secret Archives of the Vatican Library to all serious scholars (January 1881).

16. A. Firmin (Loisy), "Le développement chrétien d'après le cardinal Newman," *Revue du clergé francais* 17 (December 1, 1898, 5-20); cf. Alfred Loisy, *Mémoires pour servir à l'histoire religieuse de notre temps* (Paris: Nourry, 1930) I, 448-51.

17. Henri Brémond, *Newman: La psychologie de la foi*, Paris: Bloud et Cie, 3rd ed., 1906.

and about the implicit, never adequately formalized reasoning ("illative sense") which rightly leads one to believe with certitude, even though the grounds for faith don't seem to amount to more than so many converging probabilities. Brémond, however, was not as impartial an interpreter as he claimed to be: [18] in fact he was of a polemical anti-scholastic tendency, as the course of the controversy between him and Léonce de Grandmaison, S.J., shows.[19] Therefore the severe judgment of Bacchus and Przywara after the First World War on the disservice done to the Newmanian cause by Brémond was not altogether unjustified.[20] The conclusion we draw from this is that Newman's treatment of faith and reason enjoyed a vogue partly because of its merits in approaching the problem in a way which appealed to modern minds, and partly simply because he was a non-scholastic thinker whom authorities in the Church were under obligation to respect by reason of his papal honor, the cardinalate.[21]

But this is only half the story of this second vignette. For when the decree *Lamentabili* and the encyclical *Pascendi* appeared in 1907, followers of Newman were disheartened to find some of their master's distinctive notions there censured, for example development (D 2054, 2059, 2089) and convergence of probabilities as rational grounding of faith (D 2025).[22] Word

18. Cf. George Tyrrell in H. Brémond, *The Mystery of Newman* (tr. H. C. Corrance, London: Williams & Norgate, 1907) xvii.

19. Cf. Dupuy, *art. cit., OS* 167, see below note 24.

20. Francis Bacchus, "Newman's Oxford University Sermons," *The Month* 140 (July 1922) 1; for Przywara see note 25.

21. However, it must be recognized that apart from hard-line repristinators like Ehrle, Billot, Maritain and Gilson there were Neo-Thomists of a different sort (Mercier and others) who were determined to open traditional scholasticism to modern thought (cf. Paul Archambault, "La philosophie catholique en France," in Henri Brémond (ed.), *Manuel de la littérature catholique en France de 1870 à nos jours* (Paris: Spes, 1939, 371-73). Foremost among these until he was killed in the war (1915) was Pierre Rousselot who did in fact study Newman and adopt Newmanian insights into the basically Thomist orientation of his treatment of faith (*Les yeux de la foi*, 1910; cf. Roger Aubert, *Le probleme de l'acte de foi*, [3rd ed. Louvain: Warny, 1958] 468-69 and Dupuy, *art. cit., OS* 167 note 3).

soon came from Rome that no censure of the revered Cardinal's thought had been intended, even though some Modernists had taken shelter under Newman's mantle and used his words in a Modernist sense.[23] All this had the effect of putting Newman back under that cloud from which only the cardinalate had delivered him, not, to be sure, in respect to his person, but in respect to his distinctive teachings. Pére de Grandmaison had just the previous year expressed essentially the same reserves about Newman's usefulness in theology which Franzelin had hinted at, and now his judgment seemed to be confirmed by events: Newman will be read with great benefit, said Grandmaison, as a spiritual writer, but he is unsuitable as an intellectual "formateur"; he is "too original, too personal a thinker to be followed with safety." [24]

Newman's theology, then, was looked at askance until in the 1920s quite a little Newman renascence took place, connected with the names of Matthias Laros, Theodor Haecker, and the young Jesuits Erich Przywara and Otto Karrer.[25] Of these Przywara was doubtless the most promising. His book comparing Max Scheler's efforts to put Catholic thought on a more adequate foundation with Newman's explanation of the psychology of faith in ordinary, uneducated people shows a mind able to grasp not only traditional, but also modern thought in the context proper to it, and what is more to turn this wealth of erudition to good account in the contemporary situation (*Religionsbegründung*, 1923). Josef Trütsch, in the new manual of dogmatic theology being put out in Switzerland in several volumes, *Mysterium Salutis*, has characterized the role of Newman's the-

22. Cf. note in Denzinger-Schönmetzer at no. 3401; also Maisie Ward, *Insurrection versus Resurrection* (New York: Sheed & Ward, 1937) 260-88 and Émile Poulat, *Histoire, dogme et critique dans la crise moderniste* (Tournai: Casterman, 1962) 107.

23. Maisie Ward, *op. cit.*, 275.

24. Léonce de Grandmaison, "Newman considérée comme maître," *Études* 110 (1907) 69; cf. Dupuy, OS 169.

25. Cf. Werner Becker, "Newman's Influence in Germany," OS 178-82. Of special note is Erich Przywara's work, *Religionsbegründung: Max Scheler — J. H. Newman* (Freiburg: Herder, 1923).

ology at this stage with a very precise phrase: Newman, he says proved helpful in the assimilation of a newer personalist way of thinking into a Catholic understanding of faith.[26] "Newman proved helpful in assimilating" a method of thought developed by others after his death—this is not what we ordinarily mean by an author's influence, but it constitutes an important contribution in its own right, and one which Rousselot had already acknowledged in his theology of faith (see note 21).

The subsequent career of Erich Przywara is not known to me in any detail. However, I think two references I have found about him illustrate my thesis very aptly. First, in 1931, Henry Tristram of Birmingham Oratory said of him: "To him more than to any other man is due the rehabilitation of Newman."[27] Second, in the Oxford Symposium of 1966, Werner Becker of Leipzig summed him up in these cryptic words: "Przywara, who continued to plead Newman's importance, was unfortunately regarded as an outsider, not because of his advocacy, but because of the peculiarities of his thought and style."[28] "An outsider"— an English phrase which in German usage is considerably more forceful than in its native use. Once more the potential influence of Newman's thought winds up on a side track, while the theological movements which were to leave their impress on Vatican II pass by with many respectful nods to the prophetical Englishman.

I have presented these three brief accounts of Newman disciples with a view to restoring a sense of proportion to Newman studies.[29] For I believe that we situate Newman with regard to

26. *Mysterium Salutis* I (eds. J. Feiner and M. Löhrer, Einsiedeln: Benziger, 1965) 825 "ein personalistisches Denken, das viel Anregung Max Scheler und existenzphilosophischen, von der Phänomenologie her gewachsenen Gedankengängen verdankt, für deren Assimilation Kard. Newman erneut sich hilfreich erwiesen hat."

27. Cf. Robert Aubert, *op. cit.*, 571 note 20.

28. Werner Becker, *art. cit.*, OS 181.

29. Franz Michel Willam runs the greatest risk of losing his sense of proportion over the question of Newman's influence, which he sees as practically decisive both for Teilhard de Chardin ("Teilhard de Chardin und Kardinal Newman," *Orientierung* 34 [1970] 15-17 and 36-37) and for Pope John XXIII (*Vom jungen Angelo Roncalli 1903-1907 zum Papst Johannes XXIII, 1958-1963,* Innsbruck: Rauch, 1967). Willam's work

his influence on the Second Vatican Council most accurately when we see him on the margins of a struggle carried out largely within the dominant Thomistically-oriented theology of the period. Leo XIII was responsible not only for the effort to revitalize Thomist philosophy, but also for encouraging historians to tell the unvarnished and completely researched story of the Church's past.[30] Eventually the historiography of Catholic doctrine and of Thomism itself reached the point where the unhistorical self-image of scholastic philosophy had to give way (one thinks of the names de Lubac, Congar, Chenu). The naive notion of eternal verities stored up in the *philosophia perennis* began to yield, and with it the claim implicit to Leo's encyclical *Aeterni Patris* that Thomism was the one true philosophy for all times, which merely had to be refurbished and adapted to the circumstances and science of the present age.[31]

No doubt Newman could have made a contribution in this matter of historical perspective and elsewhere, but once his natural opportunities to exercise his intellectual influence in his time were choked off,[32] the lesson was learned independently of him. Christopher Butler's paradox is therefore supported by the investigation of Newman's influence between the Vatican Councils, the findings of which I have here sketched in broad strokes. Many of Newman's ideas were vindicated by the time of Vatican

is nonetheless valuable, for he does uncover evidence of the exceedingly subtle way in which the reading of Newman did have its effect on Teilhard and Roncalli in conjunction with other more important influences.

30. See note 15 above.

31. Cf. Denzinger-Schönmetzer no. 3137: (in theologia) "necesse est, ut multae ac diversae caelestium doctrinarum partes in unum veluti corpus colligantur . . . ." The historian, later cardinal, Franz Ehrle, S.J. brought this out in no uncertain terms in his contemporary commentary, "Die päpstliche Enzyklika vom 4. August 1879 und die Restauration der christlichen Philosophie," *Stimmen aus Maria-Laach* 18 (1880) 15 (newly edited by F. Pelster: Rome, Edizioni di storia e letteratura, 1954).

Without hedging on this anti-pluralist principle, Leo and Ehrle were confident that Thomism would be equal to the tasks of the present age: cf. James Collins, "Leo XIII and the Philosophical Approach to Modernity," in Edward T. Gargan (ed.), *Leo XIII and the Modern World* (New York: Sheed & Ward, 1961) 206 note 1.

32. Above, note 4 and the Duchesne incident.

II, but then so were many of Lamennais', Montalembert's, even Mazzini's.[33] The fact that Newman always remained loyal to the Holy See and was in his old age honored with the cardinalate saved him from being disowned outright, as the Liberal Catholics were, but could not effect the necessary insertion into professional theological circles which had been denied him in his prime during the reign of Pius IX.

33. Cf. E. E. Y. Hales, *Pope John and His Revolution* (Garden City, N.Y.: Doubleday, 1965) 165.

17   Cardinal Newman and Doctrinal Development

TERESA M. DEFERRARI

John Henry Cardinal Newman once said, "There is no one aspect deep enough to exhaust the contents of a real idea, no one term or proposition which will serve to define it." [1] So too, when one is given the awesome task of discussing Newman's development of doctrine, there is no "one word or phrase" which can be said to fully explain his conceptualization of the development of doctrine. If, however, one desires to understand the breadth and depth of Newman's development of Doctrine, the best "hint of his message" can be gained from viewing his personal life. In discussing Newman's life the first impression one has is the amazing interaction between Newman's personal life and his intellectual life. Did Newman live in a static or dynamic age? It can be said by the fact of the society's questioning of the "static mentality" which had dominated, although not exclusively reigned in their collective minds, that the "dynamism" of Newman's age was not only a response to the environment but also a development of it. Newman internalized the "dynamism" of his age, so-to-speak, and in so doing entered into dialogue with himself. Internal conflict, a high level of religious experience in the sense of conscious recognition of the place of the Transcendent in his own life, caused Newman to question deeper the facts of his environment. His particular environment was Oxford University. While a student of Church history, Newman became an admirer of the High Church movement of the seventeenth century. On July 14, 1833 when John Keble delivered his address

1. John Henry Newman, *An Essay on the Development of Christian Doctrine,* London: Longmans, 1920, p. 35.

entitled "National Apostasy," at St. Mary's, Oxford, Newman said of the speech that it was to be the start of the religious movement of 1833. The movement referred to was the Oxford movement which has also been referred to as the "Oxford Reawakening." John Moody [2] in his book *John Henry Newman* stated that the Oxford Reawakening was the "constructive movement to bring to light, and place in the ascendancy in the Anglican Church, those forgotten truths regarding the genesis and mission of Christianity." Newman's role in the formative stages of the movement at Oxford was to act as a catalyst in encouraging agitation by individuals of like mind to himself to engage in discussions, writing, preaching and correspondence in order to revitalize the Christian message.

Newman saw that the Church, like other social living organisms changed with the circumstances of men. What was once a principle of doctrine which had for a long time been deemphasized could, due to the circumstances of men, be revitalized. We read: "to live is to change and to be perfect is to have changed often." [3] Therefore the development of doctrine was a very natural occurrence for a living organism to undergo.

Taken in the social context of Newman's environment and training, and man's lack of evolutionary theories at his point in time, Newman was somewhat of an intuitive scholar leading others to evolutionary perspectives.

In specific regard to development of doctrine, Newman emphasized that the masters of the Church doctrine were the apostles. "In theory the apostles could have answered all the questions which the Church has answered in the course of time ... (but) the Church does in fact make answers that the apostles did not make. It is therefore correct to say that the Church of today does in fact know more than the apostles did." [4] However, this statement is possibly one of the most discussed ontologically-oriented controversies of many ages.

2. John Moody, *John Henry Newman*, New York: Sheed & Ward, 1945, p. 45.

3. *Ibid.*, p. 121.

4. Günter Biemer, *Newman on Tradition*, New York: Herder & Herder, 1967, p. 62.

In his Essay *On the Development of Christian Doctrine*, which is probably the single most notable work to reveal Newman's conceptualization of the development of doctrine, he states: "Doctrines expand variously according to the mind of the individual in whom they are received; and the peculiarities of the recipient are the regulating power, the law, the organization, or, as it may be called, the form of the development. The life of doctrines may be said to consist in the law of principle which they employ." [5]

The infallibility of the pope is touched on by Newman in the Essay *On the Development of Christian Doctrine*. He advocated the universal nature of infallibility insofar as the members of the Church were of one shared collective mind. Newman in discussing infallibility never separated the need for one head of the Church in order to see that infallibility has "an official outlet and means of expression." In his Essay Newman stated that "a political body cannot exist without government, and the larger is the body the more concentrated must the government be. If the whole of Christendom is to form one Kingdom, one head is essential; at least this is the experience of the last 1800 years. As the Church grew into form, so did the power of the pope develop; and wherever the pope has been renounced, decay and division have been the consequence." [6] Thus, we have in Newman's own words the importance of the existence of a pope for the Church, in order to accomodate the form which the Church has assumed.

However, just because doctrine and tradition have been passed on from generation to generation since Apostolic times, this is no excuse merely "to accept without discussion" every particular facet of doctrinal and papal matters. Newman states: "It is characteristic of our minds to be ever engaged in passing judgment on the things which come before us. No sooner do we apprehend than we judge: we allow nothing to stand by itself: we compare, contrast, abstract, generalize, connect, adjust, classify: and we view all our knowledge in the association with which

5. Newman, p. 178.
6. *Ibid.*, p. 154.

these processes have invested it." [7] In other words, every action has a certain time, place, audience and function. Newman felt that in order to understand the "latent manifestations of the Church" (to use the phraseology of Talcott Parsons) one must see action of a living organism *in toto;* only then will he have a total perspective.

7. *Ibid.,* p. 33.

IV   The Religious Experience of the Student and the Responsibility of Theologians

18 The Religious Experience of Students as the Starting Point for Teaching Theology

MARCIA McDERMOTT

An important part of the student search is in the area of the religious experience, a phenomenon observable on most campuses. This search for the religious experience embodies many disparate elements, including experimentation with drugs, Eastern religions and meditation, acid rock music, hippie communes, tarot cards, ouija boards, witchcraft and magic.[1] Despite its various forms, the search is on. Most students are aware of the depersonalizing effect of technology. In reaction to the rational, impersonal force of technology in their lives, students have opted for the less rational, more personal form of the religious experience. Opting for the religious experience helps them feel they have more control over their lives. Perhaps this is due to the fact that they can more closely relate it to their experience of life.[2]

Within the college situation students very often find their search for the religious experience better articulated in sociology, literature or philosophy classes than in those of theology. Why is this? I believe this situation is related to the two prevalent views of theology held by theology instructors: (1) theology as a science, a body of the truths of faith, and (2) theology as a discipline to evoke faith. Students generally reject both of these views.

1. See Andrew M. Greeley, "There's A New-Time Religion on Campus," *New York Times Magazine*, June 1, 1969, pp. 14-28.
2. For further reference see Andrew Greeley, "The Sacred and the Psychedelic," *The Critic*, April-May, 1969, pp. 24-32.

Scientific, rational theology is rejected because the student cannot relate the truths of faith presented in class to his experience of the religious, which is often pre-rational. Theology as faith-evoking is rejected because it is based on the assumption that faith rests upon prior intellectual knowledge, which amounts to scientific theology. Often coupled with the rejection of theology as a discipline is the further rejection of a rather intolerant attitude some theology teachers have in presenting the truths of faith. Generally students have enough knowledge of psychology to understand why people become intolerant. Shestov articulates the problem of intolerance this way:

> The great majority do not believe in the truths of the religion they profess. . . . It is only from their environment that they draw the force of their convictions. And the less convincing the revealed truths appear to them the more important it is to them that no one doubt these truths. It is for this reason that people who believe the least are ordinarily the most intolerant. . . . The truths of faith are to be recognized by this sign. . . . These truths are given freely, they are accepted freely . . . they do not make anyone afraid, and they themselves fear no one.[3]

Consequently, the student writes off theology classes as completely irrelevant, and does not know where to turn in his search, in the need even to articulate that for which he is searching.

But what do students really want in this search for the religious experience? In my opinion they need religious experiences in order to achieve truth and to live that truth, a truth that will make them free. It is not in the first place a search for right answers, not a search for a theological system, nor for institutional religion. If I may put it another way, I believe the search is for faith.

Usually the student ends up after a theology class with a body of the truths of faith and no personal experience of same.

How can theology relate to the need of students to interpret

3. Lev Shestov, *Athens and Jerusalem*. Trans. Bernard Martin (New York: Simon and Schuster, 1966), p. 425.

the experience of the need for the transcendent in their lives?
A possible method is to begin in theology class with the experience of the student. The realm of a student's experience may
include knowledge of movies, novels, plays, music, social problems. These areas of experience are not gimmicks to attract
the good will or attention of the students. Rather they serve
as the point of departure for an understanding of the experience
of the need for the transcendent. Once an atmosphere of freedom, not intolerance, is created in class and the students learn
to trust their own experience, they will be able to articulate their
experiences freely and honestly.

Merely articulating experiences, though, is not sufficient. The
theology instructor must help students interpret their experiences
in terms of the experience of the need for the transcendent. This
experience of the need for the transcendent should then be
generalized, should be seen within a larger context, of if you
wish, in an historical perspective. At this point the theologian's
knowledge of theology comes into play. Here precisely the instructor can help the students gain new insights into their experience
and to get a new slant on the truth that makes one free. Finally,
the student should formulate a theory about his experience. This
demands that he be concerned with the truth of his experience.
I realize many students hold for complete subjectivity of truth
or seem to be indifferent to it in matters of religion. However,
how to achieve truth must be discussed.

Let me give an example of how theology can relate to the
experience of the need for the transcendent, and I will interpret
this need in terms of the phenomenon of love, a universal experience of students. My example will be the experience of human
desire and the experience of love, not as a phenomenon of man's
outer world, but as a phenomenon of his inner world.

Looking at the experiences of our inner world, we soon discover that what we experience is our desires and that any
desire goes beyond itself. What our students have seen in movies,
read in novels, or heard in songs only affirms this experience.
In fact they have only to look within themselves for this experience. Take a man's desire for a woman. "Love and jealousy
can not be reduced to the strict desire of possessing a *particular*
woman," they are transcendent, they go beyond themselves, "but

these emotions aim at laying hold of the world in its entirety through the woman." [4] In a way, they even aim at God. "In each inclination, in each tendency the person expresses himself completely, although from a different angle.... But if this is so, we should discover in each tendency, in each attitude of the subject, a meaning which transcends it." [5]

I believe, as Sartre says, that every human reality experienced in man's inner world is a passion in that it projects losing itself so as to establish being. "Man loses himself as man in order that God may be born." [6] Do we lose ourselves in vain? Is man a useless passion? Theology has to raise that question, too, and go into the experience of the absurd.

The experience of love is transcendent. It goes beyond itself. Boris Pasternak describes it thus:

A young girl, she leaves the house. What does she think of doing? She has already been receiving letters.... She has let two or three friends into her secret. Let us admit all this: she is going to have a *rendez-vous*.

She leaves the house. She would like the night to notice her, the heart of the air to be wrung at the sight of her, the stars to find something to say of her. She would like to be as remarkable as trees and fences ... when they exist in the open air and not in the mind alone. But she would laugh in reply if anyone ascribed such desires to her. She is not thinking of anything like this.... She loves the lustihood of nature sanely and does not admit that the balance of accounts between her feelings and the feelings of the universe never leaves her for a moment. [7]

She does not yet admit the transcendency of her desires. Yet her desires do go beyond themselves and are transcendent.

4. Jean-Paul Sartre, *Being and Nothingness*. Trans. Hazel E. Barnes (New York: Washington Square Press, 1953), p. 719.

5. *Ibid.*, p. 720.

6. *Ibid.*, p. 784.

7. Boris Pasternak, *Safe Conduct*. (New York: New Directions, 1949), p. 139.

Spring, a spring evening, old women on the benches, low garden walls, weeping willows. Winegreen, weakly distilled impotent pale sky, dust and the fatherland, dry, brittle voices. . . .

To meet her comes a man along the road, the very man whom it is natural for her to meet.

Notice that even yet she does not admit the transcendency of her desires.

In her joy she keeps repeating that she has come for him alone. Partly she is right. Who is not in some measure the dust, the fatherland and the quiet spring evening? She forgets why she has come out but her feet remember. He and she walk on. And as she loves the man she has met with all her soul, she is distressed at her feet not a little. But they bear her onwards and the two lovers can hardly keep up with one another. . . .[8]

But if she loves, at some point she will begin to realize, as Rilke says, that she has undertaken the infinite, she has undertaken God. Yet Rilke adds, "Of course, when we love, God is not an object of love. God is a direction, not yet an object of love."[9] He connects this experience of love with the experience for the need of the transcendent more directly in a highly descriptive way.

Was there not always a time around spring when the bursting year struck you as a reproach? A desire to be glad was in you, and yet, when you stepped out into the spacious open, an astonishment arose outside in the air, and you became uncertain in your progress, as on a ship. The garden was beginning. But you dragged into it winter and continuation. While you waited for your soul to take part, you suddenly felt the weight of your limbs, and something like the possi-

8. *Ibid.*, pp. 139-140.
9. Rainer Maria Rilke, *The Notebooks of Malte Laurids Brigge*. Trans. M. D. Herter Norton (New York: W. W. Norton and Co., 1949), p. 208.

bility of becoming ill invaded your open presentiment. You
blamed your too light dress, you threw your shawl round
your shoulders, you ran up to the end of the drive: and
then you stood, with beating heart, in the wide turnaround,
determined to be at one with all this. But a bird sang and
was alone and denied you. Alas, should you have been dead?
Perhaps. Perhaps it is new, our surviving these: the year
and love. Blossoms and fruit are ripe when they fall; animals
are self-aware and find each other and are content with this.
But we, who have undertaken God, can never finish.[10]

Those who are loved live poorly and in danger. Ah, that
they might surmount themselves and become lovers. Around
those who love is sheer security. No one casts suspicion on
them any more, and they themselves are not in a position
to betray themselves. In them the secret has grown inviolate,
they cry it out whole, like nightingales, it is undivided.
They make lament for one alone, but the whole of nature
unites with them: it is the lament for one who is eternal.
They hurl themselves after him they have lost, but even with
their first steps they overtake him, and before them is only
God.[11]

St. John says the same thing in yet another way: ". . . everyone
who loves is begotten by God and knows God. Anyone who
fails to love can never have known God, because God is love"
(I Jn 4.7-9).
Theology has much to offer students if it starts with the
realm of their experience. One of the greatest needs of the
college student today is a forum in which he can freely and
honestly articulate his search for the religious experience, for
the role of the transcendent in his life. Theology classes could
be this forum, if the religious experience of the student is the
initial point of departure. The use of the method suggested in
this paper demands that the student be concerned with the
truth of his religion, while it also demands that the theologian
critically evaluate the personal value and direction of theology.

10. *Ibid.*, p. 199.
11. *Ibid.*, p. 198.

19 The Counter-Culture and Academic Reform

MYRON B. BLOY, JR.

The conflict between the academic high culture and the counter-culture of the young is deeper and more abiding than many of us, including myself, had suspected. Tenured department heads and S.D.S. leaders used to share an assumption that, however great their ostensible differences, if they dug deep enough they would eventually come to the common ground on which they could join to build the new academic Jerusalem. Even if liberalism—no matter how left-leaning—and radicalism could hardly be called synonymous, they *did*, we argued, share an aversion to the war, racism, and exploitation, and a contempt for the philistine values of the bourgeoisie. Those halcyon days of easy hope are over now. Most student counter-culturalists, concluding apparently that higher education is irreformable, have come to see the university as little more than a base for political forays and cultural experimentation. David Riesman, a peripatetic teacher, sees in classrooms everywhere an escalation of despair and a decline of curiosity. On the other hand, many faculty, unable to keep their own passion for academic change alive without their erstwhile student allies and goads, sink quietly back into their old routines, riding out the storm. Thus, academic reform languishes.

We (The Church Society for College Work) recently gained some first-hand knowledge of the difficulty of finding common ground for the academic and counter-cultures. We devised a project in which a team of articulate students—political and cultural radicals and blacks—would help seminars of senior faculty and administrators understand counter-culture values and devise more adequate educational responses to them. Although the project was planned with great care and the commitment of all the participants to our series of weekly six hour seminars was high, not much learning took place. Our student faculty, despite their articulateness and manifest leadership abilities among their peers, had little pedagogical imagination; they tended to lay on the same heavy, authoritative rap that they had experienced in the classroom. On the other hand, the faculty and administrators listened to their student teachers with polite— but, in the end, patronizing—care, apparently willing to mollify the counter-culture enough to preserve the basic assumptions of the educational establishment but unwilling, even hypothetic- ally, to entertain seriously the radical import of these new values. Our experience corroborates Michael Novak's recent description of the state of educational reform today:

> All around the country, those involved in experimental edu- cation report similar findings: the quality of work goes down; lassitude rises; petty bickering dominates school politics; both student and faculty morale sags; displays of hysteria, rage, and incredibly sloppy reasoning multiply; and self-criticism sinks in the marsh of moral complacency.[1]

Although a shrewder methodology might have improved the possibilities of communication between students and faculty in our project, I believe the fundamental logjam was caused by an inability to uncover the profound epistemological issue which is implicit in the conflict between the academic and counter cultures. In the first place, this issue was obscured by the blatant differences in life-style—in rhetoric, clothes, mores, etc.—between the representatives of the two cultures: establishment repre- sentatives seemed repressed, secretive, defensive, and, in a word, "uptight" to the radical students, who, in turn, seemed to the faculty to be frighteningly anti-intellectual, flamboyant, and, in a word, "irresponsible." But the issue was obscured even more by the tacit agreement of all concerned that the epistemological assumption of the academic high culture—namely that learning

1. Michael Novak, "Education for What?", *Christianity and Crisis*, Vol. XXX, No. 2, February 16, 1970, p. 23.

and acting, objectivity and passionate commitment could and should be separated in space and time—is an eternal given. The revolutionary challenge of the counter-culture to higher education *per se* can never achieve its proper joining until that epistemological assumption is demythologized for both cultures.

The difficulty of breaking through this impasse from the side of the academic high culture—and that, after all, is the intellectual turf on which I most naturally stand—can be seen clearly in the retreat which Michael Novak has recently beat. In *A Theology for Radical Politics,* he seemed to be striking for pay dirt when he said:

> It is important to make clear that the protest of the reformers is not merely a protest of activists against theoreticians. The student Protestants are saying the old *doctrines* are wrong, the theories are inadequate, the professors are blind to too many realities of life. The reformation is theoretical as well as practical. We have to revise our *conception* of knowledge and the role of science, our *view* of ourselves and of our world.

The issues involved, in fact, sound like metaphysical or theological issues.[2] Novak went on to argue that their "conception of knowledge" had a bias towards the present which had yet to discover a language adequate to its articulation; he said,

> They do not *wish* to be anti-intellectual, but the one available intellectual language is abhorrent to them. Moreover, it is impossible for them to return to the classics, the great books, or the humanists—the recovery of a tradition that has now lapsed would turn them into historians, whereas it is the present and the future they most want to absorb and to comprehend. Had they the language, one feels, many of them would like to articulate clearly what is happening now, and thus produce new classics expressing our own cultural era.[3]

2. Michael Novak, *A Theology for Radical Politics* (New York: Herder and Herder, 1969), p. 86.
3. *Ibid.,* p. 87.

Another aspect of their bias was, he said, towards the joining of reflection and action; in describing this bias, he said,

> The road to personal liberation is not private or through meditation, but political. Awareness grows through conscious, reflective, accurate action. The separation between thought and action, which present university life enforces, seems to the students illegitimate. . . .[4]

The role of teachers in relation to this new conception was suggested by Novak when he said,

> The radical students need help. Specifically, they need fresh theories, new intellectual tools, openness to breakthroughs and readiness for originality. In many cases, all they need is someone to help them to articulate what they have already experienced and cannot quite say.[5]

All in all, Novak's analysis last year of the counter-culture's challenge to the academic culture and his program for response were clearly on the right track, but last year he became another faculty drop-out, saying that "the youth culture and high education are at almost diametrical cross-purposes."[6] "To be sure," he adds in a small caveat,

> there are still good schools in which traditions are so strong and standards so solid that students have been able to sound a creative note, voicing insights that have not been voiced. But it would be rash to leap to the conclusion that 'the youth culture' or 'the counter culture' truly cares about educational reform, about the intellectual life, about critical habits of mind. In carefully modulated contexts, *some* of their rage may be 'constructively' channeled. But what the youth culture is up to, really up to, is not educational reform.[7]

4. *Ibid.*, p. 88.
5. *Ibid.*, p. 87.
6. *Op. cit.*, p. 23.
7. Michael Novak, "Do Students Want Education?", *Commonweal*, Vol. XCII, No. 1, p. 11.

Novak's idea of educational reform, which was formerly daring and open-ended, has now been confined to some hoary pieties; here is how he now asks and answers the question of the university's purpose:

> What is the university *qua* university? To my way of thinking it is an end and not a means, an institutional home for those who delight in fidelity to their native drive to understand; a home for those who, through giving rein to that drive, have tasted the nothingness beneath all human forms, concepts, symbols; and who through that drive debunk all present dominations and powers, and invent new possibilities for the future.... It is a home and preparatory ground, but it is not a base of operations for agents of social change. It is a home for those who otherwise have no home in any concrete social or political situation.[8]

The same man who was pleading for a new conception of knowledge based on the youth culture's sensitivity for the present moment and on their commitment to the unity of thought and action has reverted to the patronizing posture of the traditional academic culture, falling back on ontological assertions about "the university *qua* university." What happened? Although I can only infer from a number of similar metamorphoses of former allies of the counter-culture, I suspect that Novak may be among those who, while using the language of intellectual revolution, were *really* expecting a modest reformation and then felt betrayed when it turned out that what the counter-culture is about really *is* revolution. When that realization sinks in, years of socialization in the academic tradition is often more determinative of imagination and loyalty than uncertain and uncomfortable visions of brave new educational worlds.

As I indicated above, the revolutionary thrust of the counter-culture is perceived largely at the stylistic level. Notice Novak's rhetoric: insights are to be "voiced" rather than demonstrated, only "carefully modulated" inputs can be tolerated, and, most importantly, the university is repeatedly described as a "home,"

8. *Op. cit.*, p. 23.

moreover a home for those who, unlike the foxes with their holes and the birds with their nests, have no "concrete social or political situation" to lay their heads. The outrageous young, refusing to allow their life style to be carefully modulated by the mores of scholarly society, their voices forever spilling over into action, are fouling the only home left in this philistine world for those who give themselves to pure understanding. But if the counter-culture has moral insight into our society, as Novak was previously ready to grant, then his implicit complaint about its manners, its harsh judgments, its rage, is misplaced. One recalls Jesus' little lecture to an audience which had apparently found the Baptist's manners too uncouth for their taste; Jesus said to them, "What did you go out into the wilderness to see? A reed swaying in the breeze? No? Then what did you go out to see? A man wearing fine clothes? Oh no, those who wear fine clothes are to be found in palaces. Then what did you go out for? To see a prophet? Yes, I tell you. . . ." Jesus is, of course, reminding his audience that prophets have never been known for their couthness—that, in fact, the truth they bear is partially authenticated by the very *un*couthness of its bearers. Although I don't want to make too much of this aspect of the academician's retreat from the youth culture, I have no doubt that academic culture has become over-delicate, a kind of glass menagerie of arcane and brittle customs which threatens to break under the jostling of the prophetic style of the young.

But, obviously I think, the conflict in manners between the academic and youth cultures is really an expression of fundamentally differing spiritual assumptions. A recent film review in a student newspaper opened with this paragraph:

> In case you haven't heard, there's a revolution going on in this country. It's not just a 'generation gap' and it's not just a 'stage' that the kiddies are going through. Just as the renaissance brought Europe out of an intellectual vacuum, and the industrial revolution brought the west out of economic stagnation, the youth revolution is trying to carry America out of a spiritual abyss.

Although the writer's historical analogies could use some serious qualification, few close observers of the youth scene can doubt his assessment of the extent ("revolutionary") and character ("spiritual") of the change which the young struggle to accomplish in themselves and in the world—including especially the world of higher education. But neither the youth culture nor the academic culture have joined the issue on ground which brings together both the spiritual assumptions and the phenomenological realities of the two cultures: the ground is usually either so cosmic and spiritualized that the debate lacks real concretion, or so simplistically political that the spiritual roots of the conflict are never exposed. When Novak said that a revised "conception of knowledge" or "a new model of intelligence" must be the basis of educational reform, he laid bare the ground on which the issue can most profitably be joined. The pity is that he did not press substantially ahead on that ground when he had the heart for it.

In fact, it seems to me that Paul Tillich's early (1929) essay on "Realism and Faith"[9] is an extremely useful tool for describing our epistemological impasse and for suggesting a possible future basis for higher education. He builds his analysis on this assumption:

Knowing is a union between the knower and the known. The cognitive will is the will of a separated life to unite itself with other life. Theoria is not detached observation, although different degrees of separation and detachment are a necessary element in knowledge; but theoria is union with the really real, with that level of a thing in which the "power of being" is situated.[10]

The key question then concerns the operative vision of reality which determines where and how the "really real" is expected to be discovered. Tillich describes the three major Western realisms and their consequent epistemologies; the first two have their roots in Greek thinking. He says,

9. Paul Tillich, "Realism and Faith," *The Protestant Era* (Chicago: Phoenix Books, 1957), pp. 66-82.
10. *Ibid.*, p. 68.

It is characteristic of Greek thought that from the beginning it sought the power of a thing, the "really real" of it, in that element which can be grasped by the "logos," the word, the speech, the notion. The "rational" (that which is susceptible to the logos) is the really real. The power of a thing is to be discovered in that which can be grasped by word and concept.[11]

Tillich then shows how this "unity of rationality and the power of being may be interpreted in different ways":

Since the power of being is discovered by thought, the thinking subject may become, intentionally or unintentionally, the bearer of all power. . . . From the critical and ethical schools of Greek philosophy this attitude is transmitted through late nominalism to modern technical science and the technocratic world view. One concedes to things only so much power as they should have in order to be useful. Reason becomes the means of controlling the world. The really real (ousia) of things is their calculable element, that which is determined by natural laws.[12]

Tillich called this attitude "technological realism" and saw positivism as its most recent philosophical form. He then went on to describe another way that "reason as the way of grasping the power of things may be understood":

The power of being within reality may be preserved also in a rationalized and spiritualized form. In this case the true being, discovered by the logos, becomes a matter of contemplation and union. . . . Mere vital existence, the control and transformation of reality, practice generally, and even physical and mathematical knowledge are transcended, and the eternal essences and their unity and ground are sought.[13]

11. *Ibid.*, p. 69.
12. *Ibid.*, p. 69.
13. *Ibid.*, p. 70.

Tillich calls this attitude, which was dominant in the high Middle Ages, "mystical realism." It is still with us, however:

> Theories of intuitive knowledge, classicist and romantic revivals of ancient medieval forms of thought, phenomenology, the philosophy of life (aesthetic or vitalistic), the 'theory of Gestalt,' some types of the psychology of the 'unconscious'— all these seek for the inner power of things beyond (or below) the level at which they are calculable and dominable.[14]

The problem with both technological and mystical realism— the dominant forms of epistemology in the West—is that neither looks to concrete existence, the here and now, to seek the power of reality, but rather "They abstract from it—technological realism for the sake of means and ends, mystical realism for the sake of essence and intuition." [15] Only "historical realism" looks for the really real "in time and space, in our historical existence, in that sphere from which all Greeks had taken flight." [16] Tillich summarizes this third perspective, which is rooted in the prophetic-Christian interpretation of history, in these terms:

> For historical realism the really real appears in the structures created by the historical process. History cannot be understood in terms of technological realism. It cannot become an object of calculation and control like some levels of natural objects. History, on the other hand, cannot be grasped in a mystical contemplation of its essence. It is open to interpretation only through active participation. We can grasp the power of historical being only if we are grasped by it in our own historical existence. Detached observation of historical events and registration of assumed historical laws removes us from the possibility of approaching history.
> Historical realism transcends technological, as well as mystical, realism. Its decisive characteristic is consciousness

14. *Ibid.*, p. 71.
15. *Ibid.*, p. 71.
16. *Ibid.*, p. 71.

of the present situation, of the "here and now." It sees the power of being, in the depth of "our historical situation." It is contemporaneous, and in this it differs from the technological, as well as the mystical, idea of reality.[17]

The importance for cognition in historical realism is that it "makes participation in the whole of human existence a condition of true knowledge, [and] this applies to the personal, as well as the social, reality of man in history." [18] Tillich argues the case in the following terms:

Nobody is able to penetrate into the deeper levels of his personality. Knowing the really real of our historical existence presupposes the knowledge of the really real in ourselves. But knowing one's self on this level is transforming one's self. Detached observation of one's self is here impossible. And knowing our historical situation on this level transforms our historical situation. Detached observation of our historical situation is here impossible. He who knows in terms of historical realism is he who is creative in himself and in history.[19]

His conclusion is that "The ideal of knowledge in historical realism is the union of scientific objectivity with passionate self-interpretation and self-transformation . . [and] with a passionate understanding and transformation of the historical situation." [20]

Through this analysis, Tillich finally arrives at his notion of "self-transcending realism," which is, he says, "the religious depth of historical realism," a depth without which historical realism remains comparatively unrealistic. Using a beautiful image, Tillich explains himself:

Self-transcending realism is based on the consciousness of the "here and now." The ultimate power of being, the ground of reality, appears in a special moment, in a concrete situation,

17. *Ibid.*, p. 72.
18. *Ibid.*, p. 73.
19. *Ibid.*, p. 73.
20. *Ibid.*, pp. 74-75.

revealing the infinite depth and the eternal significance of the present. But this is possible only in terms of paradox, i.e., by faith, for, in itself, the present is neither infinite nor eternal. The more it is seen in the light of the ultimate power, the more it appears as questionable and void of lasting significance. So the power of a thing is, at the same time, affirmed and negated when it becomes transparent for the ground of its power, the ultimately real. It is as in a thunderstorm at night, when the lightning throws a blinding clarity over all things, leaving them in complete darkness the next moment. When reality is seen in this way with the eye of self-transcending realism, it has become something new. Its ground has become visible in an "ecstatic" experience, called "faith." [21]

This, then, is Tillich's argument in rough outline, and I expect it is already apparent how useful it can be for uncovering and breaking through the epistemological impasse between the academic and counter-cultures.

Tillich, in fact, exposes the dominant epistemological tradition of higher education and, in the process, reveals the meager parochialism of the "two-culture" analysis and debate. The fact is that, although professional and technical institutions may function primarily on the assumptions of technological realism and liberal arts colleges on those of mystical realism (according to their catalogues, at least), these differences are insignificant compared to their common flight from the here and now as the place where the really real is discovered. Surely when Novak exalts the university as "a home for those who otherwise have no home in any concrete social or political situation," he is solidly grounded in one or the other aspect of the Greek epistemology, and if the business of those in this home is to taste "the nothingness beneath all human forms, concepts, [and] symbols" then this retreat from the contemporary is also a safe bastion from which to undermine the possibility that history can ever be the bearer of the power of being. Tillich has also exposed the irony in Novak's assertion that "there is no use making universi-

21. *Ibid.*, p. 78.

ties into baby-sitting establishments for the youth culture": [22] while the young are willing to engage the risky present in order to uncover meaning, the epistemological ground of the traditional academic culture makes the university a baby-sitting establishment for those who are afraid to run the risk of self-transformation which engagement of the here and now necessarily entails. Anyone who has not been totally socialized by the academic high culture knows that the nose-tilted negativity of the academic style is usually less prophetic engagement than spiritual cop-out.

If Tillich has implicitly demythologized the academic culture, exposing its *a priori* commitments so that it becomes merely ethnocentric to speak of the "university *qua* university," he has also provided, in his development of "historical realism," a theoretical instrument for understanding the educational implications of the counter-culture. The counter-culture young already instinctively realize that the gaining of any knowledge worth the name must involve "passionate self-interpretation and self-transformation and passionate understanding and transformation of the historical situation." If they do not yet fully accept the fact that "scientific objectivity" is the other necessary ingredient of historical realism's epistemological mix, then it is largely because too many of their academic mentors and the system itself have told them that higher education is *only* interested in objectivity, that severe repression of *any* passionate self or social transformation is the price of knowledge. As the early Novak suggested, the counter-culture young need the help of experienced intellectual hands to work out their implicit epistemology and the educational shapes it might take, but these hands should recognize that modest reforms in "carefully modulated contexts" cannot contain or manifest this new consciousness, that the only way through this particular eye of the needle is a revolutionary way. New wine needs new wineskins. When we accept historical realism as a valid and useful ideal for knowledge today, we implicitly challenge such sacred academic traditions as the architecturally and psychically detached campus (the "home" away from history), that only those who have run the full gaunt-

22. Novak, "Education for What?", p. 24.

let of higher education are capable of helping others press reality for its meaning, that man's nature is dualistic with only the rational aspect as capable of cognition, that learning is a basically individualistic and competitive enterprise in which dominance and control are the appropriate attitudes, or that time is a rationalistic rather than a human reality. Although I haven't the foggiest notion of what counter-culture education would look like, I am sure that any academician who is willing to accept Tillich's assumption that the really real is discovered only through entering deeply into the contemporary moment—through abandoning oneself to an open-ended odyssey of personal and historical transformation—will find himself on the other side of the current impasse, sharing with the counter-culture young their struggle to find the appropriate educational theories, shapes, and styles for their new consciousness. For those academicians who stand in the tradition of Genesis 1 and John 1, this choice must be at least a serious possibility.

20 The Catholic Religious Experience and the Students of the Seventies

Geoffrey E. Wood

During the nineteen-sixties there has been a disruptive Catholic religious experience. I suggest that the reform of our theology departments should be at least as much the conscious consequence of that experience as it is the consequence of any intelligent assent to an academic case for reform. And I think this an important point to make, for I am convinced that a reformation based on religious experience promises to be more radical and definitive than one based only upon some prevailing argument or upon some urgent need to keep up with the Ivy League. And I am concerned that the reform of our departments be radical and definitive.

Before going into the religious event of this past decade, however, I should define or describe in a general way what I mean by religious experience. I could mean ecstasy. Religious experience has to do with ecstasy. It draws a man to stand outside himself, or beyond his ego. Religious experience disorients and reorients a man, moving him from what he thought was the center of the universe, namely his own conscious vantage point, his centripetal point of view, to the true center of the universe, wherein and whence he feels at one with all things and their source; and wherein he feels for the first time in his life at one with himself. This is ecstasy. A man has found a new place and a sure place to stand, a new center of dynamic peace.

Still, passage to that new center must not be taken lightly or enthusiastically. For, given the fathomless nature of that center, it can just as well swallow one up as supply one with a firm foundation. And, indeed, many people pursue the religious dimension for that very purpose—to swallow it whole or to be swallowed up by it—to disappear back into the womb of the universe. Such religious experience stands in direct opposition to the new birth and genuine measure of religious integrity which true mystics speak of. These have no desire to usurp the center nor do they believe that it is the center's will to swallow them up, considering the fact that it has already given them birth. Instead, they approach the center in order to experience there their true being and becoming, to merge the flux of their ego-existence with the solidity of reality and to experience the pressure of divine energy upon the closure or reluctance of their ego-existence. They enter it with a profound awareness of their relativity but also with a profound appreciation of the absolute value of a relative being. Equipped with these virtues they are able to remain in the center—to *ex-ist* there and to grow in every direction, upward and in depth and in horizontal scope. And the cross is an excellent symbol of both the centering nature of true religious experience and its expansive consequences.

Let me withdraw the term *ecstasy* because it encourages our Western habit of religious extroversion. Let me stand by the notion of centro-version and conclude that religious experience has to do with a man's painful passage from his centripetal ego-center, which would swallow the universe, to the true center of the universe whence we came and which lies not *simply* here nor there nor *simply* in the symbols of our traditional religious panorama, but beneath our ego, at the center of that self and body we are so ignorant of—a center somewhere amid the infinite space within us, yet a center which gives us more intimate and immediate contact with the objective world about us than our fingers ever could—a center which transforms our sense of touch and taste and hearing and sight to perceive transfigurations. Or rather, to perceive reality which comes across like a transfiguration because we see it so rarely.

The Catholic Religious Experience of the Sixties

Out of the nineteen-sixties we have at last a great opportunity to grasp that radical religious integration of opposites which constitute wholeness. We have this opportunity because at long last we have opposition within the community. Vatican II set up a pole opposite the imbalance which understandably issued in and from Vatican I. But my fear is that in simply opposing Vatican II and Vatican I in simply rallying around the values expressed in one or the other of these events, we shall miss our opportunity, our kairos, for religious wholeness. To be explicit, I am afraid that those who legitimately but only insist on Being, Unity, Eternity, Stasis, Heaven and Masculinity will simply be opposed by those who legitimately but only insist on Becoming, Multiplicity, History, Flux, Earth and Femininity until both part company and constitute not a communion of saints but like all the world, a communion of sinners bound tightly together by mutual mistrust, united inseparably in their contradiction.

Catholicism in essence has nothing to do with polarization except in cases where it runs into some polarized force that needs counterbalancing. Catholicism in essence has to do with wholeness, a cruciform (+) union of Being (I) and Becoming (−), Unity (I) and Multiplicity (−), Eternity (I) and History (−), Stasis (I) and Flux (−), Heaven (I) and Earth (−), Masculinity (I) and Femininity (−). Essential Catholicism has to do with the center of the cross and the whole man who both hangs in there and reigns there—the new Adam, neither regressive nor split but grounded in the center, yet *ex-isting - outstanding;* capable of distinction yet fully aware of the relativity and therefore the relationship of all human distinctions.

Essential Catholicism has always sensed that too great an emphasis on Eternity or Stasis or Transcendence could dismantle the cross, simplify life, end in infantilism or oblivion; it has always kept a watchful eye on mystical extremism, spiritual enthusiasm, gnosticism. Of course, in reacting to such transcendental extremism on behalf of the temporal, rational, material side of creation, it has been accused of worldliness, rationalism and materialism. On the other hand, essential Catholicism has also —instinctively—condemned overemphasis on secularity, fluidity, materialism, and exclusive rationalism. And consequently, to the secularist, materialist and rationalist Catholicism has come across as too other-wordly, a ridiculous Don Quixote. Don Quixote to the rationalist, Sancho Panza to the mystic—as Miguel de Una-

muno put it. But that's the truth of it: essential Caholicism is
both Don Quixote and Sancho Panza—*simul justus et peccator*—
a companionship of Self and ego, instinct and consciousness,
faith and order, prophet and priest. Essential Catholicism means
to express that wholeness which can only arise out of a reverent,
affirmative relationship with that bottomless center and source
of all Being and Becoming.

Historically Catholics have not always been essentially Catholic. They have allowed themselves, under the tension of the
times, to be drawn off-center. At Vatican I and throughout the
decades following, the Church, faced with a world that worshipped flux and multiplicity, history and matter, came down
hard and frantically for stasis, unity, eternity . . . to the point
where all flux and variety and historical development were suspect and condemned.

There can be no doubt that Vatican I had something important to say to the modern world. It saw the world off-center
and it insisted that the world come back to its true center—
as represented and administered by the priesthood of the West.
With a truly courageous obstinacy it struck history with dogma.
But it struck so hard that it was thrown off-balance itself and
Vatican II became an historical necessity. Vatican II was more
essentially Catholic than Vatican I or perhaps I should say,
it was more consciously Catholic than Vatican I, although I'm
not sure *how* consciously. Vatican II relaxed Catholic reaction
to flux and history and variety. During the nineteen-sixties we
witnessed and experienced a now hesitant, now headlong, here
timid and there enthusiastic affirmation of becoming and plurality. If this reaffirmation can be maintained without a simplistic
repudiation of the opposite values nervously upheld by a Church
caught amid the crossfire of the Reformation and Enlightenment,
then hopefully we have come close to that center wherein the
mature, essential Catholic experience lies and has always lain,
like a pearl of great price, a treasure hidden in a field, like
a sheep, which a man lost, and leaving the ninety-nine went
in search of it and when he found it returned rejoicing.

A centering experience, then. This is what lies open to Catholics as they emerge from the sixties. But because they are
emerging from the nineteen-sixties and not from the thirteen-

sixties or the eighteen-sixties they should know that radical centroversion means introversion. Catholics today can no longer pretend to be only the children of Trent or the Middle Ages. They are in fact the offspring of the Reformation and all the philosophical and psychological developments of the past four-hundred years. They are more or less aware at this stage in human development that the religious center which all religious symbols and sacraments serve is most immediately discovered and appropriated within or beneath oneself.

Religion sets up any number of external poles or centers of attraction: a holy people, a holy land, a holy city, a holy place, a holy of holies, a cross, a celestial father and mother, a Pope, an altar, a nimbus, a monstrance, the Eucharist, a rose-window, a last judgment, to draw man out of his discordant ego-centricity into personal, social and universal harmony. As men of the twentieth century we should realize that all these poles of attraction are to a serious degree projections describing a center that lies within us and not exclusively beyond some distant horizon. We have inner horizons. The whole apocalyptic and salvation-history panorama can be and should be spread across the darker regions of our soul—to be a chart of our psychic universe and its source as much as it is a chart of the universe outside us. And all the figures in that panorama can be and should be seen as facets of our composite self. It is about time we followed this symbolic, sacramental guidance into or out of our personal labyrinth, for if the source and goal of the universe does lie somewhere immediately beneath our conscious and unconscious self, then the eschaton is indeed closer than we thought—and an eschatological grounding and life style the issue of a personal wellspring and not merely the distant object of a quest or patient expectation. But then, men who lived long before the twentieth century knew that. Somewhere in Deuteronomy it is written: *For this commandment is not far off. It is not in heaven, that you should say, "Who will go up for us to heaven, and bring it to us." Neither is it beyond the sea, that you should say, "Who will go over the sea for us, and bring it to us."* But the word is very near you; it is in your mouth and in your heart. And Jesus in John spoke of our belly and living waters.

And so the nineteen-sixties, and the imbalance leading up to them, have conditioned Catholics to experience a religious centroversion toward a point or opening that rests dynamically at the base of our psyche. The God within, the frameless context out of which we live and move and have our being and become context-makers; within which we are radically at one with every seemingly external person and object around us. A *personal* Catholicism or wholeness beckons the Catholics of our times.

I don't want to deny that our habitual *conservation* and *cult* of the open center of the universe is a fine thing. Religion has always undertaken this. It has visibly and tangibly oriented people toward that center and taken seriously man's tendency to move away from it—to disintegrate himself and his world. But a conservation that simultaneously blocks participation in that center betrays its purpose and stands to lose its own integrity in the process. My belief is that Catholicism cannot lose its integrity, for the center is where the center chooses to be (*ex opere operato* tries to say that). And I believe that a variety of events like the prosperity of Lourdes and St. Anne de Beaupré, and the liturgical, biblical and ecumenical movements and the presence of men who write of the Divine Milieu and much of the content of the documents of Vatican II suggest that Catholic Christianity is still very much within the center's grasp. My point is that out of the nineteen-sixties both the Catholic institution and its members stand to be grasped by the center in a radical way. And my hope is that this will happen, for the well-being of theology departments in Catholic colleges.

The Translation of this Experience into Department Change

A radically centered department should feel the impulse of that center. It should feel the magnitude and pressure of it.

Nor can the radius, under pressure of the center, stop there. It must be allowed to move past theology and the philosophy of religion to touch upon and include other sciences which study and express our central concern. The Gentiles must have their court. A sociological, historical, psychological understanding of religion should be available to the students of the nineteen-seventies. This, of course, brings within the domain of the department a vast amount of material which has hitherto been neglected, even though it constitutes the stuff of religion. The tight theological emphasis of departments in the past tended to exclude attention to the rich fascinating products of religious imagination: myth, legend, poetry, hagiography—and the rich, fascinating, significant phenomena of religion: religious art, architecture, symbols, iconography, spiritualities, sanctuaries, grottos, pilgrimage, music, monasticism, mysticism, priestly religion and prophetic religion, sacramentals, the stuff of religious culture. It is true that the biblical and liturgical movements brought much of this out of its accessory stage into respectable treatment, but it seems to me we have been mainly pragmatic and narrow in this and have therefore hardly begun to unveil this dimension of religious study.

But our radius, now become dynamic, must press on. Until recently, the Catholic college has almost exclusively offered courses covering Western Christianity and its direct antecedents. The sphere of religion includes more than that. If the Catholic college department is really in touch with its central concern then its sphere must grow to include data and discussion of the varieties of world religion, secular and civil religion, etc.; if it is to be a truly catholic or whole department, it must deal respectfully with all that issues from the center it serves and knows.

The departmental sphere must grow. But insofar as it has become a sphere, the department can now begin to appreciate the *depth* dimension of its center. In other words it can admit the psychic aspect and value of theology, religious events, symbols, rituals, dogmas and apparitions, myths and odysseys of apocalyptic scenes and cathedral portals. Its own radical centering must alert it to its responsibility to this dimension of religion.

And here is where, especially, the students of the seventies will put a strong demand upon us. A mere multiplication of theologies, religious panoramas, and material could only bewilder them more than they are. It could only reinforce their convictions about the irrelevance of religion. The student who is really a student gives a certain priority to self-understanding and he is rightly convinced that meaningful self-understanding has to take into account current scientific, existential, evolutionary, psychological estimates of the human situation. If the dogma and data of religion cannot be translated into these terms, then he will not be interested in religion and we shall be free to spend our time with a diminishing number of disciples who experience a regressive security in observing and hearing magic sights and sounds.

Of course, the dogma and data of religion can be translated into terms that suit the modern cosmos and psyche, for the dogma and data of religion have to do with the ground of the cosmos and psyche, whether ancient or modern. They have to do with radical cosmic and self-understanding and to the degree that modern cosmic and psychological systems touch upon or are apt to convey radical self-understanding, they may legitimately take the baton from traditional religious expression and carry its weight forward—at the same time rendering the traditional material transparent and vital. And even where they fall short, they do no disservice, for they afford the student an opportunity to see the truly radical nature of the self-understanding religion teaches—a self-understanding that entails a last judgment upon every form of penultimate self-understanding, a self-understanding that insures freedom and permanent self-possession. What could be more relevant than that?

A radically centered department will appreciate all this— the scope and depth, openness and profundity of its sphere. But perhaps a radically centered department is too much to ask. Radical religious experience as a basis for reform? Yes—the history of religion indicates that that happens. But as a basis for departmental reform? If the answer to that is no, then I suppose we shall have to settle for a strictly academic rationale for reform. This is all right. I am sure it would result in a department with something of the scope and depth outlined above. But not quite. And would it be Catholic?

21   New Forms of Prayer for Contemporary Christians

How should—how may the contemporary Christian pray? Anthony Padovano says that "there cannot be an historical spirituality univocally applicable to all ages, any more than there can be an avocational spirituality suitable to all walks of life." [1] Since the *Honest to God* breakthrough by John A. T. Robinson, with its train of implications, and because of other newer theological and Scriptural insights, it would seem that we must explore the possibility of new forms of prayer in order to prevent religious schizophrenia. Otherwise we find ourselves still addressing a Supreme Being who is outside our "world" or somewhere that we are not—one to whom we "go" in order to make contact with him. Yet, if God is conceived of as the Ground of Being, if he is Ultimate Reality, and if he is Love, then it seems that we would do better to meet him in the depths of our own consciousness and in the Truth and Life which is found within us (yet is other than us) and also in the "in-betweens" of our saving, interpersonal relationships, which are indispensable to our personal Truth and Life.

In a time when we are struggling to bring our expressions of Christianity to adulthood and intelligibility in an open confrontation with what is happening in our world and with our present understanding of God and man, I have been wrestling intellectually (and also personally) by searching for a form of prayer consonant with our theology. In preparing to share my questioning with others, I invited college students to answer a questionnaire which concerned itself with their ideas, expe-

1. *Who is Christ?* (Notre Dame: Ave Maria Press, 1967), p. 63.

riences, and habits of prayer. Using the results of this questionnaire, I then reversed my procedure and began searching out some theological principles to support the forms of prayer which they exposed as theirs. This presentation, therefore, has emerged from thinking searchingly from both directions.

What follows is not for those who are already "caught up into the third heaven" but for the ordinary but enlightened Christian who needs prayer that will be suitable to his contemporary life-style. Hopefully, much of this can be related to liturgical prayer; but liturgy has been by-passed because of the need to economize on space.

From the evidence supplied by the college students who answered my questionnaire, I perceive three trends which lead to some characteristics of prayer today: social involvement; a search for greater self-awareness, identity and personal meaning; and an attraction for the sacred and the occult. Social involvement—a daily living of the Christian life in witness—is considered by many young people to be a form of prayer. It gives impetus, on the one hand, to a conventional prayer-form with, perhaps, a new flavor. It becomes "talking to God" spontaneously about one's personal life, commitments, problems, the persons affected by them, and the need for God's "being there" in this redeeming activity. Malcolm Boyd—among others—gives us published examples of this kind of prayer.

The second and third trends afford opportunity and give meaning to prayer which might be labeled "experience": experience of oneself, of one's surroundings, and of one's God.

Experiencing personal life as a form of prayer seems to have two hinges which open the door to communication with God, which is the essence of prayer. These two hinges are "presence" and "awareness." The concept of God as "Presence" has biblical roots. Israel had no images of Yahweh because he couldn't be depicted. But his *presence* was felt by them and was associated *with* certain places and objects. He was known by them in their history because he was actively present in their national history and in the history of their individual lives. Yahweh was "He who Is Always There"—"God with us"—the God who went before them but was always in their midst. Conceiving God as

"Presence" rids us of harmful caricatures of him and assists us to find him in the sounds of the now grubby, now glorious business of living in this *real world* rather than in some "beyond." God as "Presence" in our history enables us to communicate with him without necessarily addressing him but by *receiving* him and *experiencing* his presence.

"Openness" is a key word here because "presence" necessitates a degree of openness which prohibits one's hiding behind a smoke-screen of recited prayers. Like the psalmist they express their true feelings even if what they express might not sound very "nice" to pious people. Experience of "presence" involves also dual awareness: that of oneself and that of the Other.

The revealing presence of another promotes our own self-awareness.

I propose that experiencing one's *wholeness;* i.e., explicit consciousness of one's *whole self* can be a form of prayer. This "felt" experience and awareness of one's total self involves an openness to the total environment and to all that makes a human to be a person—his, because man is essentially a related creature. To the degree that one can experience his whole self, *feel* his presence to himself and what is around him, is he not to a correlative degree in communication with God? God's presence to the person is necessary for the person's *being* at all.

In deep interpersonal communication with another, if one is aware, he can find that the experience embodies far more than the sum total of the human I and thou. It is an experience also of the Transcendent Other, and the aware person can recognize the creative, redemptive growth or exchange which is taking place. I propose that genuine, charitable communication with another should also be included because it is a loving activity more often than not a work of mercy. One student expressed this when he wrote:

Prayer is communication with God. One can accomplish this in many ways; some are traditional and some are not. You can communicate with God through other people. For example, if you take time to talk with someone who is lonely, sad, or disgusted, and you help love for God through another person.

I place rather heavy emphasis upon loving interpersonal communication as prayer also because it is creative and redemptive. Could it not be a means of God's "calling each by name"? Where creation and redemption are taking place, surely God is touching the person and the person is open to receive this touch. Prayer? Why not?

Human love can be rather ordinary, but it can also be "peak" moments and experiences which reach into the mystical and ecstatic. No matter. God must, in human love, be communicating his life, and if it is personalizing at all, the individuals are open and aware. These are the ingredients for prayer. An act of love for another can be an act of love for God. Throughout the Bible we see that God reveals his love and communicates his life through events more than through words.

Creative dance can be prayer. Here is another activity which offers the possibility of involving and experiencing the whole self. One through which a person "pulls out all the stops" and opens himself to his environment, to his own deep interior self (and if the faith dimension is explicit—to God), and expresses himself in bodily movement. Too often, conventional prayer is only from the chin up. Creative dance can involve the entire body-person and can communicate his individual truth and life while, simultaneously, he may be becoming aware of it. Celebration of life is, in addition to the above, a praise of God the Giver of Life.

Any genuine aesthetic experience is an experience of the True, the Good, the Beautiful: absolute perfections which God does not *have*, but which God *is*. Therefore, in openness, presence, and awareness, it would seem that an aesthetic experience can be a form of prayer. The young people who responded to my questionnaire unanimously agreed that contemplating the beauty of nature is for them a form of prayer. God is present in and to his work, his creation. When this presence is received, communication has been established. Is it not possible that present-day exclamations such as "Great!" "Magnificent!" "Wonderful!" "Beautiful!" etc., are up-dated "Alleluias"—expressions of joy, delight, praise, wonderment, and surprise? We "wonder" at the beauties of nature, of music, of art, and of other good, true, beautiful things. In wonderment a person is filled with awe. We wonder at that which "overtakes" us. This forces us to admit of the transcendent; for only something or someone other than we can overtake us. When it is the Divine Transcendent which overtakes us in an aesthetic experience, we are in communication with God.

In moments of decision-making a person is called to open himself to the creative future. All real decisions are made in some darkness and in some hope. To make a decision affecting one's future is to throw oneself into the arms of Divine Providence and respond "Yes; Amen" to the unknown future to and from which our God "who goes before us" is calling us. Is this not an act of hope? Is it not God calling to us in a situation and is it not his love making a demand on us? Is not our decision a response to him? Is not our courage to take the risk a way of affirming the reality of God's Providence—an act of faith in him? And is this not prayer?

Scripture reading can be dialogue between God and the man of faith. God's presence is by means of the words which speak to us, and our presence to him is through our openness to hear his message and through the response we make in our hearts.

This is somewhat of a "do it yourself" age. The creative urge may be considered a call from God to become more human and to participate in his work. It would seem that this urge is the Spirit of God infusing us with or at least activating in us an affinity to God: a desire to participate in his power and activity. Often, upon completion of a project we implicitly praise God by the very delight and satisfaction we feel and express when we view our work. In the astonishment which we often experience at the creative products of our own mind and hands there comes, it would seem, a recognition of the Transcendent. Is it not possible that this could be recognition of God's presence to us as well as praise and thanksgiving?

A significant number of students indicated on the questionnaire that music can be for them a kind of prayer. One young person commented:

Contemporary music lyrics contain many values and relate

many messages to me. Spending a quiet evening listening to Simon and Garfunkel or Joan Baez is a real prayer; I find it moving and inspiring.

Why would not one's response—whatever form it may take: emoting, promise, openness to this musical "word of the Lord" which comes through the modern day prophetic minstrel be prayer?

The current search for identity, desire for experience of oneself, stretching to achieve greater self-awareness can be perceived in a scriptural, poetic way. It is a probing of the *deep*. It is the Spirit of Life and Truth hovering over the abyss —the formless chaos. It is an effort to stir the waters with the expectation of bringing forth a creation: the self—perceived as fruitful; a new creation. "Surely God is in this place." Surely, it is, as Gerard Manley Hopkins says, the Spirit searching the deep things of God. One who is open to the Spirit is in communication with God.

One may be inclined to ask, "But isn't all this mere humanism?" The phenomenon of mere humanism in a world where the Incarnation is a reality is controversial. But, assuming that the possibility exists, it seems only honest to confront it.

As indicated in the presentation of various activities which I perceive as forms of prayer, the explicit faith dimension—awareness of God's presence—is obviously desirable and enriching to the Christian's experience but not absolutely essential. This conclusion is based upon the theology of the anonymous Christian. If it is possible for a person to live unknowingly in and by the Holy Spirit of Christ, some form of communication with God must sustain and nourish this life. At least *some* of his activities, then, must be prayer or his living of the Christian life would not be possible.

The fruits of the Spirit: joy, peace, charity, are empirical signs which manifest the presence of the Holy Spirit. True, they can be ambiguous, but it is reasonable to presume that when they are consistently observable in a person's life there must be some communication with God whether the person knows it explicitly or remains unaware of the true nature of this reality.

Many persons who do not "talk to God" manifest evidence of his presence in their lives.

Nearly all of the forms of prayer presented in this essay are, in one way or another, the "inbreaking" of God into a person's life. They have been spoken of in terms of God's call and our response. The call of God—the "inbreaking"—can come *anytime*, not just at set times for formal prayer. College students made this point emphatic on the questionnaire (although they did not by any means rule out the need to "go apart" into a quiet place to pray at times). As Scripture tells us, God takes the initiative. His personal presence to us is an inbreaking into our lives and *he overtakes us in our life experiences*. In every life-giving event, the hand of the Lord is upon us, touching us in our here and now life. We may, in faith, be aware of the fact that it is the call, the touch of the Lord; and our part in the communication may then be an explicit affirmation of his presence—an act of faith in him and his being there. But does our recognition of the Lord *have* to be explicit for it to be prayer? Is it perhaps enough that we are open and responsive to the touch so that we let something happen to us? In the meantime, perhaps we can remember that even though we can say "Father" only if the Spirit addresses him through us, still the Spirit breathes where he will. Often we are surprised. Maybe, on the subject of prayer, there is a surprise in store for us.

22   Christian Mysticism in the Classroom?

APRIL OURSLER ARMSTRONG

Mysticism has often been considered embarrassing, threatening, and irrelevant to the study of theology. Yet mysticism, from St. Paul through Teilhard, has been an experience profoundly shaping theology. Mysticism is important, not merely to the pious oddball but to theologians and to the whole People of God. Human hunger for experience of the transcendent restlessly orients people in and out of the visible Church toward both real and false mysticism rather than toward arid intellectualizing.

It is my thesis that theologians and teachers of theology can find in the study of mysticism a lens first to clarify the reason for theology's existence, and secondly to expand genuine involvement in theological questions, and thirdly to sharpen ecumenical understanding.

There has been, traditionally, reluctance to dignify mysticism with study except as a sideline. What academic courses in mysticism there have been in the past ordinarily fell into the "how-to" category—they were part of spiritual reading, guides to self-improvement in prayer, or, more rarely, guides to counseling and directing souls. But such an approach is not theological, any more than a map of virtuous practice can be said to be theological.

I see two main reasons for this reluctance to study mystics seriously. The first is the preference in the past for what we may call "tidy" theology. The exuberant delight which theologians took in wearing "rational" costumes, in playing Aristotelian games, in working with geometric models, would have suffered in contact with raw experience which is seldom rational, Aris-

totelian, or geometric. It is tidy to argue the nature of God and
the Trinity from the data of past councils, scripture, and Thomistic logic. It is very untidy to have to include the experience
Meister Eckhart had of God-beyond-God, or of Theresa's mystical marriage. Only when the theologian himself was open to
mystical experience—as, for example, in the case of Bonaventure,
do we find the impact of experience taken seriously as data in
the construct of theological conclusion. The careful ignoring of
mysticism may also be due to a second, closely related factor—
a mistrust of emotionalism or feeling in religious experience.

To my utter fascination, when I entered the Catholic Church
as a convert some twenty years ago, I found deep discrepancy
between the basic teaching of this Spirit-guided community and
the basic practice of most of its spokesmen. On the one hand,
Christianity in scripture, in catechism, in sacrament spoke of a
personal, and at times verifiable, intimate, and integrally revolutionary union of each one of us with God through Jesus and
the Spirit. On the other hand, it was not considered practical—
or humble—to aspire to such an experience. Union with God
was presented as a fact to be believed, but most assuredly not
felt. Any "feeling" or "experience" of God's presence was presumed to be a sign of childishness, of womanish weakness, as in
hysteria or self-delusion, or of a lower form of religion such as
revivalism or evangelism, *a la* holy rollers.

To this day, if a student in my college course in mysticism
approaches a pastor with a question about the "dark night" of
the soul, he must do so warily. Not even one who advocates
ordination of women meets such an angry and suspicious cold
shoulder as the one inquiring—even abstractly—about mysticism.
Catholics, who could boast of the greatest mystics, have never
been officially happy about them, at least while they were alive.
Whatever the reason for our traditional mistrust of emotionalism
or sensationalism—be it Manicheeism, Jansenism, or a Hellenic
heritage—we do not approve those who say they have walked
and talked with God in any way apart from the genteel structure of prayer and sacrament.

And prayer and sacrament—which in themselves testify to
the accessibility and permeability of our God—we have in practice sociologically structured so as to make mystic experience

almost impossible. Look, for instance, at our first communions in the past. We taught the child that this bread is in truth now become the real presence of God, and that God would become one with him through his reception of communion. Then we told him he would not "feel" anything. We taught that a dynamic personal existential difference would occur within him, and concentrated on drilling him in static impersonal gesture. To be that concerned with the inauthenticity of conformity in marching and kneeling made it almost unthinkable for an interior experience to be noted.

Much the same with Confirmation: there we said that the first apostles received the Spirit with tongues of fire, and so much of an emotional impact that other citizens thought them drunk. Then we said that they were not to expect anything out of the ordinary, and since they had seldom if ever seen any grown Christian Spirit-intoxicated, they believed us. If a child did intuit an experiential presence of the Spirit he wouldn't dare say so in his fancy rented red robe!

Catholics have tended to equate the practice of the faith with good manners. Good manners in prayer militate against mysticism, or appreciation thereof. Mystics, like the primitive Christians, balance the feeling of the holy with the confidence sprung from incarnation. They unabashedly say what they feel about God. Theresa of Avila knew humility and reverence, but she could also say to Jesus: "If this is the way you treat your friends, no wonder you have so few!" From that voice of experience came enough theological expertise to qualify her as a doctor of the Church.

In diametric opposition to the bias toward rationality and away from experience, toward respectability and away from authenticity, is current student enthusiasm for mysticism in its most loose definition. The occult in all its forms is undergoing a boom unheard of in several centuries in the west. Accompanying this is an interest in religious mysticism, formal and experimental. Pentecostalism would fit loosely under this rubric. Understandably, in the face of Christian discomfort with the topic, most of the student search for information is in the direction of Eastern religions, and the smaller more eccentric cults of this country. There are even, as reported in *The New York Times*, groups calling themselves "Jesus Freaks" —ex-hippies, once freaking out on drugs and acid, now proclaiming that the one true experience is the experience of Jesus. Living in communes, sharing property, they are picketing with their long hair and granny glasses in the name of decency and morality. Actually in a wave of modern puritanism, they carry signs of protest in front of topless dancer establishments. Predictable, perhaps, that those who look for a way to "freak out" might learn of a way to the inner mansions. Predictable too that the Church should shrug in offended amusement and draw back instead of guiding, as it draws back so often from experience-oriented modern Christians engaged in cursillos, in Pentecostal happenings, or the pursuit of private mystic experience.

Current student enthusiasm may be a fad. It is definitely related to the surge of anti-intellectualism. To those who object to any logic or communication not following the grammar of the past, this is proof that it is dangerous and wrong. To those who are aware that there are other logics besides our Western one which is based on the principle of non-contradiction, and to those who personally can communicate in the language of symbol and event and sensation as well as the language of academe, it is a heartening sign.

Whether or not student enthusiasm for "mysticism" is a fad, it is clearly related to the drug orientation of the present time. The question is how. Those who see drug fascination as entirely based on escapism, immaturity, rebellion and crime, cannot help but be frightened when the same generation expresses interest in mysticism. I am, personally, repelled and alarmed by the drug problem. But, from experience with college students, I suspect that *some* of the rendezvous with drugs and chemicals springs from genuine, vital hunger for experience with the transcendent not recognized or satisfied by the Christian establishment. I read the works of the famous and the unknown in this turned-on world, from Alan Watts to some of my more intelligent students, and find they seek, and in small measure discover, the experience which men of faith have found before them. The experience, sadly, had been kept undercover and unheard for too long.

Current student enthusiasm may also be a healthy reaction

against what we might call "second-hand theology." Second-hand theology is the kind which when translated into teaching or catechism, answers questions which have never arisen in the religious experience of the student, or even, perhaps, in that of the teacher. Teaching on the Trinity falls into this category most of the time. To someone who has never experienced the Holy Spirit in action, the question of whether the Spirit is God or not is meaningless.

Experimentally, in a course on Christian systematics, I have attempted to restage, *ad lib,* major councils of the first five centuries. It is a device which works rather well on Christology, for the heresies of the past not only make sense to today's students, but perdure and are familiar. It does not work well when we get into the question of three persons and one God, even when *personae* is carefully exegeted. This generation, like many of its parents in America, is not conscious of the Spirit as active in the Church, or in their personal lives, Confirmation notwithstanding. When one tells them some early Christians defined Jesus as God because he poured forth the Spirit, they are baffled. To tell them that Christians at early councils were defending and attempting to elucidate their own experience of the Spirit, is to run up against total lack of understanding. The students can remember what second-hand theology had to say about the role of the Spirit, the gifts, the fruits. But they cannot be curious about the Spirit, or about the theology which insists on explaining to them this unknown God. If the same theology then attempts to relate the Spirit to infallibility, or authority, or collegiality, the relation is too tenuous to be retained.

But in this dilemma the current student enthusiasm for experience of the transcendent may be the key to opening the door to their personal involvement with the divine. That in turn—and only that—can lead to genuine interest in theology. A person who does not know others are around him will never be interested in the science of communication, let alone in psychology. He who does not know there is divine reality cannot be interested in the science of that reality, or in the community which celebrates it.

Before exploring how the study of mysticism may be helpful to our students, it is time to define the term. What is mysticism?

Two answers are obvious. First, that there are many possible definitions, and many possible forms of mysticism. Second, that whatever else mysticism is, it is primarily an *experience*.

Evelyn Underhill defines mysticism as knowledge and activity leading to an effort to reorganize the whole interior and exterior life to harmonize with the transcendental order apprehended in the experience. Taken apart, that definition means that the one who is called mystic does experience a way of seeing the transcendental order which demands *metanoia*—the conversion of all one's life orientation to harmony with the new vision of truth. Both knowledge and action are bent to this effort. But I myself would use a working definition of that experience something like this: a mystic experience is one of vision of relation between the person and Ultimate Reality or, in a Christian model, between creature and God, which goes beyond rationality and into affectivity, thereby unifying and integrating the whole person. Rationality, as such, plays an insignificant role in the experience, coming into play later in certain attempts to communicate the experience. *Vision* is the primary word here—vision, taken only occasionally in the sense of pictorial—vision in the sense of penetration and awareness of relation.

The vision experience called mysticism in my definition produces not only a world-view, but invariably produces also attempts to communicate to others the first-hand experience of God. The sense of discovery—of a new gestalt—produces an urgency not only to harmonize with the Real but also to guide others to the same vision. In this sense, mysticism is much like conversion, an enactment of enthusiasm.

The definition is deliberately loose. It can embrace experience from all religions and from none, from shepherds in a Portuguese pasture to Carmelites in cloister, to people eating mushrooms.

But within the Christian structure, mystic experience has often and obviously affected theology. St. Paul's experience on the road to Damascus clearly is related to his concept of the mystical body of Christ. Actually, it may seem that the relation between his writings on the mystical body and his experience of Jesus on the road is clearer than the relation between later official teachings on the mystical body and the writings of Paul.

What he saw clearly in vision he expressed in enthusiasm which was not always amenable to severe rationality and the logic of deduction. Another example of mysticism influencing theology in our own day is the work of Teilhard—again, not a work of systematics, but rather of enthusiasm beginning to communicate the model of new vision.

To understand why there is such a thing as rational theology one presupposes urgent relevance to the subject matter. One presupposes that someone, somewhere, sometime, desperately cared to explain a vital conclusion compelled by experience. Theology is not a game, rearranging concepts to form ever more dazzling mosaics, but too often this is how theology appears to our students. If theology has any purpose, theology must be the answer to *incarnate questioning*, that is, to questions rising from experience. That those questions can arise from experience is something our students do not seem to know, and that our theologians, frankly, at times tend to forget. To define the Trinity or outline a Christology, as I said, to someone who has not experienced Trinity or Christ is irrelevant nonsense. Assume however *any* mystical experience of Christ, and see what questions instantly arise.

Immediately is posed the experience of relation between human and divine. When Francis of Assisi encounters Jesus, or Mary Margaret encounters the Sacred Heart, what is this two-pronged relation between human and divine? First, in what way *can* dialogue take place between Francis or Mary Margaret and the Christ? Second, in what way can the Jesus they encounter be said to be human and God at the same time?

Secondly are posed innumerable other questions of relation: What is the relation between time and whatever is not time, whether you call it eternity or aeviternity? If I am a mystic and I am in time, how do I explain the intersection of what is not in time with me? If I am in the dimension of place and limited with a body, how explain the experience of an incarnate God who may enter the dimension of my space? For some students, awareness of the reality of someone's encounter experience may arouse genuine concern with the mythological statement of "ascending into heaven and sitting at the right hand of the

Father," leading them on to examination of what resurrection and glorified body might mean, the relation between history and supra-history, between commitment to this world and transcendence of this world.

Assume *any* mystical experience of the Trinity, any personal new awareness in encounter with the three-in-one. The door is flung open to all the paradoxes of God: Of how unity and multiplicity can be the same. Of the meaning of personal and suprapersonal. Of the logic of contradiction, in which opposites coinhere. An experience of the reality that three are one because there is no other way for there to be one except by being three demands re-examination of all our understanding of reality. What men like Dewart call the dehellenization of dogma, what I would call enhanced vision of the "creative union" of Teilhard, or of the unutterable revelation of the 5th dimension—the primal tension of relation—all this becomes not game-playing but relevant necessity in the face of such mystical experience.

It is important, considering our broad definition of mystical experience, and the experiences available to our people, to compare such typical Christian mystic emphasis with that of modern drug and chemical mysticism. Here we find important similarities and differences. One similarity not always obvious to those uncertain about drug culture is that in both religious and drug mysticism body-aids often induce the experience. It is obvious that mescaline, peyote, LSD and the like change the body's chemical situation and thereby open the person to altered perception and consciousness. Less obvious is the fact that traditional religious methods of preparation for spiritual ascent can alter body chemistry to alter consciousness.

Fasting is normal among ascetics and many mystics. Prolonged fasting alters blood sugar levels and body chemistry, which in themselves can alter consciousness and perception. The well-known Hesychast tradition of the Eastern Church, in which one sits with chin on chest, concentrating on the heart while repeating the "Jesus" prayer, also alters body chemistry. Blood circulation to the brain is affected, as is breathing. Oxygen and carbon dioxide levels change. Biochemical analysis of the effects of such prayer methods is now becoming possible. (We do have analysis of the Trappist monks' body chemistry, for instance, reporting the totally abnormal composition of the monks' sweat, which may be due to diet, or to other facets of their contemplative life). But it is clear to even an unpracticed observer that certain traditional Christian accoutrements of prayer—the posture, the beads, the phrase repetition, the candles, the incense can be a sensory overload, and semi-hypnotic aids to the altering of consciousness. Interestingly, many mystics eventually required no aids, and became able to rise or be raised to altered consciousness without them.

The work of Masters and Houston, research psychologists, as reported in *Varities of Psychedelic Experience*, involved meticulously controlled laboratory experiments administering LSD to tested and evaluated subjects. An unusual few, who rated high on tests for maturity and stability, did in the LSD experience reach high levels of experience in altered consciousness which compare remarkably with Christian non-drug mysticism. Reading the transcription of their conversations and recollections under the influence of LSD one must be struck by intense similarity with Spanish mystics, or the author of the *Cloud of Un-Knowing*. But I wish to draw attention to two salient factors. One is that those subjects who reached higher levels of vision did not wish to venture more into LSD, feeling it superfluous for the future. The second is that each subject, carefully followed up for testing in years ahead, showed significant evidence of personal transformation. Self knowledge, a kind of basic unification and re-orientation, produces enduring changes in lifestyle such as cure of alcoholism, cure of a despaired marriage, ability to concentrate on a career. It is suggested that such rare chemical experiences in certain prepared and suitable individuals effected a conversion-type experience similar to that seen in some religious mystics.

A third similarity between religious and chemical mysticism quite evident in the Masters and Houston research is the genuine possibility of self-delusion. In reading Christian mystics it is evident many of them would use as a criterion of valid experience the subject's awareness that self-delusion is possible. This would include those aware of the possibility of devils masquerading as divine. The same is apparently true of the LSD subjects of Masters and Houston. Many of what we might call lower-level experiencers seem to supply from their own desires, or from accessible levels of the immediate subconscious, effects which please them. Reading transcriptions of these and comparing them with more unitive experiences, one finds radical difference in value. And those who operate on this lower level, like pseudo-religious mystics, do not evince significant transformation afterwards. A fourth similarity between religious and drug mystic experience is that on higher levels one finds in the subject both missionary zeal and the spirit of love for all persons and all creation intensified.

What differences are then apparent? Most obvious is the degree of personal and communal safety. Religious mystics do not ordinarily threaten their survival in the course of spiritual adventures. Many are apparently opened to strength to overcome fasting weakness and loss of sleep, although it is true that many are not always healthy by any means. Religious mystics do not, presumably, alter chromosomal structures. And, speaking communally, religious mystics pose small danger to society. There is no record of a religious mystic trying to drive a car while in rapture.

Chemical mysticism can lead to inadvertent suicide when, on a bad trip, a subject believes he can fly. What the relation of this is to levitation of Christian mystics I do not presume to say. It is hard to apply scientific criteria to reports of Joseph of Cupertino flying around the Church, or Theresa of Avila hovering above the floor. But perhaps someday it may be said that while drug mystics think they can fly yet fall down, Christian mystics do fly. At least they do not kill themselves under delusion.

A second obvious difference is the degree of personal initiative and self-discipline involved. Religious mystics do not always begin with personal work. St. Francis can be surprised by dreams and a voice from a crucifix but to persevere in prayer, fasting, reformation and dedication is hard labor. Francis on Mt. Alvernia was not waiting for a sugar tablet of LSD to dissolve. He was groaning in spirit and body, driven by his motto, "My God and my all."

Both types of mystics are given to joy, even joys of the flesh. The dying Francis asks for almond paste cakes, and Theresa, faced with a royal dinner, reminds a less relaxed and unified nun that there is time for penance and time for pheasant. But the religious mystic recognizes, agonizes under, and respects those periods known as dark nights—times when God seems inaccessible, seems totally vanished. In these times the religious soul grows and strengthens; faith, hope and charity are refined and deepened. There is no parallel to this in chemical mysticism, for even a bad trip is an experience, and one can, according to some authorities, avoid a bad trip by the right setting and guide. No setting or guide prevents the anguish of the dark night.

A third difference, which can be challenged in the cases of men such as Aldous Huxley or Alan Watts, is that generally the chemical mystic has less desire to share the world activity, and less desire for self-alteration in the future. At least those who are more commonly found in chemical experiences, those who would not rate high on the Masters-Houston scale, are more prone to a loving acceptance of what is, rather than to a loving desire to change or redeem what is. The chemical mystic, though he remain in the world, is often, it seems to me, more withdrawn than the religious hermit. Physically present, he is less involved in the dialogue of good and evil, or of that strange mystery we call suffering.

There arises then, from consideration of these few suggestions, the question of whether we can consider chemicals and drugs as being normal aids to spiritual development in the future. As many good Christians ask, will it not be the same to take chemicals to speed spiritual growth as it is now to use a car for travel? Is not our fear or disdain for LSD or mescaline or marijuana at root a fear of the unknown, and an unnecessary dislike of anything "artificial"? I decline to answer. Like the question of the Pill, this one is susceptible to one answer in theory, but in practice medical evidence is not sufficient. Comparing chemicals to cars may be a good analogy. Cars in themselves do not seem immoral, but ecology poses serious questions about their effect on environment and health. There are now many ways of praying, and the life of the Trappist is not for me. Perhaps the same may be said of chemical mysticism: it is not for me. It is also, incidentally, illegal, whether it should be or not.

What I would borrow from the chemical mystic is awareness

that in Christianity we need a theology of abundance. Our teachers of mysticism have often in the past lived with a theology of bereftness: the world was bereft of goodness in many ways, and what goods it had to offer were delusive and temporary and inferior to those of heaven. Theirs was often therefore a mysticism of withdrawal, of enthusiasm for the transcendent to the exclusivity of today. The saints usually contradicted them. But the theory remained operative, and therefore discouraging to the average Christian. Christian mysticism theory needs to deepen with awareness of that love which Teilhard held for the world, the cosmos, the earth, the rock, the man. Marijuana smokers proclaim the same thing and seduce us with a message that is rightly ours.

As a theologian I am more interested in the experience data of mysticism than in the means by which it is achieved. Studied objectively, this data challenges those who are in dialogue with Ultimate Reality, and the people of God, to new response. Read, for instance, Allan Watts' *Joyous Cosmology,* an LSD-based hymn to creation which belongs in the same genre as Francis' *Canticle to the Sun* or Teilhard's *Divine Milieu.* Lay the three side by side, and you can determine a plausible method of studying mystics in relation to systematic theology. All three report an understanding close to pantheism, yet deliberately removed from it. All three report an understanding that all things are of God and in God, or of Jesus and in Jesus, or of the Ultimate Reality and in it. All three sing the joy of discovering the fabric of relation between the created and the uncreated. Yet in each is a different model, a spectrum from Francis who saw God and Christ as up there and out of the current world, though accessible and loving, to Teilhard who finds a kind of identity between the evolving world and the Christ, to Watts who does not see Christ, but only the impersonal reality.

How to relate these? What plausible method can study mystics? First, we make sure that we read the mystic's own work, not works about him. Second, we situate the mystic in context of his own culture and world experience, become aware of popular and theological trends in his time, the symbols and language available to him. Then we must try that peculiar feat I call *identification* — the feat which enables students to walk in his moccasins for a mile, to determine what *he* thought he was saying, what *he* intended, in relation to his contemporaries, as well as those before him.

Then it is possible to draw out the model the mystic was operating in, to picture forth the way he visualizes reality. On the most obvious level of model we see that Francis of Assisi lived in a flat world, with heaven above him, and God in that heaven. Teilhard lived in a different universe, not only round, but seething with energy and evolutionary direction. Both have an experience of God sacramentally within his creation, but both must see that vision differently physically, spiritually, and historically. Watts lives in a world model which does not contain the notion of God as given. It is easier to translate from one familiar model to another, so most theologians can detect the proper translation of the Franciscan vision into the Teilhardian model, but not the grammar of translation from Teilhard to Watts. Only by comparing models, and by the process of identification drawing out the grammar and vocabulary of the vision can any evaluation be properly done.

For example, in the study of mysticism it is well to determine what model is used to represent the relation of creator or world force to creation or universes; the relation of what we call body and what we call spirit; the relation of time and eternity, or any of the four dimensions and a non-dimensional reality; and of what men call good and what men call evil.

The next step then would be to relate the model and experience to previous or current rational structures of theology and observe the interaction. Some mystics work with the model given them by the theological culture in which they live—as with Theresa of Avila, and the mystic experience is indeed conditioned by that model. Others work primarily from the model provided by their experience, and their theology is conditioned by that model. So, for example with St. Gregory Palamas. In an attempt to defend the Hesychast mystical experience, in which the Hesychasts claimed to penetrate and be penetrated by the uncreated Light, which they termed Tabor Light, Palamas faced an apparent conflict of truths in theology. Western investigators were accusing the Hesychasts of heresy because, in the western model, their claim meant that they were seeing the beatific vision, which was deemed to be impossible to man alive on earth. To answer this, Palamas created another model of God drawn from the vision—a two-level God, one level being accessible to man and called the energies of God, and another level inaccessible, which might be called the Godhead.

In that case, conflict of models with experience produced not too fruitful an outgrowth of dogma development, because translation between the models was not undertaken. Yet, interestingly enough, two-level models of God can be found in such diverse sources as Sankara the Hindu, Meister Eckhart the Christian, and in several chemical and psychological mystics. It may be that the true dogma development along that line has not yet come about, waiting on more Christian experience of vision and of model translation.

Awareness of different models within the mystics' communication is an important reminder that no study of the mystics can attempt to compel them to report the same truth. They cannot be forced into one hypothesis. Attempts may be made to sort them into categories, if you will, as Zaehner has done, separating "profane" mystics from "religious" mystics. They can be catalogued as "nature" mystics, a la Wordsworth, and cosmic mystics, a la Huxley, for convenience sake. What is vital is to reverence the data of their experience and communication, and listen to it. Even more primary is the need to accept their testimony of the reality of experience.

Then at least these four goals can be accomplished: First, the study of mystics can help demonstrate the primacy of experience in religion, and consequently in theological development. Second, the study of mystics can make the history of religion and the comparison of religions more intelligible and useful. Third, the study of mystics can serve as a corrective to over-rationalizing in producing new theories of theology. Fourth, the study of mystics can establish an atmosphere in which theology and experience can flourish together. That alone would be a tremendous dehellenizing achievement, bringing about a real theology of hope, establishing a divine milieu. The Spirit might be able to speak more clearly if intelligent souls were well enough integrated to accept the darkness which is light.

23   Theology Should Be Required of All

WILLIAM J. SULLIVAN

It is a legitimate and even necessary part of the life of a university or college that it define itself. Unless one wants to work on the supposition that there is somewhere an ideal essence labeled "university," the task of defining the university and its nature is part of the work of the university itself. What the university is or what it does will undoubtedly vary in different ages, different cultures. For this reason, self-definition is an on-going task.[1]

1. There is very little material in print on the specific question of theology as an academic requirement. This paper is in sequence with two previous studies which I have done: "The Catholic University and the Non-Catholic Student," *Religious Education,* Vol. LXIV, No. 3 (May-June, 1969), 188-193; and "Theology for Undergraduates," *America* Vol. 121, No. 16 (Nov. 15, 1969), 463-66. The first article deals with background considerations; the second gives a parallel but alternate argumentation for this proposal.

Cf. also Christopher F. Mooney, S.J., "The Role of Theology in the Education of Undergraduates," a paper delivered at the Jesuit Educational Association Workshop, Regis College, Denver, Colo., August 6-14, 1969. A collection of papers from this Workshop, edited by Eugene E. Grollmes, S.J., was published in late 1970 by B. Herder Book Co., St. Louis, under the title, *Catholic Colleges and the Secular Mystique.* An important product of the JEA Workshop from the point of view of the question under discussion here is the consensus paper entitled, "Theology and the Jesuit College: A New Rationale."

A selection of items from the periodical literature on these topics would include:

A) *On the nature of the Catholic University*:

The principle and background papers contained in the *Proceedings* of the Denver JEA Workshop referred to above constitute a major source of contemporary reflection on this question.

One limit of the definition is that the understanding will be focused upon or centered around the academic. In moving toward this intellectual-academic self-definition, one of the prime factors is a set of values to which the given university or college may commit itself. There is a common rhetoric of the university

A most perceptive study of the nature of the Catholic university and one to which I am much indebted is: Quentin L. Quade, "The Catholic University: A Christian Perspective," *America*, Vol. 120, No. 14 (Apr. 5, 1969), 392-96. Quade has also written "Academic Planning and Leadership: Problems and Potentials of Catholic Universities," an as yet unpublished paper delivered at Marquette University, Jan. 10, 1970. Quade is also the principal author of "University and Catholic: Final Report of the Special Committee on the Christian Character of Marquette University," a special report delivered to the administration of Marquette University on Dec. 10, 1969. This "Quade Report" is now under discussion at Marquette University; it is to be hoped that the general sections of the Report will be given wide national circulation.

Another important essay on the nature of the contemporary Catholic university is: William J. Richardson, S.J., "Pay Any Price? Break Any Mold?" *America*, Vol. 116, No. 17, (Apr. 29, 1967), pp. 624-642. Richardson has two papers in the Denver JEA *Proceedings*.

Two studies of the legal aspects of the status of the Catholic university are: Charles M. Whelan, S.J., "Catholic Universities and the Gelhorn Report," *America*, Vol. 119, No. 16 (Nov. 16, 1968) 474-74; and *item*, "Catholic Colleges on Trial," *America*, Vol. 122, No. 5 (Feb. 7, 1970) 122-24. Neil G. McCluskey, S.J., has followed the evolution of the relations between the Catholic universities and Rome in: "Rome Listens to the Universities," *America*, Vol. 121, No. 3 (Aug. 2, 1969) 58-60 and "Rome Replies (Act II)," *America*, Vol. 122, No. 12 (March 28, 1970) 330-34.

For an expression of the Cassandra complex on this question, cf. John Cogley, "Catholic Universities: 'The Future of an Illusion,'" *Commonweal*, Vol. 86, No. 11 (June 2, 1967), 310-316, and *ibid*. "Identity Crisis in the Catholic College," *Saturday Review*, Vol. 50 (June 17, 1967) 68ff.

B) *On the academic role of theology in the university*:

Important background material on this question comes from two sources. The first is the series of *Proceedings* of institutes sponsored by the Jesuit Educational Association over the past 20 years. The Institutes in question are: Institute on College Religion, Holy Cross College, Worcester, Mass. 1951; Institute on Philosophy and Theology, Loyola University, Los Angeles, Calif., 1962; and the Workshop on Jesuit Colleges and Universities, Regis College, Denver, Colo., 1969. The papers and proceedings of these institutes are available through the national office of the "Jesuit Edu-

which presents it as a place of unbounded, unlimited, intellectual activity. Those who work exclusively from this notion or rhetoric emphasize the notion of the university as un-committed, as value-free. I do not find it terribly realistic. To be a place of intellectual activity: yes. To be devoted to the search for truth wherever it may be found: yes. But therefore to assume and maintain a neutral, value-free stance: no. This is not theoretically necessary for a university, nor is it so clear that it is practically possible.

A university may be legitimately built upon a certain set of values or truths.[2] If this were not possible the search for truth

cational Association" in Washington, D.C.

The second general source is the *Proceedings* of the "Society of Catholic College Teachers of Sacred Doctrine," predecessor of the "College Theology Society." The Annual Conventions during the first years of the S.C.C.T.S. D. centered around the nature and role of theology in the university. Cf. *Proceedings First Annual Convention* (1955) Ed. by Urban Voll, O.P., Dunbarton College, Washington, D.C., 1956. *Proceedings Second Annual Convention* (1956). No editor listed. Reprinted Regis College, Weston, Mass., 1964. *Proceedings Third Annual Convention* (1957). Ed. Brother C. Luke, F.S.C., Reprinted Regis College, Weston, Mass., 1964. Also several articles in *Proceedings Tenth Annual Convention,* (1964). Ed. M. C. Wheeler, R.S.C.J., Regis College, Weston, Mass., 1964.

Cf. also Bernard J. Cooke, "The Problem of Sacred Doctrine in the College," in *Modern Catechetics,* Ed. G. Sloyan, New York: Macmillan Co., 1963. *Ibid.,* "The Place of Theology in the Curriculum of the Catholic College," *NCEA Bulletin,* Vol. 63, No. 1 (Aug. 1966), 210-213. Robert A. McDermott, "Religion as an Academic Discipline," *Cross Currents,* Vol. 18, No. 1 (Winter, 1968), 11-33. Christopher F. Mooney, S.J., *op. cit.* and "College Theology and Liberal Education," *Thought,* Vol. 34 (1959), 325-30. G. Sloyan, "The New Role of the Study of Religion in Higher Education," *Journal of Ecumenical Studies,* Vol. 6, No. 1, (Winter, 1969), 1-17. F. X. Shea, S.J., "Theology as an Academic Discipline," in *The Role of Theology in the University,* eds. J. Frank Devine, S.J., and Richard W. Rousseau, S.J., Milwaukee: Bruce Publishing Co., 1967, pp. 13-93.

2. In his *America* essay Quade asserts that the purpose of the university is "not to 'confirm the beliefs of the like-minded' but to testify to the relevance of values to social and personal action, and to exemplify one value structure in its relations to the many human problem areas." (Quentin L. Quade, "The Catholic University: A Christian Perspective," *America,* Vol. 120, No. 14 (Apr. 5, 1969), 392-96.

which, in the rhetoric alluded to above, characterizes the university, would be a rather bootless adventure. As someone has expressed it: That the only value is to search for value is as patently absurd in morals, philosophy, and theology as it is in physics and medicine. There is such a thing as truth discovered, affirmed, incorporated, witnessed to, and transmitted. I would argue that commitment to a set of truths does not contradict the nature of the university provided that the genesis of the position is rational, that commitment remains open, and that its maintenance is in accord with the university's mode of existence and operation.

The question can be raised whether this situation of commitment to a set of values is not true of all universities. Those who use and profess the "value-free" rhetoric often have a commitment to a certain perspective of life, a certain understanding of reality which is as definite, as marked as that of those who explicitly acknowledge their value base.

Among the values that a university may incorporate are those of the religious or spiritual dimension of man's existence. If it is possible and legitimate for a university to incorporate and emphasize humanistic or societal or personal or scientific values, it is very hard to see why it may not do this with values that relate to the religious or the spiritual. Different religious traditions would have different sets of values; and so presumably the university which reflected these various value-sets would have a slightly different configuration. I would not say *a priori* that every religious perspective could have a university incorporation. If it were a tradition that were inimical to intellect or to humanistic values, it would be difficult to imagine how this would relate to the university. But *e converso*, this is the very reason why the central Catholic tradition in Christianity with its strong emphasis on intellect, on the positive relation of nature and grace, on the nobility of man, has always found the university a locus in which to incorporate and express itself. To continue the line of reasoning, the incorporation of value which we are speaking about here must take place—because we are talking about a university or college—primarily and fundamentally in the intellectual or academic mode. It is not enough that it express itself in an extra-curricular fashion, i.e., campus ministry, or by the presence of a certain number of religious persons.[3]

Because the university is essentially an intellectual academic institution, its values must be expressed in this way. It is at this point then that we arrive at the conclusion that it is legitimate and even necessary for the religiously oriented and committed university to express itself in theological activity, in a school or department which through research and teaching studies and develops the understanding of this aspect of man. Theological activity in this sense of the term becomes one of the "legitimate academic alternatives"[4] of a Catholic university. By "legitimate academic alternatives" is meant the programs or courses or institutes by which a given university expresses its orientation and so its specificity.

Theological activity—research and teaching—is a legitimate, coherent aspect of the life of a Catholic university. It is one of the activities that specifies it academically. It is therefore legitimate that a Catholic university community demand the continuing and vigorous presence of a theological school or department. And it is also legitimate that that community demand the participation of the student body in that activity. In plain words, it is legitimate that there be a theology requirement for the students.

One more step: Since the values that the theological activity is trying to explore, express, and develop are—in the Catholic tradition—universal values, it is logical and legitimate that it should demand that all students be in contact with this activity and these values. The spiritual dimension of man, his religious life is not something that is limited in the Catholic perspective

3. Cf. the divergent position on this question taken by two articles published in the 1969 NCEA Convention Issue of *America*, (Vol. 120, No. 14, Apr. 5, 1969). The first is Quade's essay "The Catholic University: A Christian Perspective." Quade argues the necessity of the incorporation and expression of values through academic programs, institutes, etc. The second article is Ladislas M. Orsy, "The Catholic University: A Catholic Presence." In his article Orsy espouses the rather curious position that a given university is Catholic because of the presence of a certain number of Catholics in the university community. A stronger contrast in positions could hardly be imagined.

4. The phrase is Quade's and is found in and explained in the two unpublished papers referred to in Footnote No. 1.

to religious people, to a certain limited group of men, e.g., Catholics, or Christians. The affirmations about man are universal affirmations.

The problems to which these affirmations address themselves are seen as universal problems. The experiences of man which reflect the problems, the search for solutions, and the reactions to the solution offered by the Christian affirmation—all of these have a general, universal aspect and not simply a parochial one. Somehow or other there is even here a reflection of that great Catholic truth of the universal salvific will of God.

All of this means that it is legitimate and logical to require contact with the religious dimension of man of all students. It means that it is illogical to require it only of the Catholic students. Such a policy can mean that *either* the institution regards religion and Christianity as relating to a certain delimited class of men, those who are officially Christian, *or* that the university is performing a custodial religious education function and not an intellectual, academic one. Both of these alternatives I find very unsatisfactory.

It is not being argued here that theology must be required in a school which no longer has academic requirements in other departments. Such a stance would show very much of the confessional or custodial attitude which is behind the present practice. The general educational stance of the institution with reference to academic requirements will be a prime factor in determining the specific policy in the theology area. For example, if a school operates on a track system or with an area requirement or a contract program, the requirements in theology would be in the same mode as those in other departments. But if the institution has maintained academic course requirements in other areas, for example, Biology, or modern languages or English, then corresponding requirements are legitimate and—it is argued here—necessary in the theology area.

In the first place, a number of Catholic colleges and univesities have already adopted this policy, or one roughly equivalent to it.[5] There is no intention or pretention here of lecturing

5. An extremely useful source of information on this matter is the "Brescia College Report," prepeared by the Rev. Joseph M. Mills, Chair-

these institutions on something that they have already done. But the rationale for this position has not been worked out in detail, or at least has not been widely and publicly discussed. And such a discussion is very important. If for no other reason, it is important because the counter position has received wide coverage over the past few years.

Secondly, another element of relativity that must be kept in mind is that any educational policy depends upon practical and concrete circumstances. It depends upon the history and traditions of a department; it depends upon the attitudes of the members of the department; it depends upon the number of courses which, practically speaking, the departments are able to offer. And therefore the implementation of the position that is proposed here must grow out of the concrete situation of the department or college. It is for these reasons that this proposal is not to be understood as monolithic or inflexible. It is a position that involves general educational philosophy which must necessarily be fitted to the practical realities of the individual college or university.

The reflection on the question of theology requirements for undergraduates has been occasioned by widespread student—and perhaps faculty—unrest with present requirements. The precise focus of dissatisfaction to which I have pointed is that of the confessional nature of the requirement. This is clearly not the focus of the dissatisfaction for the students. They have been opposed to theology requirements because they do not find the courses stimulating, relevant and interesting. In many instances, though by no means all, the students have voiced their resentment at being required to take second-rate courses. It seems that this resentment is perfectly legitimate. The only rationale for requiring a course at all is the judgment that it makes an important contribution to the overall education of a student. A poor course in whatever discipline makes no contribution at all. And therefore it should not be required. However, the proper response

man of the Department of Theology at Brescia College and presented at the 1970 Annual Convention of the College Theology Society. According to the Report, approximately 18 schools have a general, i.e., non-confessional, requirement in some form.

to student opposition to taking poor or irrelevant courses is not to drop the requirement but to improve the courses. And it is not clear that this avenue has always been carefully or thoroughly explored. Why is this true? Very simply, because it is much easier to drop requirements than to reform a department.

It is at least probable that the student opposition to theology courses—to the extent that it is precisely focused on theology—will be minimized or neutralized by offering a set of interesting, relevant, intellectually stimulating and educationally developing courses. It may be argued that if these kinds of courses are offered, then no requirement of any kind is necessary. This argument has been made frequently. I am not sure that this is true. And the reason for my doubt is the following: if theology requirements are dropped for this reason—that is that interesting and stimulating courses will attract the students—it is very probable that other departments will simply increase their requirements and that the students will not have the options and the leisure to take advantage of these theology courses. It is the experience of many who teach in the humanities area of universities that any lowering of requirement in these areas occasions an increase of the requirements in the area of the sciences. And therefore it may be necessary even with stimulating and challenging courses for the humanities department to insist upon requirements for two reasons: first, their conviction of the intrinsic importance of their discipline to the overall education of the student, and secondly, their realization that a requirement is a necessary means of assuring that the student is exposed to this discipline in the practical give-and-take of the university or college setting.

There is another type of argument that has been advanced for dropping the theology requirement in Catholic schools. The argument runs as follows: you must not require students to take theology because this is too personal a matter. It is much too intimate and too personal a thing to be treated in an academic way. This is the same kind of argumentation that is used to say that one should not give grades for a theology course: "How can you grade someone on his religious life or his relation to God?" This argument can be rejected because it is based very simply on a confusion between theology and religious education.[6]

Religious education is life education. It is oriented directly toward the Christian life. For that reason a great deal of religious education is practice, in the literal sense of the term. It consists of introductions into the life of the Christian community, into its rites and sacraments. Theology is focused primarily on understanding. Its immediate object is not the *practicum* but the *intellectum*. It is knowledge, a very special kind of life that has an intrinsic relation to life because it is value-knowledge; but it still remains knowledge.[7] Nothing is gained by confusing religious education and theological education. And when it is a question of university life, something very important is lost by the neglect of reflection, research and teaching the *intellectum* of Christian faith. Therefore such academic items as course listings, grades, credit point averages, term papers, course requirements, major programs, etc., are legitimate for and suitable to the theological enterprise within the university context as an educational, academic enterprise.

There is political implication of the proposal being made here which should be explored briefly. One of the concerns of Catholic educators throughout the country is the possibility of public financial aid for Catholic institutions of higher education. This is a very delicate and a very complicated matter. It is certainly not my intention to offer any detailed comments in this area which involves court decisions, interpretation of the Constitution, etc. However, the proposal being made here has a major positive element with regard to the possibility of government aid.

An objection to public aid for Catholic institutions is based on the claim that they do engage in specifically religious activities

6. For discussions of the particular nature of religious education, cf. Frank McQuilkin and Gabriel Moran, "Religious Instruction: Two Views," *Commonweal*, Vol. 86, No. 2, (March 31, 1967), pp. 48-54; and "A Statement on Teaching Religion," *America*, Vol. 116, No. 1 (Jan. 7, 1967), 16-20.

7. For a very careful discussion of this complex question, cf. William J. Richardson, S.J., "The University and the Formation of the Christian," an unpublished paper included among the background material for the Denver JEA Workshop, Aug. 1969.

and in the promotion of religion. The theology departments and theology programs of these schools are pointed to as an indication of this. This argument is incorrect since it is based on a misunderstanding of the nature of theology. But it is true that the present posture of many institutions, that is, requiring theology courses only of the Catholic students, lends support to this accusation. There are two possible positions which could be taken in the face of this objection. One would be to drop the theology requirement entirely. And this move has been made by certain institutions, thus adopting a "low profile." However, this policy seems to run contrary to the basic orientation of the Catholic university and its commitment to the religious dimension in man. Another possible response would be to define the theological activities as academic and to demonstrate this by making participation in theology learning a strictly academic requirement, that is, applicable to *all* students. Without pretending to offer a judicial opinion on the matter it does seem that such a posture would be much more acceptable than the present "confessional" type of requirement.

In support of this opinion there is the type of argumentation that Fordham University has offered to the State of New York in its application for public funds. The application indicates that the theology department and its activity are part of the regular academic program of the University and points to the general theology requirement as a demonstration of this. A recent statement of the Rev. Charles Whelan, S.J., points in the same direction. Commenting on the recent Connecticut cases, Fr. Whelan observed that the position of the Catholic colleges who were defendants in this case would have been much stronger if their theology programs and theology requirements had applied to all the students in the colleges and not simply just to Catholic students.[8] Any department of theology which adopts

8. "I left the courtroom, however, still wondering whether the judges would interpret the exemption of non-Catholics from certain subjects as a sign of religious sensitivity on the part of the defendants or as a sign of some ulterior purpose with respect to Catholic students. If religion and theology are to be credible as academic subjects, exemptions, in my judgment, should be based on strictly academic grounds." Charles

this stance should be able to offer a variety of courses which would include "confessional" or "commitment" courses in the Catholic tradition, but also courses of a more descriptive or phenomenological variety.

I am not arguing—in fact I would assume rather the opposite position—that the department of theology in a Catholic university must be a neutral department. By neutral department I mean one that would offer only descriptive courses. This is the position which the departments of many public and private institutions have taken. Their "religion" or "religious studies" courses are all descriptive, non-confessional, non-commitment. I would argue that the department of theology in a Catholic institution does not have to and should not move into this position. The course offerings of the department can precisely be eclectic. As I indicated above, some of the courses could be "commitment" courses in the Catholic tradition. This does not exclude the possibility of a "commitment" course in some other tradition. Other courses could be descriptive or phenomenological, for example, Introduction to Religion, Comparative Religions, etc. In any case, the student would be permitted to fulfill his theology or religious studies requirement by selecting courses from these two types of offerings.

Because this is an issue of considerable importance, I will explain the distinction between a commitment course and a descriptive course as I understand it.[9] The focal point of the distinction is on the issue of truth claims. Any course, whether it be in history, geography, philosophy, theology, will make truth claims. The distinction between a commitment and a descriptive course in the area of theology or religious studies

M. Whelan, S.J., "Catholic Colleges on Trial," *America*, Vol. 122, No. 5 (Feb. 7, 1970), 122-24.

9. In my *America* article, "Theology for Undergraduates," *America*, Vol. 121, No. 16 (Nov. 15, 1969), 463-66, I used the very unsatisfactory terminology of "confessional" and "non-confessional" to describe these two types of courses. The terminology was poor because these terms are not common in the Catholic tradition and because they have a different meaning in the Protestant traditions in which they are used. Further, the *America* article does not make clear the basis of the distinction.

is that in the commitment course, truth claims are made which are based precisely upon the faith posture of the one making the claim. For example, an assertion is made that Jesus Christ is God-man; an assertion is made that the Christian God is a triune God; an assertion is made that Christ is really present in the Eucharist. This type of assertion which is based upon the faith commitment of the one making it must be distinguished from a descriptive assertion. For example, the statement is made that the Christian tradition holds that Jesus Christ is the Son of God, or the Lutheran tradition holds that *Sola Scriptura* is the rule of faith. These statements are also truth claims, but strictly speaking they are not based upon a faith position. They are claims that are arrived at through the methods of the history of ideas, through the study of documents, and so forth.

The Catholic theology department may, and I think should, offer both of these types of courses. It does not have to adopt a neutral or non-commitment stance. If a variety of both types of courses are offered, the choice of specific courses should probably be left to the student. Certainly commitment courses in the Catholic tradition should not be required of the non-Catholic student. And in the present student situation, it is probably better that such courses should not be specifically required of the Catholic student. He, too, should be left to choose, from the whole range of courses which will fulfill the requirement, those which interest him.[10]

The position taken here on the question of theology requirements in the Catholic university represents a differentiation or distinction from two other positions which have been widely discussed in recent years. This proposal, as I argued in the first part, is based on the notion of the Catholic university as an intellectual center representing, reflecting upon, and developing a given tradition, that is, the central Roman Catholic tradition.

This notion of the Catholic university is very different from

10. The rationale for not requiring specific courses in the Catholic tradition of the Catholic student is discussed by Mooney in his paper, "The Role of Theology in the Education of Undergraduates." Cf. Footnote No. 1.

the older "custodial" notion of the Catholic institution.[11] According to this rationale, the primary purpose of the Catholic college or university was to preserve the student from the nefarious effects of the secular society in which he lived. In this understanding of the Catholic college, religion or theology was an integral part of the education, but for a very different reason. It served to indoctrinate the young student in his tradition, to inculcate him with certain principles and attitudes which were part of the protective panoply against the society in which he lived. The argument that is being made here is not based upon this custodial notion of the college or university.

More importantly, this position also distinguishes itself from that of those who could argue that the Catholic university is a contradiction in terms. This argument has been made in several forms by the self-appointed Catholic intellectual establishment of this country. Working on a very superficial understanding of the notion of the university, and highly impressed by certain rhetorical phrases, some have argued that you cannot have a university which represents, embodies, and develops the Catholic tradition. The argument about the Catholic university as contradictory is another argument but, in any case, this present proposal rejects this notion as being insufficient, as not truly reflecting the nature of a university in its depth.

It is argued here that a university has the right and the obligation to define itself academically, that in that definition it can express a commitment to certain values and specifically to religious values. When the Catholic college or university so defines itself, theological activity is an important aspect of its academic work. Thus it has the possibility and the right to require a participation in that theological activity of its students. This position is consistent with and flows from the notion of the Catholic university as the active, intellectual center of a tradition which sees the spiritual dimension as basic to the life of man, which sees spiritual values as universal to the situation of man, and which sees a rational dimension to the religious life of man.

11. For a discussion of this, cf. Gerald Fogarty, S.J. "The Question of Catholic Schools: Past and Future," *America*, Vol. 119, No. 9 (Sept. 28, 1968), 254-57; and Michael Buckley, S.J., "The Function of a Catholic University," *U.S. Catholic*, No. 34 (Sept., 1969), 47.

Contributors

GEORGE DEVINE (Editor) is currently Assistant Professor of Theology at Seton Hall University.

APRIL OURSLER ARMSTRONG (Mrs. Martin F. Armstrong, Jr.) is author, theologian, wife and mother, residing in Stamford, Connecticut.

GREGORY BAUM, an Augustinian teaching at St. Michael's College, Toronto, has published many books, including such recent offerings as *Man Becoming* and *Faith and Doctrine*.

SEELY BEGGIANI, currently Rector of Our Lady of Lebanon Maronite Rite Seminary in Washington, D. C., is also on the religious education faculty of the Catholic University of America.

MYRON B. BLOY, JR., an Episcopal priest, is Executive Director of the Church Society for College Work.

NAFTALI CHAIM BRANDWEIN occupies the Rose B. and Joseph H. Cohen Professorship of Modern Hebrew Literature in the Department of Near Eastern and Judaic Studies at Brandeis University, where he is Chairman of the Council of Humanities.

JAMES C. CHERESO, another Dominican Father, is Assistant Professor of Systematic Theology at Loyola University of Chicago.

TERESA M. DEFERRARI has taught both undergraduate and graduate courses at St. John's University, New York, where she has been an Associate Professor for the past several years.

JOHN P. DOYLE, a member of the Congregation of Christian Brothers, is Editor of *Theology Notes,* a publication of the Theology Department of Iona College, where he is Assistant Professor of Theology.

MARY PATRICIA FRANZ, a Dominican sister, has been a Professor of the Old and New Testaments, Patristics and Ecclesiology at St. Thomas Aquinas College in Sparkill, N. Y., and headed the Theology Department there. She is progressing towards a doctoral degree in religion at McMaster University.

AGNES REGINA HALL, a sister of St. Joseph, is currently Assistant Professor and Chairman in the Department of Theology at St. Mary of the Plains College.

BELA KRIGLER was ordained a member of the Piarist Order and received his M.A. in Budapest, Hungary. He later came to the United States and is presently teaching theology at Rosary Hill and Medaille Colleges in Buffalo.

MARCIA MCDERMOTT teaches theology at Marymount College in Salina, Kansas.

JEREMY MILLER, who belongs to the Eastern Province of the Dominican Order, is currently Assistant Professor of Religious Studies at Ohio Dominican College.

PAUL MISNER, Assistant Professor of Systematic and Historical Theology at Boston College, has contributed articles and book reviews to several professional journals.

ROBERT E. NEALE has gained much pastoral experience since his 1954 ordination by the Bennington Association of the Vermont Congregational Conference. He has a B.D. and Th. D. degree from Union Theological Seminary, where he is presently Associate Professor in Psychiatry and Religion.

RAYMOND PANIKKAR, ordained a priest in 1946, left Europe for India in 1954, becoming senior research fellow in the universities of Mysore and Varanisi; commutes each spring to Harvard, as visiting Professor of comparative religions.

WEBSTER T. PATTERSON, formerly chairman of the Theology Department at Seattle University, he now teaches at Loyola College in Baltimore. Dr. Patterson is the author of two books on Cardinal Newman.

PHEME PERKINS is now a member of the religious studies department of Canisius College.

CARL F. STARKLOFF, a Jesuit priest, is presently Assistant Professor of Theology at Rockhurst College, having taught in the summers at St. Louis University.

THEODORE M. STEEMAN studied for the priesthood in the Franciscan Philosophicum and Theologicum respectively in Venray, Alverna and Weert, Holland, prior to his ordination and is presently a lecturer in the Department of Theology at Boston College.

WILLIAM J. SULLIVAN, a priest of the Society of Jesus, is now Assistant Professor of Theology at Marquette University, and a member of the Board of Advisors of *Theological Studies*.

JOHN CARROLL WHITE is Assistant Professor of Theology at LaSalle College, and is currently pursuing doctoral studies in Christian Origins at nearby Temple University.

GEOFFREY WOOD has been Professor of Sacred Scripture at Catholic University and at Swarthmore College, and taught courses in Scripture and Catholicism at Bucknell University, prior to his present position as Associate Professor of Religion at Loyola College in Baltimore.